Clear Grammar **4**

2nd Edition

Clear Grammar 4

2nd Edition

Keys to Advanced ESL Grammar

Keith S. Folse
Deborah Mitchell
Barbara Smith-Palinkas
Donna M. Tortorella

Ann Arbor
University of Michigan Press

Thanks to the readers and contributors of exercises—Laura Monroe, Ekaterina Goussakova, Shawn Pollgreen, Marshall Mitchell, Ximena Lozano, and Dorothy Zemach.

ISBN-13: 978-0-472-03244-0

2016   2015   2014   2013   4   3   2   1

Contents

To the Teacher

The purpose of a grammar book for English language learners (ELLs) is to help our students acquire the patterns of English. Simply put, grammar is nothing more than patterns. Some of these patterns are relatively easy (e.g., adjectives precede nouns), while others are more difficult (e.g., prepositions or articles). To help our students acquire these patterns, the four books in the *Clear Grammar* series feature a unique combination of useful grammar information written in simple language with activities that promote more accurate and fluent writing, speaking, reading, and vocabulary.

Clear Grammar 4 offers students and teachers solid presentations of grammar information and useful practice activities for lower-advanced students. It is part of a four-volume corpus-informed series of grammar books for all levels of students of English as a second or foreign language. Book 4 covers grammar points for lower-advanced non-native speakers of English, including noun clauses, adverb clauses, past perfect tense, and conditionals.

Clear Grammar 1 begins the series with basic grammar points, such as simple present and simple past tenses, count and non-count nouns, and prepositions. *Clear Grammar 2* continues with grammar points such as irregular past, articles, and modals. *Clear Grammar 3* continues with grammar points such as phrasal verbs, passive voice, infinitives vs. gerunds, and adjective clauses.

Clear Grammar 4 contains exercises that provide relevant practice in basic grammar points for ELLs at the lower-advanced/advanced level. It assumes that students have knowledge of basic English grammar, including simple sentence structure and verb tenses (past progressive, present perfect, future) and modals. It is designed to be used by adult learners—high school age and up. It is suitable for either intensive or non-intensive programs.

Important features of all four new editions of *Clear Grammar* include:

1. clear grammar explanations with user-friendly charts
2. a grammar discovery task using students' inductive learning skills
3. a large number of activities (about 190 in this book), as well as a wide variety of activities (fill in the blank, sentence completion, scrambled sentences, matching, error ID, editing, original writing, reading, and vocabulary)
4. many more grammar activities at the longer discourse level
5. corpus-informed vocabulary items connected to a unit's target grammar
6. reading skills: each unit includes a critical reading activity and a sentence-reading exercise in which the target grammar is featured
7. writing skills: each unit concludes with two writing activities, one on editing student writing and the other for original student writing
8. vocabulary quizzes: each unit includes at least two vocabulary reviews, one of which focuses on collocations

9. communication skills: each unit includes one to five speaking activities that require students to speak and listen to each other while using the target grammar

10. online extra practice activities that are indicated within each unit

The books in the *Clear Grammar* series have eight main goals:

1. to teach the basic grammar points necessary for ELL students

2. to expose students to a substantial amount of useful, high-frequency, corpus-informed vocabulary that is related to the grammar point being studied, including words, phrases, and idioms

3. to provide ample written practice in these structures at the multi-sentence and dialogue levels

4. to provide practice at varying cognitive levels (i.e., not just rote grammar knowledge and comprehension but also synthesis and evaluation)

5. to engage ELLs through a variety of activities and games

6. to improve students' writing, speaking, reading, and listening

7. to provide ample opportunities for students to check their progress while studying these structures

8. to serve as a grammar reference that is written with language and terms that an ELL at the upper-intermediate or advanced level can understand without teacher assistance

The units may be done in any order. However, it is recommended that the general sequencing of the units be followed whenever possible. An attempt has been made to recycle material from one unit into following units where appropriate. For example, once past tense for irregular verbs has been covered, many of the sentences in subsequent exercises in other units include irregular past tense for further reinforcement.

Although a great deal of variety of material exists in the book, there is a general pattern within each unit.

If you see a key in the right margin in a grammar lesson, it means that this grammar point is featured as one of the 15 keys in *Keys to Teaching Grammar to English Language Learners* by Keith Folse (2009).

Unit Organization

1. **Discover Grammar Task.** In many grammar classes, the teacher simply presents the grammar lesson to the students. Another effective technique is to involve the students in an inductive grammar discovery task that begins each unit.

   Students work together to read a short passage or conversation of one to two paragraphs that are rich in examples of the target grammar and then answer a series of questions about the structures in the text. These questions focus on grammar and meaning.

   Students may or may not be able to actually figure out the grammar issue, but this creates a teachable moment in response to the learners' need to know. Your goal is to pique the students' curiosity about the lesson's grammar. After completing the task in their books, students should discuss their answers as a class before beginning the actual lesson. Some students are better able to remember information that they themselves have worked with, so involving students in this kind of discovery task may ultimately benefit their learning.

2. **Grammar Presentation Charts.** Simple, easy-to-follow charts explain the target grammar, which often features corpus-based vocabulary connected to the grammar point.

3. **List of Potential Errors with Corrections.** This section of the unit includes a list of several of the most common errors made by learners. Following each error is the corrected form so that students can see not only what they should avoid but how it should be corrected. Our students represent a wide range of linguistic groups, and every effort has been made to take this into account in selecting which kinds of errors to include here.

4. **Written (as opposed to Speaking) Exercises.** Teachers and students want a large number of written exercises to allow for ample practice of the newly learned structure. The exercises have been sequenced so that the early exercises require only passive knowledge of the grammar point. For example, students circle one of two answers or put a check mark by the correct word. These exercises are followed by others that are more cognitively demanding and require active production of the language structure. In this way, students can comfortably move from passive knowledge to active production of a structure.

   The written exercises in this book are short enough to be done in a small amount of time, yet they are thorough enough to provide sufficient practice for the structure in question. These exercises may be done in class or as homework. Furthermore, they may be checked quickly either by individual students or by the class.

5. **Grammar at the Discourse Level.** As often as possible, the written exercises in this book consist of connected sentences related to a single topic, with the title of the material indicated just before the grammar activity. This connected discourse helps ELLs improve their overall English fluency while focusing on the target grammar items.

6. **Extra Online Practice.** After students have practiced a structure, they are directed to do corresponding interactive activities on the website that accompanies this series (**www.press.umich.edu/elt/compsite/cleargrammar/**). Students record their scores for these activities in their books, which gives teachers who so desire an opportunity to see how students are doing on a particular grammar item.

7. **Mini-Conversations.** Instead of unconnected single-sentence exercises, this written exercise consists of dialogues that require students to recognize or use the target grammar in a broader context than single sentences.

8. **Editing.** Students need to become proficient at editing their own grammar. To that end, a special activity in each unit allows ELLs to be the judge of whether or not a given sentence does or does not contain an error with the target grammar items.

9. **Sentence Study for Critical Reading.** In this activity, students read a sentence that contains the target grammar and then must choose which of three sentences

that follow are true based on the information in the original sentence. To improve critical-thinking skills, one, two, or all three of the statements may be true, so students must read all three and carefully consider their veracity.

10. **Speaking Exercises.** Each unit has at least one interactive speaking activity that provides an opportunity for students to practice the grammar and build fluency.

11. **Two Review Tests.** Equally as important as the teaching of a given grammar point is the measurement of the learning that has taken place. Near the end of every unit are two review tests. These review tests have various kinds of questions to assess learners' ability in different ways.

    Review Test 1 contains multiple choice questions. It is important to discuss not only why the correct answers are correct but also why the distractors are not correct. Review Test 2 is Production and Evaluation. Part 1 of this review test requires production of the grammar, usually through a fill-in-the-blank activity. Because editing grammar is such an important student skill, Part 2 requires students to edit material that contains typical ELL errors.

12. **Reading Practice.** This longer reading activity generally consists of 200–400 words of text followed by several comprehension questions. The target grammar has been underlined to reinforce students' knowledge and awareness of the grammar.

13. **Two Vocabulary Practices.** Grammar knowledge without expanding vocabulary knowledge is useless, so vocabulary must be practiced and learned. The units overtly present new vocabulary to help students increase their vocabulary as much as possible. To this end, two vocabulary practice activities help solidify students' knowledge of vocabulary.

    Word Knowledge features 25–35 key words from the unit and two answer options. Students should select the one word that is clearly related to the target vocabulary word.

    Collocations features 25–40 key phrases or word combinations that are used frequently. Here students choose the one word that best completes the phrase. Examples include *a* _____ *menu* with *sauce* and *special* as answer choices, and *in* _____ with *fact* and *menu*.

14. **Writing Practice.** The writing practice at the end of each unit has two parts. Part 1 provides additional editing practice as students must edit a student writing sample according to a list of errors that have been identified. These errors represent the most typical ELL errors for this proficiency level and grammar point. In Part 2, students are to write a short assignment based on something similar to the passage written for Part 1. Teachers may elect to have their students write sentences or paragraphs depending on the curriculum in their program.

15. **One-Minute Lesson Notes.** A unique feature of this series is the inclusion of numerous student notes, which appear in two small shaded boxes in each unit. These notes contain important information on an array of language areas, including grammar, vocabulary, pronunciation, capitalization, punctuation, and learning strategies, which teachers may discuss with the whole class or just point out to students for additional information.

Keys to Using This Book for Students

 Grammar Lesson

These charts have useful grammar information. Learn this information. If you do not understand something, ask your teacher.

 BE CAREFUL!

These mistakes are common. Do you make these same mistakes? Study these mistakes and the corrections very carefully.

 Editing Practice

Editing practice is offered in several places within a unit. This exercise practices the grammar by asking you to recognize errors.

 Connecting Grammar and Vocabulary

This symbol indicates a box explaining how vocabulary is tied to a specific grammar text. Content is based on real language samples.

 One-Minute Lesson

These boxes have important information about grammar, vocabulary, spelling, or language usage.

 Online Exercise

This symbol means that there is an extra practice activity online. Be sure to write your score in your book.

 Speaking Practice

Doing exercises on paper is not enough. In these conversations and speaking activities, you must try to use your new grammar as much as possible. Listen to other students' grammar.

 Review Tests

Each unit has two review tests. The first one has multiple choice questions, and the second has other kinds of questions.

 Reading Practice

As you do this practice, be sure to notice the underlined grammar examples in the reading.

 Vocabulary Practice

Grammar is important, but you need to have a large vocabulary. Pay careful attention to the two vocabulary practices.

 Writing Practice

Part 1 works on editing. You need to be able to write correctly, so this part is very useful. In Part 2, you can write original work.

Unit 1

Subject–Verb Agreement

 ## Discover the Grammar

Read the 12 items. The subjects and verbs are in bold. Some subjects and verbs are singular and some are plural. Circle S or P to indicate if the subject is singular or plural. Then answer the questions that follow.

Item Number	Sentence	Singular or Plural
1	A **flag is** a piece of fabric used as a symbol or signaling device.	S P
2	**Flags are** usually rectangular, displaying a distinctive design.	S P
3	The **flag** of the U.S., as well as the flags of many other countries, **is** red, white, and blue.	S P
4	The **Netherlands and France have** red, white, and dark blue striped flags.	S P
5	Our **class is studying** the reasons for the design and color of the U.S. flag.	S P
6	**Every symbol and color has** specific meaning.	S P
7	Two popular colors in flags are green and yellow. **Neither** of those colors **is** in the U.S. flag, however.	S P

Item Number	Sentence	Singular or Plural	
8	The **news** sometimes **carries** pictures of patriotic citizens waving flags.	S	P
9	Even when two countries' flags share the same colors, there **are** **differences** in design.	S	P
10	A **number** of countries' flags **are** red, white, and blue.	S	P
11	The **"Stars and Stripes" is** a popular name for the U.S. flag.	S	P
12	Of all the countries' flags **that are** red, white, and blue, the **flag** of the U.S. **is** the only "Old Glory."	S	P
		S	P

1. Why is the verb in Number 1 *is* but *are* in Number 2?

   _____

2. The word *France* is singular, so in Number 4, is *France has* possible?

   _____

3. In Number 5, *class* is a word to describe a group of people. If the subject of this sentence is talking about a group of people, why is the verb *is* and not *are*?

   _____

4. In Number 6, there are two nouns (*symbol, color*), so why is the verb singular?

   _____

5. In Number 7, the word *colors* is clearly plural. Can you explain the use of *is* in this sentence?

   _____

6. In Number 8, is the word *news* singular or plural? How do you know?

   _____

7. In Number 9, why does the verb come before the subject?

   _____

8. In Number 10, the subject is *number*. How do you know that flags cannot be the subject? The subject looks singular, so why is the verb plural?

_____

9. In Number 11, *stars* is plural and *stripes* is plural, so why is the verb singular?

_____

10. In your own words, how do you know when to use a singular verb or a plural verb?

_____

 # Grammar Lesson

Subject–Verb Agreement

Subjects and verbs agree in number. Singular subjects require singular verbs, and plural subjects require plural verbs. Some agreements are easy to understand, but others are trickier. Compare these three examples.

Examples of Subject-Verb Agreement	Subject	Verb
1. easy: The **answer is** B.	answer	is
2. a little difficult: The **answer** to Question 5 **is** B.	answer	is
3. tricky: The **answer** to the first six questions **is** B.	answer	is

<u>Rule 1</u>. An –s or –es ending does opposite things to nouns and verbs: It *usually* makes a noun **plural,** but it *always* makes a present tense verb **singular.**

   A frog lay<u>s</u> its eggs in the water. (singular)

   Frog<u>s</u> usually **lay** hundreds of eggs. (plural)

<u>Rule 2</u>. Subjects and verbs must agree in number even if other words or phrases come between them.

   Registration for courses **begins** on Monday. (singular)

   The **requirements** for this course **are** complex. (plural)

<u>Rule 3</u>. When a prepositional phrase adds items to a singular subject but starts with **with, along with, in addition to, as well as,** or **including** and is set off with commas, the verb still agrees with the singular subject.

   My cat, as well as her kittens, **has** two white front paws.

<u>Rule 4.</u> Compound subjects joined by **and** usually take a plural verb. However, when the parts of a compound subject form a singular idea or refer to a singular person or thing, they take a singular verb.

> **Alaska and Hawaii are** the newest states. (plural)
>
> **Peanut butter and jelly is** my favorite sandwich. (singular)

<u>Rule 5.</u> When a compound subject is preceded by **each** or **every**, the verb is usually singular. However, when **each** comes after a compound subject, the verb is usually plural.

> **Every man and woman has** to show a form of identification before boarding a plane.
>
> The **men and women each have** to go through a metal detector.

<u>Rule 6.</u> Singular indefinite pronouns take singular verbs: **-one, -body, any-, either, neither, each**. Plural indefinite pronouns take plural verbs: **both, few, many, several**.

> **Anything is** possible. (singular)
>
> **Somebody loses** his or her keys every day. (singular)
>
> **Few know** the answer. (plural)
>
> **Both have** already left. (plural)

<u>Rule 7.</u> Indefinite pronouns are either singular or plural, depending on the meaning of the word they refer to: **all, any, more, most, none,** and **some**.

> **All** of the money **was stolen**. (singular)
>
> **All** of the coins **were retrieved**. (plural)

<u>Rule 8.</u> When parts of a subject are joined by **or, nor, either . . . or,** or **neither . . . nor,** the verb agrees with the subject nearest to it.

> **Either** John **or** his **parents are going to** meet you at the airport. (plural)
>
> **Neither** the plumbers **nor** the **electrician knows** how to repair it. (singular)

<u>Rule 9.</u> When a collective noun acts as a unit, it takes a singular verb. When a collective noun acts as individual members of a group, it takes a plural verb. (Some collective nouns are *army, audience, class, committee, crowd, family, group, team.*)

> The **team practices** every Tuesday. (singular, as a group)
>
> The **team wash** their own uniforms at home. (plural, each individual)

<u>Rule 10.</u> When **the** comes before **number**, it is singular. When **a** comes before **number**, it is plural.

> **The number** of people **wasn't** verified. (singular)
>
> **A number** of people **were watching** the game. (plural)

Rule 11. Subjects plural in form (ending in –s, –ics) but singular in meaning take a singular verb. For example: nouns like *athletics, acoustics, politics, news, measles, mumps;* course names such as *linguistics, physics,* etc.; place names such as *the United States, Wales,* etc.; and words for time and money.

> **Mathematics is** a required course for my major. (singular)
>
> The **news was** not good. (singular)
>
> **Nine dollars is** a great price for that book.
>
> **Forty minutes is** a very short time to make a connecting flight.

Rule 12. Subjects and verbs agree in number even when the subject comes after the verb, for example, in inverted word order or with **there** or **here.**

> Here **is** the **map** you lost. (singular)
>
> There **are** many **details** to be aware of. (plural)

Rule 13. When the subject of the clause is **who, which,** or **that,** the verb agrees with the number of its **antecedent,** which is the word the pronoun is referring to.

> John is the **man who is wearing** a black shirt. (singular because *who* refers to *man*)
>
> Those are the **cars which are selling** fast. (plural because *which* refers to *cars*)

Rule 14. Be careful with **one of the.** Remember that **one of the ____s who/that** is **plural,** but **the only one of the ____s who/that** is **singular.**

> Rex is **one of the** dogs **that always win** a ribbon at the show. (plural)
>
> Rex is **the only one of the** dogs **that wins** a blue ribbon every year. (singular)

Rule 15. Titles and words named as words take singular verbs.

> The **Buccaneers is** the football team from Tampa. (singular)
>
> *The New York Times* **is** a popular newspaper. (singular)
>
> *We* **is** a subject pronoun. (singular)

BE CAREFUL!

Common Learner Errors	Explanation
1. The men ~~was~~ were astonished.	Irregular plural subjects take plural verbs.
2. The homework ~~were~~ was easy.	Non-count subjects take singular verbs.
3. She ~~cans~~ can go out tomorrow night.	Modals are always in the same form. Modals are verbs, but they do not agree in number.
4. Most of the facts ~~was~~ were misstated.	When an indefinite pronoun is used with a plural count noun, it takes a plural verb.
5. Most of the information ~~were~~ was correct.	When an indefinite pronoun is used with a non-count noun, it takes a singular verb.
6. It ~~were~~ was gloomy and cold yesterday.	The subject it always takes a singular verb even if the topic seems plural, as with two adjectives.

EXERCISE 1. Subject-Verb Agreement in Context

Circle the correct form of the verb that agrees with the subject in number.

Kung Fu Fast Facts

1. Kung fu (is, are) a type of martial arts, and most types are associated with a region that (denotes, denote) its fighting style.

2. Many schools have specific colors that (indicate, indicates) their particular kung fu style.

3. Oftentimes schools will have an animal that (symbolizes, symbolize) the philosophy or fighting style of their school.

4. Students of kung fu (is, are) all trained in the same basic stances and conditioning techniques, which they often do together in each class.

5. Kung fu students often (uses, use) meditation techniques to help develop their focus and calm their breathing.

6. A number of Chinese weapons (is used, are used) in some of the more advanced techniques.

7. One of the most famous kung fu practitioners (was, were) Bruce Lee.

8. Other famous kung fu artists (is, are) Jet Li and Jackie Chan.

EXERCISE 2. Subject-Verb Agreement in Context

Circle the letter of the correct answer.

Red, White, and Blue

1. The colors of the American flag _____ red, white, and blue.

   a. is   b. are

2. The *Stars and Stripes* _____ one of the names of the flag.

   a. is   b. are

3. The stars and six stripes _____ white.

   a. is   b. are

4. The background for the stars _____ blue.

   a. is   b. are

5. Purity and innocence _____ represented by the color white.

   a. is   b. are

6. The stripes of the flag _____ symbolic of the rays of light that _____ from the sun.

   a. is . . . come   c. is . . . comes

   b. are . . . come   d. are . . . comes

7. The seven red stripes and six white stripes _____ the original 13 colonies.

   a. representing   b. represents

8. There _____ 50 states, so there _____ 50 stars.

   a. is . . . is   c. is . . . are

   b. are . . . is   d. are . . . are

EXERCISE 3. Subject-Verb Agreement in Context

Underline the correct form of the verb that agrees with the subject in each sentence.

The Murphy Family's Trip to Seattle

1. The Murphy children (have, has) never been to Seattle before.

2. Their mom and dad (thinks, think) that the city would be a great place to visit on spring break.

3. Neither the parents nor the kids (knows, know) what they want to see first in Seattle!

4. The Space Needle (is, are) one of the attractions that they have read about.

5. The family also (want, wants) to visit the Pacific Coast, but they will need a car for this.

6. A popular, large sculpture (exist, exists) under a bridge that the kids want to see—and it's a sculpture of a Halloween monster!

7. The Mount St. Helen's monument (is, are) another site that the family (hope, hopes) to visit.

8. Both of the parents (wants, want) to visit the beautiful Japanese Garden.

9. Mr. Murphy (have, has) always wanted to visit the coffee shops in Seattle.

10. Whatever the family (decide, decides) to do, they will be happy to be together on the trip.

 Do Online Exercise 1.1. My score: _____ /10. _____ % correct.

EXERCISE 4. Editing: Is It Correct?

If the sentence is correct, write a check mark (✔) on the line. If it is not correct, write an X on the line and circle the mistake. Then make the change above the sentence. (*Hint:* There are eight sentences. Two are correct, but six have mistakes.)

Ordering Food for an Event

_____ 1. Almost everyone has attended a special event where food was served.

_____ 2. Very few, however, has ever had to organize such an event.

_____ 3. Ordering food for a large number of people are a challenge.

_____ 4. First, the number of guests have to be determined.

_____ 5. In addition, decisions about the food has to be made.

_____ 6. One factor in choosing the food is how much money is available.

_____ 7. Another are the type of event.

_____ 8. A number of other factors is also important to consider, which is why this

task can be so difficult for most people.

Do Online Exercise 1.2. My score: _____ /10. _____ % correct.

EXERCISE 5. Mini-Conversations

Circle the correct words in these mini-conversations.

1. A: The flight from Tokyo to the Philippines (are, is) about five hours.

   B: Really? I thought it took longer than that.

2. A: Do you need one stamp or two to mail that letter to Peru?

   B: The exact number of stamps needed (are, is) hard to say.

3. A: What is the most popular car color in the U.S.?

   B: I don't know, but the parking lot (has, have) a lot of gray cars.

4. A: Why did you decide to go to Michigan and then Wisconsin to study English?

   B: My main reason for going to Michigan and Wisconsin (was, were) to be in cold weather.

5. A: What do you know about Central America?

   B: I think the main export of Nicaragua, Costa Rica, and Guatemala (are, is) coffee, but I could be wrong. What do you think?

6. A: Can you ask your father or your brothers to help you tomorrow?

   B: I have already asked all of them. Unfortunately, neither my brothers nor my father (is, are) available tomorrow.

7. A: I paid ten dollars for my lunch today.

   B: What? Are you kidding? Ten dollars (is, are) too much for a simple lunch.

8. A: When you play tennis, do you prefer playing singles or doubles?

   B: I prefer doubles because singles (is, are) too difficult for me at my age.

ONE-MINUTE LESSON

Some nouns are often followed by a specific preposition: *the main **export** of*, *the **reason** for*, *the **flight** from/to*. These **noun + preposition** combinations must be memorized.

EXERCISE 6. Sentence Study for Critical Reading

Read the numbered sentences. Then read the answer choices and put a check mark (✔) in the yes or no box in front of each sentence to show if that answer is true based on the information in the original sentence. If there is not enough information to mark something as yes, then mark it as no. Remember that more than one true answer may be possible.

1. *O Pioneers* is the title of a book written by the author Willa Cather. *My Antonia* is another of Willa Cather's books depicting life on the prairies.

   ☐ yes ☐ no   a. Willa Cather wrote about authors in *O Pioneers*.

   ☐ yes ☐ no   b. Willa Cather wrote about life on the prairies in *My Antonia*.

   ☐ yes ☐ no   c. Willa Cather wrote at least two books.

2. Life on a college campus is confusing at times for most first-time students. Orientation is designed to answer some of the most frequently asked questions students may encounter.

   ☐ yes ☐ no   a. All first-time students are confused on the first day of classes.

   ☐ yes ☐ no   b. Students should have input into orientation.

   ☐ yes ☐ no   c. If a student has a question about college, he or she should attend orientation.

3. Americans send greeting cards to celebrate birthdays, religious holidays, anniversaries, births, graduations and cards to express congratulations or sympathy. Because the Internet is now so easily accessible, it has contributed to the prominence of e-cards.

   ☐ yes ☐ no   a. Americans are more likely to send their best wishes over social media than to use a stamp and the postal service.

   ☐ yes ☐ no   b. Ecards save time and money.

   ☐ yes ☐ no   c. The postal service uses ecards.

4. The state of Maine is famous for its lobsters and blueberries. Lobsters are most abundant and least expensive during months that end in the letter *r*. Blueberries are a summertime fruit.

   ☐ yes ☐ no   a. It costs more to order lobster in a restaurant in the spring.

   ☐ yes ☐ no   b. We do not know if Mainers eat either apples or oranges in the summer.

   ☐ yes ☐ no   c. Blueberries cost less in December.

5. Neither Bolivia nor Switzerland has a seacoast. Canada, on the other hand, has thousands of miles of coastline.

   ☐ yes ☐ no   a. Bolivia's coast is longer than that of Switzerland.

   ☐ yes ☐ no   b. Canada's coastline is longer than that of Switzerland.

   ☐ yes ☐ no   c. Switzerland has no coastline, and neither does Bolivia.

EXERCISE 7. Speaking Practice: Explaining a Monument in Another Country

Imagine you are going to interview someone from another country about a famous monument in that person's country. You are going to gather as much information as you can about the monument. Imagine that your goal is to draw a picture of the monument without having seen it. To do that, you need to ask as many questions as you can think of. Use the space provided. Write your questions, checking for subject-verb agreement and for question word order.

Your partner's country: _____

Your partner's monument: _____

1. _____
2. _____
3. _____
4. _____
5. _____
6. _____
7. _____
8. _____
9. _____
10. _____

REVIEW   **EXERCISE 8. Review Test 1: Multiple Choice**

Circle the letter of the correct answer.

1. Both France and Germany _____ the Euro as their currency.

   a. use   b. uses   c. would use

2. Every man, woman, and child born in the U.S. _____ to have a Social Security number.

   a. has   b. have   c. will

3. The cats and dogs each _____ to be on a leash.

   a. needing   b. needs   c. need

4. The package, in addition to the letters, _____ mailed on Thursday.

   a. was   b. were   c. is

5. Either Mr. Harper or his students _____ to enter the competition.

   a. are going   b. is going   c. will going

6. Mathematics _____ one of the most difficult courses at that school.

   a. is considered   b. will consider   c. are considered

ONE-MINUTE LESSON

The pronouns **everybody** and **everyone** may seem plural, but they are singular and take a singular verb: *everybody is, everyone has.*

EXERCISE 9. Review Test 2: Fill In the Missing Verb Forms

Read the sentences. Fill in the blank with the correct form of the given verb.

1. Linguistics _____ one of the required courses for English teachers.
   (be)

2. All of the food _____ eaten before we got to the picnic.
   (be)

3. *Horrible Bosses* _____ one of the funniest movies I _____ seen.
   (be)   (have)

4. There _____ so much work to do that I didn't know where to begin.
   (be)

5. Measles _____ a childhood disease that _____ almost
   (be)   (be)
   eradicated.

6. Here _____ the answers to your questions.
   (be)

7. Something _____ fishy around here.
   (smell)

8. The only one of the actors who really _____ the lines _____
   (know)   (be)
   not here today.

Do Online Exercise 1.3. My score: _____ /10. _____ % correct.

EXERCISE 10. Reading Practice: Two Games to Help with Learning Words

Read the passage. Pay attention to the underlined verbs. Then answer the comprehension questions that follow. The grammar in this unit has been underlined for you.

Pictionary and *Scrabble* <u>are</u> Jennifer's favorite board games. *Hangman*, as well as *Twenty Questions*, <u>is</u> also a favorite. These word games <u>are</u> right up her alley because she <u>is studying</u> to be a linguist. Linguistics <u>is</u> the science or study of language. Jennifer particularly <u>enjoys</u> learning about word origins, roots, affixes, phonetics, and new vocabulary—anything that <u>expands</u> her knowledge base of any aspect of language. Her father always <u>says</u>, "A good vocabulary <u>is</u> indicative of a learned person." She <u>is</u> determined to expand her vocabulary in pursuit of becoming "a learned person." Not only board games and fun activities but also music and movies <u>have contributed</u> to her development.

Because she <u>was raised</u> in a multilingual environment, Jennifer <u>can comprehend</u> and verbally <u>respond</u> to two other languages besides her native tongue. This <u>has helped</u> her tremendously in her studies of word origins. She now <u>needs</u> to work on reading and writing in these other languages so that she <u>becomes</u> fluent in them as well. Here <u>are</u> some activities she <u>is integrating</u> into her learning. See if you <u>can help</u> her generate answers.

1.

	h	e	r				s	

2.

		t		i	c	

1. A. Write five yes-no questions that you would ask to find out what #1 is.

   <u>Is this an animal?</u>

   _____

   _____

   _____

   _____

   B. Write five yes-no questions that you would ask to find out what #2 is.

   <u>Is this a person?</u>

   _____

   _____

   _____

   _____

2. Why does Jennifer like board games about words?

   _____

   _____

3. Are the games an aid or a hindrance to her field of study? Explain.

   _____

   _____

4. What are the different ways/techniques she is trying to expand her vocabulary?

   _____

   _____

5. Do you think her father is a positive influence? Why?

   _____

   _____

EXERCISE 11. Vocabulary Practice: Word Knowledge

Circle the answer choice that is most closely related to the vocabulary on the left. Use a dictionary to check the meaning of words you do not know.

Vocabulary	Answer Choices	
1. requirements	what you can do	what you must do
2. indefinite	not simple	not specific
3. bonus	something extra	something you can eat
4. a symbol	a representation	a sound
5. signify	to sing	to indicate
6. a function	a purpose	a cost
7. generate	demand	produce
8. a resolution	all people agree	most people don't agree
9. an occurrence	an event	an option
10. individual	signal	single
11. positive	not negative	not usual
12. sequence	time order	total cost
13. constant	continuous	somewhat
14. statistics	general ideas	numerical information
15. a stripe	a circle	a line
16. expand	become larger	become softer
17. a costume	everyday clothing	special clothing
18. denote	hide	indicate
19. indicate	to display	to mean
20. complex	very involved	very simple
21. compound	individualized	put together
22. precede	come before	come after
23. detect	certify	find
24. distinctive	special	down to earth
25. alternate	a1b2c3d4e5	ABCDEFGHIJ
26. a board game	for building houses	for having fun

EXERCISE 12. Vocabulary Practice: Collocations

Fill in each blank with the answer on the right that most naturally completes the phrase on the left. If necessary, use a dictionary to check the meaning of words you do not know.

Vocabulary	Answer Choices	
1. _____ well as	as	for
2. chickens _____ eggs	lay	put
3. to be associated _____	to	with
4. pass _____ your assignment	in	on
5. a connecting _____	class	flight
6. encounter _____	an answer	a problem
7. go _____ a trip	in	on
8. a ray of _____	air	light
9. X _____ with Y	alone	along
10. gather _____	information	sports
11. type 50 words _____ minute	a	by
12. _____ a competition	enter	take
13. _____ her alley	right up	left without
14. to work _____ a project	in	on
15. we have so much _____	doing	to do
16. _____ cards	greeting	greetings
17. please be _____ tomorrow	in time	on time
18. retrieve the _____	wallet	weather
19. registration _____ a course	for	to
20. _____ least	at	in
21. a _____ influence	hard	positive
22. _____ fluent	become	need
23. misstate a _____	fact	form
24. whatever you decide _____	doing	to do
25. one of the _____	attraction	attractions

EXERCISE 13. Writing Practice: Explaining a Local Attraction

Part 1. Editing Student Writing

Read these sentences about a student's description of a local attraction that many tourists like to visit. Circle the 16 errors. Then write the number of the sentence with the error next to the type of error. (Some sentences have more than one error.)

_____ a. subject-verb agreement   _____ d. preposition

_____ b. missing subject   _____ e. verb tense

_____ c. article   _____ f. singular-plural of nouns

A Local Attraction
1. My husband and I live in Orlando, Florida, one of most popular tourist destination for both young and old. 
2. People all over a world know Orlando for the big theme parks that are certainly the main attractions for the millions of tourist who visit our area each year.
3. However, one of our favorite thing to do in this area is to take a boat ride on the many lakes here because is so much fun.
4. Winter Park, which is a city adjacent to Orlando and about 15 minutes from our house in downtown Orlando, have a special boat ride tour that is well known among local resident.
5. Unfortunately, not many people from outside the area are aware by this simple but fun thing to do.
6. The boat ride leave from Morse Boulevard every hour on the hour.
7. This fascinating ride covers twelve miles and lasted for about one hour.
8. The trip takes you across three of the many lakes in our area and are narrated by your guide.
9. We like this tour in many reason, but one of the most amazing aspects is the low price of a ticket.
10. For those who decide to take this great tour, we recommended that you wear a hat and sunglasses because the sun reflecting on the lakes are often quite bright. Enjoy!

Part 2. Original Student Writing

Imagine that some people from outside your hometown area are coming to visit your city or town. Write a paragraph about one specific place that tourists should visit. Start with the name of the destination and then give details about the place. You will use a lot of simple present tense in your paragraph because you are writing general facts about the place. If you need help, study the example in Part 1. Underline the examples of subject-verb agreement so the teacher can see what you are trying to practice.

Beethoven

Presented by

The
Washington
School of
Musi**cal**
Design

Unit 2

Word Forms

Discover the Grammar

Read this conversation about a performance, and then answer the questions that follow.

Line	
1	*Ann:* Hi, Jenna. Did you read the newspaper article about the fundraising
2	concert that was held at the Washington School of Musical Design?
3	*Jenna:* No, I didn't. In fact, I never saw an announcement. What day was it?
4	*Ann:* Last Saturday. The music students gave a free performance for the
5	student body and the community. However, donations were accepted
6	at the door.
7	*Jenna:* Oh, I'm sorry I missed it. What were they raising funds for?
8	*Ann:* They need to raise money to perform in Europe next summer.
9	*Jenna:* That's great! Did your son Alan participate in the concert?
10	*Ann:* Of course he was a participant. Like every performer in the show, he's
11	been studying and practicing the selections for several hours daily for the
12	past three weeks.
13	*Jenna:* Which musical pieces did they select?

14	*Ann*:	Well, the musicians were allowed to choose from a list of compositions.
15		Making this selection was not easy, but they finally decided on the
16		famous German composer Beethoven.
17	*Jenna*:	That was quite generous yet risky for the director to leave the decision
18		in the hands of the students, don't you think?
19	*Ann*:	Well, I think it shows that he realized the students' maturity. He's also
20		very confident in their ability, so it wasn't too much of a risk.
21	*Jenna*:	Yes. I've heard that they are very mature and have genuine talent.
22	*Ann*:	It's true. They even performed Beethoven's 9th Symphony, which is his
23		most recognized piece. It received a standing ovation, which really
24		boosted their confidence.
25	*Jenna*:	Now I'm really sorry that I missed it. I'm glad the concert was success-
26		ful. I wonder how much money was donated as a result of all of their
27		hard work.

1. Most people think that the ending *–ing* is for verbs, but *–ing* can also be for nouns and for adjectives. Write the six *–ing* words, their line numbers, and their part of speech (*noun, verb,* or *adjective*).

	–ing Example	Line Number	Part of Speech
a.			
b.			
c.			
d.			
e.			
f.			

2. Write the six *-tion* or *-sion* words found in the passage, the line numbers, and their part of speech (noun, verb, or adjective).

–tion / –sion Example	Line Number	Part of Speech
a.		
b.		
c.		
d.		
e.		
f.		

3. Find the words *maturity* (Line 19) and *mature* (Line 21). How are these two words different?

_____

4. Find the words *risky* (Line 17) and *risk* (Line 20). How are these two words different?

_____

5. Which root word has the highest number of different endings in the passage? Write the word and all of its various forms. (Example: *study, student* = two forms)

_____

_____

6. What questions do you have about word forms?

_____

_____

_____

Grammar Lesson

KEY
13

Word Forms

In English, words have a base, or root, that gives a basic meaning to the word. For example, the base in the word *unhappiness* is *happy*.

If you add a **prefix** to the beginning of the word, it changes the **meaning** of the word. For example, when you add the prefix *dis-* to the word *respect*, the result is the word *disrespect*, which is the opposite meaning of *respect*.

If you add a **suffix** to the end of the word, however, it usually changes the word's **function,** also known as the **part of speech,** within a sentence (verb, noun, adjective, and adverb). For example, notice how the adjective *real* can become a noun (*reality*), a verb (*realize*), or an adverb (*really*).

Rule 1. You can often identify the part of speech of a word by its suffix. Some common suffixes that indicate the **part of speech** are –ize (verb), –tion (noun), –al (adjective), and –ly (adverb).

Example Suffix	Part of Speech	Example Word	Example Sentence
–ize	**verb**	*finalize*	Have you called Global Travel to **finalize** our vacation plans?
–tion	**noun**	*finalization*	The **finalization** of your plans depends on your ability to pay for the tickets on time.
–al	**adjective**	*final*	By the **final** week of school, we were ready for vacation.
–ly	**adverb**	*finally*	I'm **finally** ready to get out of town and relax.

Rule 2. The addition of a suffix can change the pronunciation of a word, especially the stress of certain syllables. For example, when the stress is on the first syllable of a three-syllable word, the addition of a suffix causes the stress to move to a different syllable.

Verb/Adjective	Noun
ed-*u*-*cate* (verb)	*ed*-*u*-**ca**-*tion*
sim-*i*-*lar* (adjective)	*sim*-*i*-**lar**-*ity*
ad-*ver*-*tise* (verb)	*ad*-*ver*-**tise**-*ment*

BE CAREFUL!

Common Learner Errors	Explanation
1. The investigation was aided considerably by the recent ~~discoverment~~ **discovery** of new evidence.	It is difficult to predict which ending is the correct one when creating new words. Check a dictionary when you are trying to create a new word.
2. Several committee members had a ~~difference~~ **different** opinion.	(*Difference* is a noun; *different* is an adjective.)

EXERCISE 1. Understanding Base Words and Suffixes

Write the shortest base word for these words with suffixes.

1. motivation _____
2. explorer _____
3. natural _____
4. comfortable_____
5. different _____

6. liquefy _____
7. finalize _____
8. thicken _____
9. density _____
10. randomness _____

Do Online Exercise 2.1. My score: _____ /10. _____ % correct.

Grammar Lesson

Verb Endings

KEY
13

VERBS	are actions or existence words that describe what nouns do.	
Suffix	Meaning	Example
-ate	to cause, to become, to supply with	*motivate, educate*
-en	to make something have a certain quality	*darken, soften*
-ify	to cause or make into something	*identify, solidify, unify*
-ize	to become	*generalize, finalize*

<u>Rule 1</u>. Verbs can be created from **nouns** or **adjectives** with these suffixes.

<u>Rule 2.</u> Be careful with spelling changes when adding word endings. Sometimes letters are dropped or added in unpredictable ways. When in doubt about spelling, you should refer to a good dictionary.

    2a. vowel dropped: *clear* + –ify   = **clarify**

    2b. vowel added: *different* + –ate = **differentiate**

EXERCISE 2. Verb Endings in Context

Underline the verbs in the sentences. Circle the suffixes of the verbs. Do not include helping verbs. Be careful! Some sentences may have two verbs. The first one has been done for you as an example.

Dave's Race

1. At that speed, Dave will not qualify for the race.

2. His slow speed does not justify a starting time.

3. If he quickens his pace, he may qualify.

4. Dave verbalizes his feelings in poems.

5. In contrast, his coaches articulate their feelings through long speeches.

EXERCISE 3. Building Verbs

Construct verbs from these nouns and adjectives by adding the appropriate verb suffix. The spelling may change, so use a dictionary to check the spelling of the new word. In the first column, write **N** if the original word (on the left) is a noun and **ADJ** if it is an adjective. Some words may be both.

Original Word	N or ADJ	Verb
1. class	_____	_____
2. diverse	_____	_____
3. final	_____	_____
4. alien	_____	_____
5. light	_____	_____
6. clear	_____	_____
7. apology	_____	_____
8. different	_____	_____

ONE-MINUTE LESSON

Some verbs are followed by a specific preposition: *Dave will not* **qualify** *for the race*. These *verb + preposition* combinations must be memorized.

 **Grammar Lesson**

Noun Endings

KEY
13

NOUNS	are people, places, things, or ideas.	
Suffix	**Meaning**	**Example**
–al	the act of doing something	*rehearsal, denial*
–ence, –ance, –cy	an action or process; quality, condition	*reference, performance, secrecy*
–ent, –ant	someone or something that does something	*president, participant*
–er, –or, –r	someone or something that does something	*teacher, elevator, printer*
–ese, –an, –ish	nationality or language	*Chinese, Canadian, Turkish*
–ity, –ty,	state, character, or condition of being	*equality, insanity, beauty*
–tion, –ion	act or result of doing something	*attention, impression*
–ism	a belief or set of ideas	*capitalism, atheism*
–ist, –ian	a person who performs a specific action; a person with certain beliefs	*chemist, capitalist, technician, humanitarian*
–ment	a result of doing something; a place of action	*development, department*
–ness	state or condition	*happiness, illness*
–ology, –logy	the science of; equipment for	*biology, technology*
–ry, –y	a result, activity, or place of business	*victory, carpentry, laundry*
–ship	a state or condition; an art or skill	*friendship, sportsmanship*
–th	a quality	*strength, depth*
–ure	an act, process, or result	*failure, composure*

<u>Rule 1</u>. Nouns can be created from **verbs** (*fail + -ure*), **adjectives** (*ill + -ness*), and sometimes from other **nouns** (*friend + -ship*) by adding suffixes.

<u>Rule 2</u>. Sometimes a **compound noun** is created from two nouns. Compound nouns may be separate words (*plastic cups*) or spelled as one word (*bedroom*).

<u>Rule 3</u>. **Proper nouns** are names of people, places, languages, origins, months, holidays, and product brands. They are capitalized: *Tom, Florida, Nike*. Proper nouns can have suffixes: *Tommy* (a diminutive of *Tom*), or a *Floridian* (a person from *Florida*).

EXERCISE 4. Noun Endings in Context

Underline the nouns that have suffixes. Circle the suffixes that make them nouns.

The School's Computer Lab

Mona: I'm surprised to see you at this orientation. I didn't know you were a teacher.

Joanna: Yes, this is my third year. I'm gaining more confidence with every new year.

Mona: What grade do you teach?

Joanna: I have the pleasure of being the computer specialist for all the grades.

Mona: That must be difficult.

Joanna: Not really. Actually, it's a lot of fun. We use programs with a lot of animation, which helps the students who aren't readers yet. The kids get a lot of enjoyment out of it.

Mona: Are there enough computers for each child to work independently?

Joanna: Unfortunately, no. We use a buddy system, so that means everyone has a partner. You'd be surprised at how many new friendships have blossomed.

Mona: You mean to tell me there aren't any arguments over who controls the mouse or keyboard?

Joanna: No, there's a willingness to take turns. The children have a good sense of fairness. No problems.

Mona: You're such an optimist.

EXERCISE 5. Building Nouns from Verbs

Form nouns from these verbs by adding the appropriate noun suffixes. Sometimes more than one suffix can be used to produce separate, yet related, definitions or uses. Check your dictionary for the proper spellings and possible noun forms. The first one has been done for you as an example.

1. invest   investor/investment   5. improve   _____

2. conform   _____   6. integrate   _____

3. impress   _____   7. discover   _____

4. confide   _____   8. manage   _____

EXERCISE 6. Building Nouns from Adjectives

Construct nouns from these adjectives by adding the appropriate noun suffixes. Check your dictionary for the proper spellings. The first one has been done for you as an example.

1. personal   personality   5. violent   _____

2. similar   _____   6. responsible   _____

3. weak   _____   7. brilliant   _____

4. happy   _____   8. honest   _____

Do Online Exercise 2.2. My score: _____ /10. _____ % correct.

 **Grammar Lesson**

Adjectives

ADJECTIVES	describe nouns or pronouns.	
Suffix	**Meaning**	**Example**
–able, –ible	capable of; tending to; fit for; or having qualities of	*comfortable, reversible*
–al, –ial	of or relating to something	*musical, occasional*
–ant, –ent	performing or causing a specified action/process; being in a specified condition	*abundant, persistent, competent*
–ary	belonging to; relating to	*planetary, military*
–ate,	having, containing, or having to do with something; state or quality	*compassionate, fortunate*
–ful	full of	*beautiful, prideful*
–ic, –ical,	relating to or characterized by	*periodic, organic, analytical*
–ish	having qualities of, or tending to be	*bluish, childish*
–ive	having tendency to, character of, function of, connection to	*expensive, massive*
–less	without something	*useless, fearless*
–ous, –ious	having qualities of; full of	*dangerous, gracious*
–y	having the character of	*curly, funny*

<u>Rule 1</u>. Descriptive adjectives can be made from **nouns** or **verbs** with these suffixes.

<u>Rule 2</u>. Adjectives with these suffixes can occur before a noun (*a funny story*) or after **be** (*the story is funny*). In contrast, certain adjectives (the **a- adjectives**) cannot precede nouns. Examples include *alike, alive, alone, afraid, asleep, awake,* and *aware*.

<u>Rule 3</u>. When describing something, usually no more than one or two adjectives appear in any one phrase; however, in the extremely rare instances where we use three (or more) adjectives before a noun, there is a common sequence of categories: **opinion, size, shape, age, color, origin, material, purpose.**

Example 1: **a small white paper plate**

Example 2: **competent, efficient, professional service**

Notice the commas between the adjectives in Example 2. Each adjective is from the same category. If the adjectives can be put in any order, commas are needed.

Rule 4. Some adjectives can have more than one ending. Check a dictionary as the meanings or contextual use will differ. For example, *a* **sensible** *person* is NOT the same *as a* **sensitive** *person,* and **substantial** *work* is NOT the same as **substantive** *work.* Be careful that you select the appropriate adjective ending by checking a dictionary.

EXERCISE 7. Adjective Endings in Context

Underline all the descriptive words in these sentences about a spelling bee. Circle the adjective suffixes. The first one has been done for you as an example.

Nate and Kate's Spelling Bee

1. Nate and Kate are very studious twins, but in many ways they are different.

2. Nate and Kate attend separate schools that are very competitive.

3. Nate earned the prestigious honor of representing his school in the regional spelling bee.

4. Kate came home from school very irritable because she wasn't chosen to be her school's representative.

5. Kate's negative attitude surprised Nate.

6. He thought she would be enthusiastic about his accomplishment.

7. As time passed, Kate became supportive and helpful to her brother.

8. She helped Nate practice an exhaustive list of words every night.

9. At the spelling bee, Kate was Nate's most passionate and zealous fan.

10. In the end, spelling became a wonderful way for Kate and Nate to work together.

EXERCISE 8. Building Adjectives from Nouns

Create adjectives (descriptive words) from these nouns by adding the appropriate adjective suffix. Some letters may need to be changed. Check the spelling. It is possible that more than one adjective may exist. Check your dictionary. The first one has been done for you as an example.

1. sense   _sensible/sensitive_   5. violence   _____

2. peril   _____   6. monotony   _____

3. athlete   _____   7. style   _____

4. accuracy _____   8. hero   _____

EXERCISE 9. Building Adjectives from Verbs

Create adjectives from these verbs by adding the appropriate adjective suffix. Check the spelling. Some letters may need to be changed. It is possible that more than one adjective may exist.

1. help   _____   5. create   _____

2. prohibit _____   6. observe   _____

3. envy   _____   7. accept   _____

4. depend   _____   8. obey   _____

Do Online Exercise 2.3. My score: _____ /10. _____ % correct.

Grammar Lesson

KEY
13

Adjectives Ending in *–ing* or *–ed*

A verb ending in –ing (**present participle**) or –ed/–en (**past participle**) or can also function as a descriptive adjective. However, each form has a different meaning and usage.

Adjective	Meaning/Example
interesting	Attracting attention, not dull or boring. She is an **interesting** teacher. This is an **interesting** book.
interested	Wanting to learn more about something. The boss was **interested** in our idea. This is an opportunity for **interested** parties.

<u>Rule 1</u>. Present participle adjectives (–ing) describe the person or thing creating the action/emotion.

<u>Rule 2</u>. Past participle adjectives (–ed/–en/irregular) describe the receiver of the action/emotion.

Connecting Grammar and Vocabulary

There are hundreds of possible –ing and –ed/–en adjectives in English. Here are 40 common examples listed in order of frequency. The most effective strategy is to focus on the most common forms you need.

40 Frequent Participles Used as Adjectives			
present participle (–ing)		**past participle (–ed, –en, etc.)**	
1. interesting	11. developing	1. unidentified	11. limited
2. willing	12. surprising	2. concerned	12. tired
3. growing	13. working	3. involved	13. so-called
4. following	14. ongoing	4. supposed	14. armed
5. living	15. exciting	5. interested	15. broken
6. existing	16. running	6. united	16. lost
7. remaining	17. changing	7. married	17. advanced
8. amazing	18. missing	8. used	18. complicated
9. leading	19. overwhelming	9. increased	19. unknown
10. increasing	20. continuing	10. surprised	20. scared

Source: Reilly, N. (2013). *A Comparative Analysis of Present and Past Participial Adjectives in the Corpus of Contemporary American English.* Thesis, University of Central Florida.

EXERCISE 10. Selecting the Appropriate Adjective in Context

Read this conversation. Ashley has recently been hired by a large company, and Sean is showing her around. Circle the adjective that best fits the context.

The Office Dress Code

Ashley: I've noticed that some people are wearing jeans. Can I assume that there is no ❶ (written, writing) policy on what we can wear?

Sean: No. While jeans may be ❷ (appropriate, appropriated) attire for the IT department, they are not ❸ (permissive, permitted) in the Sales department.

Ashley: But I don't work in Sales. I work in Finance. The general public doesn't even see me. Besides, when we have ❹ (stormy, storming) weather, it is a very ❺ (challenging, challenged) trek from the bus stop to the office in high heels and a dress.

Sean: Many women wear ❻ (sensible, sensitive) walking shoes and then change them as soon as they arrive in the office.

Ashley: Why change shoes? Can't we just stay in our more ❼ (comfortable, comforted, comforting) shoes and, of course, jeans? If we could wear ❽ (relaxed, relaxing) apparel, you'd have more ❾ (energetic, energizing) employees and a more ❿ (motivated, motivating) staff.

Sean: Well, I don't make the policies here.

ONE-MINUTE LESSON
Many adjectives that describe the weather end in the letter –y: *rainy, sunny, windy, stormy.*

 **Grammar Lesson**

KEY
13

Adverb Endings

ADVERBS	modify verbs, adjectives, and other adverbs.	
Suffix	Meaning	Example
-ly	in a particular way (**manner**) or times (**frequency** or **time**)	*easily, quickly* *occasionally, recently*

<u>Rule 1.</u> Adverbs of manner can be made from adjectives by adding –**ly**.

<u>Rule 2</u>. Not all adverbs of manner end in –**ly**; for example, *fast, well,* and *hard*.

<u>Rule 3</u>. Not all words that end in –**ly** are adverbs. Here are some common **adjectives** ending in –**ly**: *friendly, lively, lonely, lovely, neighborly, orderly, silly, ugly*.

<u>Rule 4</u>. Some –**ly** adverbs have corresponding –**ly** adjectives.

   daily as adjective: Our library subscribes to four **daily** newspapers.

   daily as adverb: Kumiko exercises **daily**.

<u>Spelling Rule 5</u>. When adding an –**ly** suffix to an adjective ending in –**l**, add –**ly**: *careful* = **carefully**.

<u>Spelling Rule 6</u>. When adding an –**ly** suffix to an adjective ending in –**y**, change the *y* to *i*: *happy* = **happily**.

<u>Spelling Rule 7</u>. When adding an –**ly** suffix to an adjective ending in –**le**, drop the *e*: *reasonable* = **reasonably**.

<u>Rule 8</u>. Most adverbs of manner that end in –**ly** can be placed at the beginning of a sentence, at the end of a sentence, or between the subject and verb.

   He walked into the room **quietly**.

   He **quietly** walked into the room.

   Quietly, he walked into the room.

↔ **Connecting Grammar and Vocabulary**

Here are 15 frequently used adverbs that end in **–ly.** They are listed in order of frequency. You should try very hard to add this vocabulary to your regular English usage to make your English sound more natural.

15 Frequent –ly Adverbs		
1. really	6. absolutely	11. finally
2. only	7. exactly	12. simply
3. actually	8. early	13. especially
4. probably	9. obviously	14. clearly
5. certainly	10. basically	15. quickly

Source: Corpus of Contemporary American English, www.americancorpus.org/

EXERCISE 11. Adverb Endings in Context

Underline the eight **–ly** adverbs in this advertisement. Be careful that you don't mistake an adjective for an adverb.

The Best Cleaning Product

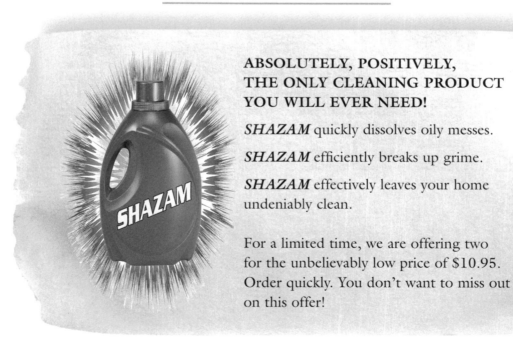

ABSOLUTELY, POSITIVELY, THE ONLY CLEANING PRODUCT YOU WILL EVER NEED!

SHAZAM quickly dissolves oily messes.

SHAZAM efficiently breaks up grime.

SHAZAM effectively leaves your home undeniably clean.

For a limited time, we are offering two for the unbelievably low price of $10.95. Order quickly. You don't want to miss out on this offer!

EXERCISE 12. Building Adverbs from Adjectives

Form **-ly** adverbs from these adjectives.

1. absolute _____
2. obvious _____
3. clear _____

4. simple _____
5. probable _____
6. basic _____

EXERCISE 13. Verbs, Nouns, Adjectives, and Adverbs in Context

Read this conversation about insurance rates. Circle the correct form of the word that completes the sentence. Use verbs, nouns, adjectives, and adverbs.

A High Insurance Bill

Manny: Hi, Jill. What's the matter? You look so (distraught, distraughtly).

Jill: You're right. I'm (miserably, miserable)! I just got my insurance bill.

Manny: Which one?

Jill: Our policy is a (combine, combination) for both house and auto insurance. You won't believe how (astronomically, astronomic) high it is this time.

Manny: I'm not very (contentment, content) with mine either. The town just (recently, recent) re-zoned all the homes within a mile of the beach as being in a (flooded, flood) zone, so that means higher insurance for certain. That includes you and me.

Jill: No wonder my (annual, annually) premium is so high. Maybe I should move.

Manny: I understand. In fact, my house is going on the market next week.

Jill: Oh? I hope you (success, succeed) in selling it soon.

EXERCISE 14. Mini-Conversations

Circle the correct words in these mini-conversations.

1. A: I hate that (dreadfully, dreadful) long flight from L.A. to Manila.

   B: Don't worry. I upgraded our tickets, and the new planes have (fully, full) reclining seats.

2. A: The tag says this shirt is reversible. What does that mean?

   B: It means that it can be (worn, wearing) with either side out.

3. A: Do you think Felipe is in (deny, denial) about his grades?

   B: Of course. He doesn't want to believe that he is not going to pass.

4. A: I heard the Strattons bought an old house. What does it look like?

   B: Oh! It's a (lovely, loving) Victorian-style home.

5. A: Why does this old (wood, wooden) table look rather gray?

   B: If you put oil on it, you will (darker, darken) the color.

6. A: Did the teacher (clarify, clarity) the instructions?

   B: I'm still a little (confused, confusing). I'll ask him about the project again tomorrow.

7. A: The professor said he appreciates Mindo's (punctuality, punctually).

   B: That's wonderful. Finally, Mindo is getting serious about his studies.

8. A: How do hospitals (prevent, prevention) their patients from contracting other diseases?

   B: They carefully (sanitize, sanitary) everything to prevent the spread of disease.

EXERCISE 15. Speaking Practice: Word Categories Game

Step 1. The teacher will divide the class into small groups (or pairs) and will determine a length of time to play, such as 15–20 minutes. Each group selects one person to be the scorekeeper and one person to begin the activity.

Step 2. Student A calls out a verb, adjective, adverb, or noun with any of the suffixes used in this unit. (No proper nouns or animals are allowed.) Student B has two choices: either change the form of the word, or use the same suffix and change the root.

For example, if Student A calls out the word *automatic*, then Student B could call out either *automatically* or *automation* as a way of changing the form. However, Student B would also have the option of using the suffix (*-ic* in the case of *automatic*) with a different root, such as *periodic*. If Student B should call out *automatically*, for instance, then Student C will have the choice to use *automation* or create a new word that ends in *–ly*. The game continues in this way. Note that you cannot re-use a word that someone has already used.

Step 3. Keep score. For each correct change in the suffix, the player receives one point. For each correct new word with the same suffix, the player receives two points. Using the example given, *automatically* would receive one point, but *periodic* would have received two.

Step 4. Challenge your opponent. If an opponent thinks that the player has used a word that does not exist, then the dispute can be settled by referring to a dictionary or asking the teacher. If the student who challenges is correct, the student gets three points and the other player loses a turn.

Step 5. At the end of the set time, add the total points for each group. The team with the highest number of points wins the game.

EXERCISE 16. Editing: Is It Correct?

Look at the two underlined words in each sentence. If the word form is correct, write a check mark (✓) on the line. If it is not correct, write an X on the line and circle the mistake. Then make the change above the sentence. (*Hint:* There are 16 underlined words. Four are correct, but twelve have mistakes.)

1st word   2nd word

_____   _____   1. Hi, Billy. I called you last night to <u>reminder</u> you that the <u>presidential</u> debate was on Channel 5.

_____   _____   2. Oh, yeah. I got your message, but I couldn't watch it; I had a <u>substance</u> amount of homework. Did anyone <u>impressive</u> you?

_____   _____   3. Three candidates were very <u>defense</u> about their positions while the other three spoke <u>calm</u> about their views.

_____   _____   4. Did they debate <u>education</u> and <u>interesting</u> rates?

_____   _____   5. Everyone was <u>supportable</u> of an increase in the <u>availability</u> of a college education to more middle class students.

_____   _____   6. I need to apply for <u>finance</u> aid next semester. Did they say anything that would be <u>beneficial</u> to me?

_____   _____   7. Four were in <u>favorable</u> of low-interest loans, and two wanted to increase the number of <u>scholarly</u> to pay the tuition of the brightest students.

_____   _____   8. Those are all <u>interested</u> possibilities. I'm <u>real</u> sorry I missed it.

Do Online Exercise 2.4. My score: _____ /10. _____ % correct.

EXERCISE 17. Sentence Study for Critical Reading

Read the numbered sentences. Then read the answer choices and put a check mark (✔) in the yes or no boxes in front of each sentence to show if that answer is true based on the information in the original sentence. If there is not enough information to mark something as yes, then mark it as no. Remember that more than one true answer may be possible.

1. The defense attorney objected to evidence that could have been advantageous to the prosecutor.

   ☐ yes ☐ no a. An objection was made by the defense against the use of certain evidence.

   ☐ yes ☐ no b. The defense's objections gave the prosecutor an advantage.

   ☐ yes ☐ no c. It was evident that the defense had an objectionable advantage.

2. Humans have varying degrees of different types of intelligences, such as musical, spatial, and interpersonal.

   ☐ yes ☐ no a. There are personal variations in the types and amounts of intelligences that each of us possesses.

   ☐ yes ☐ no b. People who are very musical often lack other intelligence.

   ☐ yes ☐ no c. Humans who have a variety of degrees are intelligently, musically, and interpersonally different.

3. When seen under magnification, all snowflakes are hexagonal crystals, yet no two snowflakes are exactly alike.

   ☐ yes ☐ no a. Snowflakes are less than magnificent if they are not hexagons like other snowflakes.

   ☐ yes ☐ no b. All snowflakes are shaped like a hexagon, but when they are magnified, none of them look alike.

   ☐ yes ☐ no c. Snowflakes magnify other crystals so that they all look exactly the same.

4. Reading to your children and allowing them the opportunity to select their own books are two important forms of parental encouragement that can help children to become better readers.

   ☐ yes ☐ no a. The importance of childish parents is seen as an encouragement to a good book selection.

   ☐ yes ☐ no b. Children who are good readers are usually children who were read to by their parents.

   ☐ yes ☐ no c. Selecting a book for a child can encourage the parents to be better readers.

5. Mechanical engineers need to be able to provide exact specifications so that electricians and plumbers can complete their jobs.

☐ **yes** ☐ **no** a. Mechanics are provided specific jobs as electricians and plumbers.

☐ **yes** ☐ **no** b. Mechanical engineers are provided with electricity and plumbing.

☐ **yes** ☐ **no** c. Exact job specifications must be given to electricians and plumbers by the mechanical engineers.

REVIEW ▶ **EXERCISE 18. Review Test 1: Multiple Choice**

Circle the letter of the word that best completes the sentences in this conversation between cousins who attend rival high schools.

A Football Rivalry

1. *Chad:* Hey, Tyrell, are you going to the game Friday night?

    Tyrell: Very funny! You know I'm the quarterback. How about you? Are you going to _____ ?

    a. attendant   c. attendance
    b. attend   d. attended

3. *Chad:* Surely you're joking. You know I'm one of the best _____ players North High has.

    a. defend   c. defensive
    b. defender   d. defensible

3. *Tyrell:* Yeah, I know. That's why South High is going to win. Our _____ can outrun your defense any day.

    a. offensiveness   b. offensive   c. offender   d. offense

4. *Chad:* You know that I'm going to _____ the ball first! Then I'll just run right past you and wave as I'm going by.

    a. interception   b. interceptor   c. interceptive   d. intercept

5. *Tyrell:* Then I'll dance over the goal line. I'm going to _____ you with my fancy footwork.

    a. impressing   b. impress   c. impressive   d. impression

6. *Chad:* The only _____ you're going make is the one your head makes when it hits the ground.

    a. impressing   b. impressive   c. impression   d. impressed

EXERCISE 19. Review Test 2: Production and Evaluation

Part 1.
Fill in the blanks using words from the word list. Change the endings of words to create the correct part of speech. There will be two plural nouns, four adjectives, and two adverbs.

word list	culture	green	mystery	observe
	frighten	history	magnet	playful

The Dancing Northern Lights

The Aurora Borealis, frequently referred to as the Northern Lights, is a spectacular blend of blue, green, and pink ribbons of light that ❶ _____ dance through the dark winter nights of the polar region. ❷ _____ fields at the North and South Poles of the Earth pull on electrically charged particles from the sun, and when these charged particles collide with oxygen or nitrogen in the atmosphere, magnificent colors are created. These ❸ _____ lights inspired a number of spooky legends and myths that were told again and again by ❹ _____ diverse groups living in the northern hemisphere. Some native tribes in northern Alaska have a ❺ _____ legend that describes the Northern Lights as devious spirits that quickly descend to earth and capture any person who whistles at them. Additionally, because of the up-and-down movements that are effortlessly made by the ❻ _____-colored Northern Lights and the bursts of red, some ❼ _____ have wondered if the legend of the Chinese dragon came from ancient ❽ _____ of these lights in the northern sky.

Part 2.

Read the short passage. Carefully look at the underlined words. There are eight mistakes. Circle the mistakes, and write the correction above the mistake.

Reading in a Second Language

Good second language readers need to be able to ❶ <u>recognition</u> a large number of words ❷ <u>automatically</u>. Weak second language readers are at a disadvantage because of their ❸ <u>limit</u> vocabulary knowledge, so they must make use of context clues to ❹ <u>inference</u> the meaning of any unknown words they will encounter. Unfortunately, it is the second language readers' very limited vocabulary knowledge that hinders their being ❺ <u>ability</u> to make ❻ <u>fully</u> use of context clues as well. In other words, ❼ <u>compared</u> to first-language readers, second-language readers' lack of vocabulary ❽ <u>know</u> forces them to guess word meanings more often; however, this very lack of vocabulary knowledge also ❾ <u>severe</u> limits second-language readers' ability to make use of context clues for guessing. One solution, then, would be to teach second language readers a ❿ <u>sufficiently</u> number of vocabulary items. The bottom line is that knowing more vocabulary can certainly improve their reading ability.

EXERCISE 20. Reading Practice: Global Warming

Read this essay about global warming, and then answer the comprehension questions that follow. The grammar from this unit, words with the same base but various suffixes, is underlined for you. Use your dictionary for words that you do not understand.

Global Warming Is Happening Now

Our changing climate is affecting how planet Earth looks. Global warming is causing dramatic changes in weather patterns, including the frequency and severity of storms, cold, heat, and drought. In turn, these changes result in differences in coastlines, mountain ranges, forestation, etc. At the North and South Poles, glaciers are receding, icebergs are breaking away, and habitats are changing—all because of global warming.

Glaciers, huge masses of ice and snow, are formed in areas where it snows heavily and summers are too brief for it to melt. Year after year, the snow and ice

accumulate. After deep accumulation, the bottom layers of heavy snow turn into solid ice; eventually, with the pull of gravity, the ice begins flowing. The face of the glacier advances when more snow and ice accumulate than melt, and it retreats when the opposite occurs: when more snow and ice melt than accumulate. When melting equals accumulation, it remains stationary. Whichever happens, advancing or retreating, glacial ice continues to descend because of gravitational pull. When a glacier flow reaches the sea, enormous blocks of ice break off and become floating icebergs.

In southeast Alaska, massive walls of ice rise majestically above the icy waters of Glacier Bay. Scientists called glaciologists study glaciers and compare historical data about their movement. In recent years, satellite images of the Columbia Glacier have shown it receding fairly consistently at about 80 feet a day, revealing clues about global warming.

Global warming is happening right now. To alleviate its negative effects, we all need to take a stand and have a <u>conscious</u> willingness to be <u>contributors</u> to solutions since we have all <u>unconsciously</u> <u>contributed</u> to the problems.

1. According to what the author writes (not what you know), describe the ways that our weather is changing. Complete this sentence (pay attention to word forms):

   Recently, our weather _____

   _____

2. What is a glacier? _____

   _____

3. What causes a glacier to recede?

   _____

   _____

4. Is *receding* a synonym for *retreating*? What do these words mean?

   _____

5. Who has reported that the Columbia Glacier is receding?

   _____

6. Some people do not believe global warming is happening. Look on the Internet for one reason to support these people's beliefs. Write that reason here.

   _____

   _____

7. Do you believe global warming is real? Discuss your reasons in class.

EXERCISE 21. Vocabulary Practice: Word Knowledge

Circle the answer choice that is most closely related to the vocabulary on the left. Use a dictionary to check the meaning of words you do not know.

Vocabulary	Answer Choices	
1. competent	capable	polite
2. go on the market	for a long time	for sale
3. remind	remember	visualize
4. a legend	a movie	a story
5. apology	I'm late	I'm sorry
6. descend	go down	go up
7. a plumber	for the bathroom	for the classroom
8. drought	no air	no water
9. brief	important	short
10. obviously	clearly	loudly
11. laundry	clothing	furniture
12. a buddy	a friend	a server
13. risky	beautiful	dangerous
14. severe	very bad	very good
15. magnify	larger	smaller
16. clarify	make clear	make heavy
17. spooky	I am afraid	I am asleep
18. drown	in air	in water
19. donate	find	give
20. devious	negative	positive
21. massive	huge	tiny
22. collide	hit	turn
23. urgent	very important	very interesting
24. accumulate	collect things	destroy things
25. hinder	negative	positive

EXERCISE 22. Vocabulary Practice: Collocations

Fill in each blank with the answer on the right that most naturally completes the phrase on the left. If necessary, use a dictionary to check the meaning of words you do not know.

Vocabulary	Answer Choices	
1. _____ a footprint	exit	leave
2. for several _____	hour	hours
3. _____ talent	article	genuine
4. participate _____ something	by	in
5. have confidence _____	of	in
6. the decision is in your _____	hands	mind
7. _____ a different opinion	have	think
8. a _____ discovery	recent	soon
9. a _____ variety of	narrow	wide
10. It's _____ fun	a lot of	much
11. a buddy _____	class	system
12. have an argument _____ something	over	under
13. an exhaustive _____ of places	job	list
14. a passionate and zealous _____	baby	fan
15. a _____ event	frightened	frightening
16. _____ clothing	appropriate	bored
17. I just _____ my bill	earned	received
18. succeed _____ doing something good	in	on
19. _____ does it look like?	How	What
20. prevent our baby _____ catching a cold	from	with
21. Which department do you work _____?	in	on
22. _____ a mile	with	within
23. a reversible _____	shirt	sport
24. financial _____	aid	kitchen
25. encourage you _____ something	to do	doing
26. a blend of _____	colors	pages

EXERCISE 23. Writing Practice: Describing the Best Skiing

Part 1. Editing Student Writing

Read these sentences about one student's opinion about growing up near a ski slope. Circle the 15 errors. Then write the number of the sentence with the error next to the type of error. (Some sentences have more than one error.)

_____ a. missing *a/an*

_____ b. incorrect or missing *–ly* ending

_____ c. missing verb

_____ d. incorrect or missing noun ending

_____ e. incorrect or missing adjective ending

The Best of Skiing
1. Snow skiing is a physical demanding sport.
2. It also financially demanding because skiing for one or two days can be quite expensive.
3. A ski resort within an hour's drive of your home is one importantly factor that increases the accessible of this sport.
4. The chances of your becoming great skier are much better if you learn during your youngness.
5. Additionally, an avid skier thrives on fresh snow, and it must snow frequently in order to prevent danger conditions from developing.
6. What if you take your long-awaited annually vacation to upscale resort only to find unfavorable conditions?
7. You would probably stay in the lodge and rest near warm fireplace.
8. I was one of those luck kids who got to ski nearly every weekend on pristine mountain in the Rockies.
9. My favorite month March because the frigid storms had passed, the crowds were gone, the lift-lines were short, the snow was ideal, and the sun shone warmly on my face.
10. I remember skiing effortlessly down the slope on the softly white sugary snow, hearing nothing but the gentle whooshing sound of my skis beneath me and feeling nothing but the warm of the sun on my face.

Part 2. Original Student Writing

Situation: You are writing a script for a movie. Who are the two main characters? What is the setting? Summarize the plot. Think about your five senses. Then describe the two characters in as much detail as you can. Use a variety of nouns, verbs, and adjectives with suffixes that you have been learning. Underline each new word so the teacher can see what you are trying to practice.

Unit **3**

Past Perfect Tense

Discover the Grammar

Read the passage about a family vacation. Then answer the questions that follow.

Line	
1	Two years ago, my family went on a fishing vacation in the Bahamas. I have
2	two friends who consider themselves experts at fishing, but the truth is that they
3	hardly ever catch anything. I just wanted to get out of Denver's cold winter
4	weather, but my friends had only one thing in mind: to catch the biggest fish!
5	Our flight from Denver left around 6 AM, so by the time we arrived at our
6	hotel in Nassau, we had been awake for almost 20 hours. Since it was already
7	dark, we weren't able to see much of the islands. The trip had worn us out, so
8	we went to bed as soon as we got into our rooms.
9	The next morning we all met for breakfast at 8:00 AM as we had agreed to
10	do the night before. Unfortunately, we were all in a bad mood. We were tired
11	because thunder had woken us up throughout the night as severe storms passed
12	through the islands. When we got our breakfast, we were thrilled to see our

13 | plates full of exotic tropical fruit, including mangos, papaya, and starfruit.
14 | Though I had seen a mango in the supermarket, I had never eaten one! It was
15 | delicious! After breakfast, the overall mood of our little group improved
16 | substantially.
17 | Happy and content, we all went down to where the boats were to meet our
18 | fishing guide. He thoroughly explained all the equipment, where we would be
19 | fishing, and what to do in case of an emergency. After the guide had explained
20 | everything, we put on our life jackets and found our places on the boat. The
21 | guide started the boat, and we sailed away.
22 | Some of us just sat staring at the amazing blue-green water, but Ned
23 | and Pete wasted no time in getting ready to fish. I had never seen them so
24 | intent or so focused before. In fact, they spent the next three hours fishing
25 | while everyone else was enjoying the ocean scenery and retelling old family
26 | stories. I had never seen my uncles so happy!
27 | For most of us, the trip was beautiful because of the scenery, and we'll
28 | always remember this great day. However, this story had a very surprising
29 | ending for one of my friends. Just as the guide announced that it was time to
30 | head back to the marina, my fishing pole bent sharply, and the guide
31 | shouted, "I've caught something! It's the big one!" Well, to make a long story
32 | short, my Ned had caught a twenty-pound wahoo, which is a kind of fish
33 | that many people want to catch in the Bahamas. From the smile on my uncle's
34 | face, this was surely the best vacation he had ever had!

1. Find the 11 examples of *had* + past participle. Write the line number, and then copy the subject and the verb phrase here.

Line	Subject	*had*	Past Participle

2. Why do you think the writer uses *explained* in Line 18 and not *had explained*?

_____

_____

3. Why do you think the writer uses *went* in Line 1 and not *had gone*?

_____

_____

4. Can you explain the use of *had ever had* in Line 34? Some students think *had had* is a mistake, but it is correct English.

_____

_____

5. The combination of *had* + past participle is called past perfect tense. Have you ever studied this tense? What do you know about it? What questions do you have?

_____

_____

_____

Grammar Lesson

KEY 3

Past Perfect Tense

Examples	Subject	*had*	Past Participle
Had you ever **seen** snow before you moved to Montreal?	you	had	seen
I **had been** on a plane only once before that day.	I	had	been
He was nervous because he **had** never **gone** to a job interview.	he	had	gone
Last summer Ashley took a course online. It was the first online course that she **had** ever **taken**.	she	had	taken
I failed the test even though I knew the material. It **hadn't made** any sense at the time, but now I know why it happened.	it	had	made
Jeff claimed that we **had taken** his keys, but this was not true.	we	had	taken
Growing up, they **had had** a very hard life.	they	had	had

<u>Rule 1</u>. In past perfect tense, a verb has one form: **had + PAST PARTICIPLE**.

<u>Rule 2</u>. The past participle of a regular verb is the same as the simple past tense form. If the verb is one syllable and ends in **consonant + vowel + consonant** (c-v-c), we double the final consonant before adding **–ed**. We do the same for a two-syllable verb if it ends in **consonant + vowel + consonant** (c-v-c) and the pronunciation stress is on the second syllable:

open → ope<u>n</u>ed	occur → occu<u>rr</u>ed
(o) pen	oc **(cur)**
[1st] 2nd	1st [2nd]
because we stress the 1st syllable	because we stress the 2nd syllable

Rule 3. The past participle of an irregular verb is impossible to predict. There are some irregular verbs with similar past participles, so you should try to learn these verbs in their groups. For example, some verbs do not change (*put, put, put*), some change *–d* to *–t* (*send, sent, sent*), and others change a vowel in the middle (*sing, sang, sung*). Studying these patterns can help you learn these verbs better. (See Appendix C.)

Rule 4. Past perfect tense has a few distinct usages. Three common usages include:

a. a past action that occurred before another past action or time (*I* **had traveled** *to France* **before** *I flew to Japan*).

b. an action that started in the past and continued until another action or event (*I* **had lived** *in New York for ten years* **before** *I decided to leave*).

c. a past action in a sentence with **if** or **wish** (**If I had studied, I would have made a better score. I wish I had studied more!**) (More information on this usage is presented in Unit 4.)

Rule 5. Common time expressions for past perfect tense include *after, already, before, by the time, ever, just, never, once, until, (not) yet*.

Rule 6. To make a negative statement, add **not** after **had**. (*We had not gone to the bank yet*.) In informal English, it is possible to use the contraction **hadn't**.

Rule 7. The question form is **had + SUBJECT+ PAST PARTICIPLE** (*Had you ever gone to that particular branch of that bank before then?*). In other words, you invert the **SUBJECT** and **had**.

Rule 8. To answer a yes-no question, use **had** for a short affirmative answer and **had not** (**hadn't**) for a short negative answer: *Yes, we had*. OR *No, we hadn't*.

 BE CAREFUL!

Common Learner Errors	Explanation
1. I went to China in 2011, but that was not my first trip to Asia. I ~~traveled~~ **had traveled** to Japan in 2009.	Use past perfect to talk about an action that happened before another action or event.
2. The flight ~~taken~~ **had taken** off by the time I got to the gate.	Remember to use **had** with the past participle.
3. By the time the teacher said, "Pens down," I ~~didn't have~~ **hadn't** finished all of the questions.	Do not use **didn't** to form the negative in past perfect tense.
4. ~~Did you have~~ **Had you** received any letters from Jacob in the months prior to his visit?	Do not use **did** in the question form in past perfect tense.

EXERCISE 1. Affirmative Past Perfect

Fill in the blanks with the correct forms of the verbs. The first one has been done for you as an example..

	work		*take*
I	had worked	I	_____
you	_____	you	_____
he	_____	he	_____
she	_____	she	_____
it	_____	it	_____
we	_____	we	_____
they	_____	they	_____
Jo	_____	Jo	_____
Jo and I	_____	Jo and I	_____

EXERCISE 2. Which Action Started First?

Each sentence has two verbs. Circle the two verbs, and then write a check mark (✔) by the action that happened first. If the two actions happened at the same time or if you cannot tell which started first, mark the third answer. The first one has been done for you as an example.

1a. When my plane (landed), the movie (had finished).

_____ land   ✔ finish   _____ at the same time or we don't know

1b. The movie had finished when my plane landed.

_____ land   _____ finish   _____ at the same time or we don't know

2a. When my plane landed, the movie finished.

_____ land   _____ finish   _____ at the same time or we don't know

2b. The movie finished when my plane landed.

_____ land   _____ finish   _____ at the same time or we don't know

3a. The game had started when the president arrived.

_____ start   _____ arrive   _____ at the same time or we
                                             don't know

3b. When the president arrived, the game had started.

_____ start   _____ arrive   _____ at the same time or we
                                             don't know

4a. The game started when the president arrived.

_____ start   _____ arrive   _____ at the same time or we
                                             don't know

4b. When the president arrived, the game started.

_____ start   _____ arrive   _____ at the same time or we
                                             don't know

EXERCISE 3. Question Form of Past Perfect

Change the sentences into questions using the past perfect. Substitute *wh-* questions for the underlined word/words.

1. Linda had made her Christmas candy <u>by November 15th</u>.

   Question: _____

2. Kumiko had seen the movie <u>twice</u> before she read the book.

   Question: _____

3. Miki had lived in <u>Idaho</u> before she moved to Tampa.

   Question: _____

4. Serhat had spent <u>14 hours</u> working on his class project before it was completed.

   Question: _____

5. Caroline had studied <u>medicine</u> before she got her MBA.

   Question: _____

ONE-MINUTE LESSON

on vs. in. In English, we **work on** something such as a project or assignment: *I'm working on my homework.* A common error is to use the preposition *in.*

Do Online Exercise 3.1. My score: _____/10. _____% correct.

Connecting Grammar and Vocabulary

Thousands of verbs could be used in the past perfect tense, but you should focus your time on learning the most commonly used verbs in past perfect tense. Study this list of common verbs for past perfect tense.

8 Frequent Verbs in Past Perfect Tense			
1. had been	3. had come	5. had taken	7. had left
2. had gone	4. had made	6. had done	8. had had

NOTE: These verbs occur with the past perfect more than 40 times per million in conversation, fiction, news, and academic prose.

Source: Biber, D., et al. (1999). *Longman Grammar of Spoken and Written English.* London: Longman.

EXERCISE 4. Studying Grammar and Vocabulary from Real English

Do a search on the Internet for four of the eight most common past perfect verbs. (For example, search for *had been* or *had gone*.) Copy the sentences here. Circle the past perfect verbs in your examples. You may work with a partner. Share your answers with the class.

1. _____

   _____

2. _____

   _____

3. _____

   _____

4. _____

   _____

 # Grammar Lesson

Past Perfect Progressive Tense

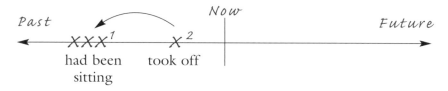

Examples	Subject	*had been*	VERB + –ing
We **had been sitting** on the plane an hour before we finally took off.	We	had been	sitting
How long **had** you **been living** in Miami before you met your husband there?	you	had been	living
By the time I woke up, it **had been raining** for several hours.	it	had been	raining

<u>Rule 1</u>. In past perfect progressive tense, a verb has one form: **had been** + **VERB** + **–ing.**

<u>Rule 2.</u> Use past perfect progressive tense (instead of past perfect tense) to emphasize the duration of an action.

<u>Rule 3.</u> Use past perfect progressive tense with action verbs like *talk, use,* and *help.* Do not use this tense with verbs that do not show an action. Four kinds of verbs that do not usually occur in past perfect progressive tense are: senses (*hear, see, smell, feel, sound*), emotions (*like, love, need, prefer, want*), mental states (*believe, forget, remember, seem, think*), and possession (*belong, have, own, possess*).

<u>Rule 4.</u> For verbs that end in –e, drop the final –e before adding –ing: take → taking

<u>Rule 5.</u> If a one-syllable verb ends in **consonant + vowel + consonant** (c-v-c), double the final consonant before adding –ing: **cut** → **cutting** (but **read** → **reading**).

<u>Rule 6.</u> If a two-syllable verb ends in **consonant + vowel + consonant** (c-v-c), we double the final consonant before adding **–ing** if the pronunciation stress is on the second syllable:

open → ope<u>n</u>ing	occur → occu<u>rr</u>ing
(o) pen	oc (**cur**)
[1st] 2nd	1st [2nd]
because we stress the 1st syllable	because we stress the 2nd syllable

BE CAREFUL!

Common Learner Errors	Explanation
1. Madison hadn't ~~been hearing~~ **heard** that song in ages.	Do not use the progressive form of past perfect with **non-action** verbs.
2. Jacob had ~~been playing~~ **played** tennis only twice before today.	Do not use the progressive form of the past perfect with actions that are **repeated** a given number of times.
3. Zachary ~~had driving~~ **had been driving** a pickup truck until his mother gave him a car.	You must use a form of **be** (**been**) with past perfect progressive tense.
4. Isabella had been ~~wait~~ **waiting** for the bus for 30 minutes when she decided to call a taxi.	You must use **–ing** with past perfect progressive tense.

EXERCISE 5. Production of Past Perfect Progressive

Use past perfect progressive tense to write a sentence about an event that was happening before another event you can think of. The first one has been done for you as an example.

1. (texting) _I had been texting before I came to class._

2. (driving) _____

_____

3. (eating) _____

_____

4. (talking on the phone) _____

_____

5. (cutting onions) _____

_____

6. (studying) _____

_____

EXERCISE 6. Negative Form of Past Perfect and Past Perfect Progressive

Write these statements or questions in the *negative* form with the past perfect or past perfect progressive verb in parentheses. The first one has been done for you as an example. Sometimes more than one tense is possible.

1. When Mom came in the door, she knew that Dad (cook).

   When Mom came in the door, she knew that Dad hadn't been cooking.

2. I went skiing yesterday, but I (be) on skis since 2004.

   _____

3. Dave and Linda (date) very long when they got married.

   _____

4. Brenda told the veterinarian that her cat (eat) for several days.

   _____

5. On his way to work, Ray suddenly remembered that he (turn off) the coffee maker.

   _____

EXERCISE 7. Time Connectors

Combine the sentences with the word in parentheses. Change one of the verbs to **past perfect** or **past perfect progressive** in order to make the sentence logical. The first one has been done for you as an example.

1. Gary photographed the whale (1st). (**before**) It dove under the water (2nd).

   Gary had photographed the whale

   before it dove under the water.

2. The children already ate (1st). (**when**) Their father came home (2nd).

   _____

3. The girls were tired (2nd). (**because**) They were working all morning (1st.)

   _____

4. The baby was sick for two days (1st). (**before**) Kerri and John both decided to stay home (2nd).

   _____

5. Sally never used the Internet (1st). (**until**) Sam taught her how (2nd).

_____

6. I read four great books (1st). (**by the time**) My vacation ended (2nd).

_____

Do Online Exercise 3.2. My score: _____ /10. _____ % correct.

EXERCISE 8. Sentence Study for Critical Reading

Read the numbered sentences. Then read the answer choices and put a check mark (✔) in the yes or no boxes in front of each sentence to show if that answer is true based on the information in the original sentence. If there is not enough information to mark something as yes, then mark it as no. Remember that more than one true answer may be possible.

1. Emily had visited Rome before she got married, so she and her new husband decided to go to Venice on their honeymoon.

   ☐ yes ☐ no a. Emily got married before she went to Rome.

   ☐ yes ☐ no b. Emily got married after she went to Rome.

   ☐ yes ☐ no c. Emily got married before she went to Venice.

2. George and Jorge had never been on a hot-air balloon ride before yesterday. They had been discussing it last summer when they saw a TV commercial about a special offer on a four-hour ride. They had made a reservation at that time, and yesterday their dreams came true.

   ☐ yes ☐ no a. The balloon ride took place yesterday.

   ☐ yes ☐ no b. The balloon ride took place last summer.

   ☐ yes ☐ no c. George and Jorge's ride was shown on TV.

3. Before the bell rang, Joan and Melissa had been arguing in the hallway. Professor Spencer had to intervene and then the bell rang.

   ☐ yes ☐ no a. Professor Spencer was arguing with Joan and Melissa.

   ☐ yes ☐ no b. Joan and Melissa stopped arguing when they saw Professor Spencer.

   ☐ yes ☐ no c. Joan and Melissa were not arguing when they went into the classroom.

4. When Grandma Lillian reached her 16th birthday, she had been sewing, knitting, and crocheting for almost ten years. It was then that she became an apprentice to the town tailor and eventually replaced him when he retired.

[yes] [no]   a. The town tailor was Grandma Lillian's apprentice.

[yes] [no]   b. Grandma Lillian learned to sew when she was a six-year-old girl.

[yes] [no]   c. Grandma Lillian was the town tailor.

5. I had washed my clothes and left them in the washer overnight. When we were having our morning coffee, a weird odor wafted in from the laundry room.

[yes] [no]   a. We were drinking coffee and smelling something odd at the same time.

[yes] [no]   b. I was washing clothes and drinking coffee at the same time.

[yes] [no]   c. I washed my clothes before I smelled something strange.

EXERCISE 9. Speaking Activity: Are You Pulling My Leg?

Step 1: On the lines provided, write six sentences using a past perfect verb with a time expression as used in the examples. Write three sentences about yourself that are TRUE and three sentences that are NOT TRUE.

Step 2. Work with a partner. Don't let your partner see your sentences. Student A will read one of his/her sentences, and Student B will guess if the sentence is TRUE or NOT TRUE (*You're pulling my leg!*). If B's guess is correct, Student A will mark the sentence ✔. If B's guess is incorrect, Student A will mark the sentence X.

Step 3. Student B reads a sentence and Student A will guess if the sentence is true or not. As in Step 2, Student B will mark A's guess as correct ✔ or incorrect X.

Step 4. Students A and B continue taking turns until all sentences have been read. Count the total number of guesses marked correct ✔. The student with the most correct guesses wins.

NOTE: When selecting a sentence to read, it is important to mix the order in which they were written.

Examples: *By age six, I had learned to ride a bike.*
             I had already traveled on five continents by the time I was sixteen.

                                                                          ✔ or **X**

TRUE   _____. _____

TRUE   _____. _____

TRUE   _____. _____

NOT TRUE _____. _____

NOT TRUE _____. _____

NOT TRUE _____. _____

EXERCISE 10. Simple Past and Past Perfect in Context

Complete the sentences with the correct form of the verb in parentheses. Use past perfect or simple past as needed.

Urashima: A Japanese Folktale

Once upon a time, a young fisherman named Urashima rescued a turtle from some boys who were teasing and hitting her with sticks. Then one day while he was fishing, the turtle swam up to his boat and said, "Urashima, you saved my life; now I have a reward for you. Please, get on my back." Urashima was surprised, but he (get) ❶ _____ on the turtle's back as she (request) ❷ _____.

The turtle dove under the water and took Urashima to a dazzling palace where he met an elegant princess. She prepared a delicious banquet for him, and together they were entertained by a host of colorful fish dancing to beautiful music. Soon he (begin) ❸ _____ to wonder how long he (be) ❹ _____ away from home.

"I need to go home now," he told the princess. She didn't want him to leave, but she complied with his wish. The turtle took Urashima back to the beach where he lived. However, things seemed different to Urashima. His house (stand) ❺ _____ near the hill, but now nothing (be) ❻ _____ there. He saw an old woman and asked her if she (know) ❼ _____ what (happen) ❽ _____ to Urashima's house. She answered, "A young man named Urashima (live) ❾ _____ in this town 100 years ago. One day he went fishing and (never come back) ❿ _____."

Urashima was very distressed. Then he remembered that he had a pearl-covered box that the princess (gave) ⓫ _____ him before he (leave) ⓬ _____ the palace. She (tell) ⓭ _____ him not to open it unless he (need) ❶❹ _____ help. Urashima sat

down and opened the box. A mysterious white cloud came out of the box, and

suddenly Urashima turned into a white crane. As he (fly) ❶❺ _____

away, he looked down and saw the turtle looking up.

EXERCISE 11. Mini-Conversations

Circle the correct words in these mini-conversations.

1. A Hey, did you know that Muhammed Ali (had won, had winned) a gold medal
   in the 1960 Olympics before he (turned, turns) professional?

   B: No, I had no idea!

2. A: (Had Julia Roberts ever received, Had ever Julia Roberts received) an Academy Award before she (had been starring, starred) in *Erin Brockovich*?

   B: No. That was her first Academy Award even though she (had had, has had)
   several hit movies prior to her role as Erin Brockovich.

3. A: Did you ever find your wallet?

   B: Yes! I thought I (had lost, was losing) it, but it was in my purse all along.

4. A: Why did you take the bus everywhere when you were on vacation?

   B: Well, that is something that we (have always, had always) done on all our trips.

5. A: (Had you visited, Are you visiting) Japan before you moved to Tokyo?

   B: Yes, twice. I fell in love with the culture at first sight and knew at once that I
   really wanted to study there.

Do Online Exercise 3.3. My score: _____ /10. _____ % correct.

EXERCISE 12. Review Test 1: Multiple Choice

Circle the letter of the correct answer.

1. Unfortunately, by the time the plane started to land, the movie _____ so the passengers were not able to see how the movie ended.

   a. had not finished   b. was not finishing   c. did not finish   d. had not finishing

2. Millions of years ago, huge animals called dinosaurs _____ in certain areas of the world.

   a. lived   b. living   c. had lived   d. had been living

3. The teacher asked Jill to be quiet. Jill kept on talking. When the teacher asked Jill for the third time to be quiet, he _____ enough. He asked her to leave the room. Jill was quite embarrassed, but she gathered her books, stood up, and left the room.

   a. had   b. was having   c. had had   d. had been having

4. In 2011, Giles went to Germany and Belgium. He _____ to either of these countries before, so he didn't know what to expect.

   a. had not gone   c. did not go
   b. was not going   d. had not been going

5. In 1500, sailors _____ Holland, Spain, and Portugal in order to search for spices on the other side of the globe.

   a. left   b. leave   c. had left   d. had been leaving

6. When Steve Fossett began his solo balloon flight around the world, he _____ that he would encounter 10 days of thunderstorms over Argentina. Consequently, his balloon was damaged, and he was forced to end his trip.

   a. was anticipating   c. hadn't anticipate
   b. had anticipated not   d. had not anticipated

7. In March 1999, Bertrand Piccard and Brian Jones _____ the first round-the-world trip in a balloon.

   a. had made   c. had been making
   b. made   d. were making

8. Alexander Graham Bell _____ on a multiple telegraph system for several years when he coincidentally discovered that the sound of a human voice could be transmitted as an electrical impulse through wires.

   a. worked   c. had been working
   b. has been working   d. had worked

EXERCISE 13. Review Test 2: Production and Evaluation

Part 1.
Read this short passage. Underline the correct form of the verb in parentheses.

My Son's Clean Room

For the past six months, I ❶ (am having, have had) a difficult time getting my teenaged son to clean his room. While I ❷ (have tried, am trying) taking away his cell phone until his room is clean, he still ❸ (won't clean, wasn't cleaning) it! I thought that I ❹ (had tried, have tried) everything to convince him to clean his room, and then I ❺ (was seeing, saw) a funny post on a parenting website. A mother ❻ (had leaving, was leaving) town for the weekend and ❼ (left, leaves) her son a note that said, "I ❽ (was hiding, hid) $100 in your room for groceries. Clean your room, and you will find it. Love, Mom."

Part 2.
Read each sentence carefully. Look at the underlined verbs. If the underlined part is correct, circle the word *correct*. If it is wrong, circle the word *wrong.* Then write the correction above.

correct   wrong   1. How long have you been waiting by the time the plumber arrived?

correct   wrong   2. The Civil Rights Act brought equality to African Americans who had been struggled with the problems of segregation and discrimination for over 100 years.

correct   wrong   3. June hadn't studied for the test, yet she passed it.

correct   wrong   4. Christopher Columbus had originally thought that he could sail west to reach Asia; instead, he had found the Americas.

 ONE-MINUTE LESSON
The expression **have a difficult time** is followed by a gerund: *I had a difficult time reading this book.* A gerund is also used with any adjective and the word **time**: *have a hard time driving, have a good time traveling, have a fun time visiting.*

EXERCISE 14. Reading Practice: A Letter of Congratulations

Read this letter of congratulations. Then complete the questions that follow. The grammar from this unit is underlined for you.

Dear Rita,

　　Congratulations on the birth of your beautiful new daughters. I <u>hadn't realized</u> you were pregnant. <u>Had I known</u>, I certainly would have said something. I <u>had left</u> a message on your voicemail about a week ago, but I never heard back from you. I can still remember your other children's births five and six years ago. How time flies! Please give them a hug and a kiss from me. I hope to see you and Jim out and about soon with all your children.

　　　　　　　　　　　　Sincerely,

　　　　　　　　　　　　Karen

---

1. Who is congratulating whom? For what reason?

   _____

   _____

2. What season do you think it is? Is there any clue?

   _____

   _____

3. What happened to the message that Karen had left?

   _____

4. Can you explain the meaning of the phrase *How time flies?*

   _____

   _____

5. How many children do Rita and Jim have? What do you base your answer on?

   _____

   _____

EXERCISE 15. Vocabulary Practice: Word Knowledge

Circle the answer choice that is most closely related to the vocabulary on the left. Use a dictionary to check the meaning of words you do not know.

Vocabulary	Answer Choices	
1. thrilled	happy	upset
2. substantially	a little	a lot
3. stare	hear	look
4. marina	an accident	some boats
5. odd	average	strange
6. consequently	although	therefore
7. comply	ask questions	follow directions
8. the flight took off at 2	it started at 2	it ended at 2
9. thoroughly	completely	slowly
10. your overall feeling	your general feeling	your specific feeling
11. previous	after	before
12. nap	eat	sleep
13. a veterinarian	for animals	for cars
14. a whale	on a mountain	in an ocean
15. a struggle	a fight	a team
16. take place	happen	steal
17. argue	disagree	discover
18. a tailor	clothes	computers
19. dive	above a map	into the water
20. an odor	a bad smell	a good smell
21. a continent	a large area of land	a small area of land
22. an interview	to get a job	to buy a computer
23. duration	a period of time	a length of distance
24. a banquet	food	information
25. at once	right away	right here

EXERCISE 16. Vocabulary Practice: Collocations

Fill in each blank with the answer on the right that most naturally completes the phrase on the left. If necessary, use a dictionary to check the meaning of words you do not know.

Vocabulary	Answer Choices	
1. an expert _____ cutting onions quickly	at	to
2. hardly _____	ever	never
3. have one thing in _____	heart	mind
4. the trip _____ me out	found	wore
5. severe _____	money	weather
6. to make a long _____ short	lesson	story
7. grow _____	down	up
8. _____ a search	do	make
9. the best night _____ there	go	go/to go
10. in _____	age	ages
11. a pickup _____	train	truck
12. to pick _____	apples	negative
13. women's _____	lefts	rights
14. a _____ offer	sometimes	special
15. _____ summer	ago	last
16. _____ a reservation	do	make
17. enroll in a _____	book	class
18. _____ an award	improve	receive
19. a _____ cookies	box	dozen
20. _____ their honeymoon	at	on
21. rescue _____	a new house	a young cat
22. _____ a trip	do	make
23. the _____ of a human voice	electricity	sound
24. over 100 _____	year	years
25. _____ in love	fall	take

EXERCISE 17. Writing Practice: Writing about a Good Event in Your Life

Part 1. Editing Student Writing

Read these sentences about something good that happened to someone. Circle the 15 errors. Then write the number of the sentence with the error next to the type of error. (Some sentences have more than one error.)

_____ a. singular-plural   _____ d. subject-verb agreement

_____ b. verb tense   _____ e. preposition

_____ c. word order   _____ f. missing *a* or *an*

An Amazing Accomplishment
1. When people think in the word *accomplishment*, they often thought of really big things such as graduating from college or getting their first job.
2. I agree that these two is certainly very important accomplishments.
3. However, I am going to write about a different kind for accomplishment.
4. Last month I bought lottery ticket for one dollar, and my ticket won.
5. I did not win the grand prize of one million dollar.
6. Instead, I have won five thousand dollars because my ticket had five of the six winning numbers.
7. When I realized I had a winning ticket, I knew at once what should I do.
8. I called the office lottery and gave them my information.
9. I take the ticket to the store where I had bought it, and then I filled out special form.
10. I knew exactly what to do because I had won the lottery before once.
11. About ten years ago, I won two hundred dollars because I guessed three of the six lottery number correctly.
12. All of my friend say that I am the luckiest person they knew, and I think they may be correct because of these two accomplishments.

Part 2. Original Student Writing

Situation: You have just won an Olympic medal, and a magazine has asked you to write a short article that tells your story. (Choose any sport.) Use these questions to help write your article: When did you first become interested in the sport? How had you become interested in it? How many years had you participated before you decided to compete with the goal to make the Olympics? How long had you practiced before you made the Olympic team? What was your best event? Who was your top rival? In what city were the Olympics held? Add any other details that you need in order to make this story interesting. Write approximately 500 words.

Be sure to practice simple past, past perfect, and past perfect progressive verbs. For example, your paper might include sentences such as *I* <u>had been dreaming</u> *about the Olympics for years when I finally met my idol, the man who coached Michael Phelps.* Underline the grammar points that you have used so the teacher can see what you are trying to practice.

Unit 4

Conditionals:
If Clauses and *Wish*

 ## Discover the Grammar

Janice and Kurt are planning their upcoming vacation. Read this passage, and then answer the questions that follow.

Line	
1	For each of the past eight years, Janice and Kurt have spent their vacation
2	time at home, either working in the garden or fixing up the house. This year,
3	however, they are planning to spend their July vacation somewhere else.
4	They've checked the Internet for weather information about areas of the
5	country they might like to visit. They are really eager to travel somewhere
6	soon. In fact, if they had free time right now, they would take their vacation
7	immediately, but they can't leave right now. They still have a couple of
8	months to explore their options.
9	So far, they have learned the following information. If they want to spend
10	their time near the water, they will have a hard time choosing among dozens of
11	outstanding beach resorts. For example, if they go to the beach in Atlantic City,
12	New Jersey, the air temperature will be in the mid-70s in July, and the water
13	temperature will be in the low 70s. That's very appealing to them. On the

74

14	other hand, if they chose to visit Miami Beach in July, both the air and the
15	water temperatures would be considerably warmer, around 85 degrees. That
16	sounds wonderful to them, too. Janice and Kurt also like to go camping, so
17	vacationing in the mountains is another option. They could choose to visit
18	the Rocky Mountains in Colorado if they wanted cooler weather. In July, the
19	temperature in the mountains can range from a high of 80 degrees to a low
20	of 40 degrees. If they go to the Rockies, they will certainly have to plan for
21	this type of weather variation.
22	It is without a doubt a tough decision that Janice and Kurt are facing. They
23	wish they were able to go to all of the places they have researched. If they had
24	more money and more time, they would be able to do exactly that. In fact, they
25	would have gone to both the beach and the mountains this year if they hadn't
26	recently spent so much of their savings on a new big-screen TV. They wish they
27	had realized this earlier!

1. Circle the eight examples of *if* and the two examples of *wish* in the passage.

2. Write the line numbers of the four *if* clauses that have simple past tense verbs. Write the subject-verb combinations from both the *if* clause and the main clause. The first one has been done for you as an example.

Lines	*if* Clauses	Main Clause
6	If they had . . .	they would take . . .

3. All four of these sentences are talking about the present time. What do you notice about the verbs in the *if* clause and in the main clause? Do you see any present tense verbs?

_____

_____

_____

4. Write the line numbers of the three *if* clauses that have simple present tense verbs. Write the subject-verb combinations from both the *if* clause and the main clause.

Line	*if* Clauses	Main Clause

5. All three of these sentences are talking about the future time. What do you notice about the verbs in the *if* clause and in the main clause? Do you see any future tense?

_____

_____

_____

6. Find the one *if* clause with past perfect tense. What time is this sentence talking about? _____

   What is the verb in the main clause? _____

7. Find the two examples of *wish*. Are the verbs after *wish* talking about present or past time? What tense are they?

Line	Verb after *wish*	Tense	Time

8. What questions do you have about this grammar?

_____

_____

 **Grammar Lesson**

Real Conditionals in the Present or Future

A conditional sentence expresses the idea that the action in the main clause (the result clause) can only happen when a certain condition (the clause that begins with **if**) is fulfilled. The **if** clause states the condition, and the main clause states the result.

Real Condition *If* Clause	Result or Main Clause	Meaning
If the weather **changes** suddenly, **simple present tense**	I **get** a headache. **simple present tense**	factual
If it **snows** a lot tonight, **simple present tense**	they **will call off** school tomorrow. **future tense**	certainty/ prediction for the future
If you **have** time, **simple present tense**	you **should visit** the local museum. **modal + VERB**	advice/ suggestion/ warning for the future
If it **rains**, **simple present tense**	**don't open** the windows. **imperative**	instructions for the future

<u>Rule 1</u>. Real conditions express situations that can happen in the present or future. They are often used when **stating facts, general knowledge, habits, predictions, advice, or instructions.**

<u>Rule 2</u>. Real conditions in the **present (factual)** use the simple present tense form of the verb in both the **if** clause and the result.

<u>Rule 3</u>. Real conditions in the **future (real possibility)** use the simple present tense form of the verb in the **if** clause + **modal or modal phrase** *(should/can/could/may/might, will, be going to, have to)* and the base form of the verb or the imperative in the result clause.

<u>Rule 4.</u> **Negative forms** of the verb can be used in the condition or result clause or both.

BE CAREFUL!

Common Learner Errors	Explanation
1. If it ~~will rain~~ **rains** tonight, I will call you for a ride home.	Do not use **will** or **be going to** in the **if** clause.
2. Tornadoes can cause severe damage to ~~a building, if~~ **a building if** they touch down.	Do not use a comma after the result clause. Use a comma after the **if** clause.

EXERCISE 1. Real Conditions in the Present or Future

Circle the real conditions from the list of items from a gardening pamphlet.

Five Sage Suggestions for Gardeners

1. If you choose the wrong plants for your garden, the plants will not grow.

2. The plants may not need fertilizer if the soil is rich.

3. If plants are covered with mulch, diseases cannot infect them so easily.

4. If weeds are not picked, the plants have to compete for water and nutrients.

5. If you put a small fence around your garden, it may help keep unwanted animals out.

EXERCISE 2. Real Conditions in the Present or Future

Circle the correct verb in the **if** clause or result clause to make a real conditional in the present or future.

Playing at the Park

Every weekend, if the weather is nice, I ❶ (will spend/spend) time outside with my children. One of their favorite things to do is to go to a nearby park. If we ride our bikes to the park, it ❷ (takes/will take) about 10 minutes. If there ❸ (is/will be) a lot of traffic, it takes a little longer. Once we get to the park, the kids choose their favorite playground equipment to play on. Jeffrey likes the climbing walls, but if he ❹ (climbs/will climb) too high, I start to get nervous. I always have to remind him, "If you're not careful, you ❺ (fall/will fall) and hurt yourself." His reaction is usually to roll his eyes at me. My daughter Cheryl loves to play on the seesaw. On the way to the park, she almost always asks me, "Mom, if there ❻ (is/will be) no one for me to play with, ❼ (do/will) you go on the seesaw with me?" If she ❽ (finds/will find) someone to play with at the park, she ❾ (will spend/should spend) the entire time on the seesaw. Sometimes I talk to the other parents who are there. After an hour or so, the kids and I ride our bikes back home. On the way, I tell them, "If the weather is nice next weekend, we ❿ (come/will come) back."

Grammar Lesson

Unreal Conditions in the Present or Future

Unreal (imaginary) Condition or *If* Clause	Imaginary Result or Main Clause	Meaning
If he **had** time, **simple past**	he **could take** a long vacation. **would/could/might + VERB**	He doesn't have time. (present)
If I **were** you, **simple past**	I **would plan** the picnic for Sunday. **would/could/might + VERB**	I'm not you. (present)
If a hurricane **hit** the town, **simple past**	it **would destroy** everything. **would/could/might + VERB**	A hurricane will probably not hit the town. (future)
If she **joined** a travel club, **simple past**	she **might** not **feel** so lonely. **would/could/might + VERB**	She has not joined a travel club yet. (future)

<u>Rule 1</u>. Unreal conditions in the present or future express situations that are untrue, not possible, or imaginary in the present and that probably will not happen in the future. Although it is possible that the situation could change and become true in the future, it probably will not.

<u>Rule 2</u>. Unreal conditions in the present or future use the simple past form in the **if** clause and **would, could** or **might plus the base form of the verb in the result clause.**

<u>Rule 3.</u> Either clause, or both, can be made negative.

 BE CAREFUL!

Common Learner Errors	Explanation
1. If I ~~know~~ **knew** the answer right now, I would tell you.	Use the past tense for unreal conditions in the present.
2. If I ~~was~~ **were** you, I would memorize this rule about unreal conditions.	Use **were** instead of **was** for the verb **be** for all persons, singular and plural, in unreal conditions in the present or future. **Was** is used only in very informal language.

EXERCISE 3. Identifying Present or Future Unreal Conditions in Context

Circle the condition that is unreal or probably won't happen.

Moving Away for a New Job

1. If I were you, I would accept the job in San Antonio.

2. I think you would regret it if you decided to stay here in Lincoln.

3. Of course we'd all miss you if you left this company, but we would all still keep in touch.

4. I'll bet you'd be more excited about leaving if it didn't mean having to pack.

5. If Alex had time, I'm sure he'd help you pack for your move.

6. If I weren't planning your going-away party, I'd help you pack, too.

EXERCISE 4. Speaking Activity: Unreal Conditionals

Form a small group. Make a chain of conditionals: The first person will offer a sentence using an unreal conditional in the present or future. The second person will change the result clause in the original sentence to an unreal *if* clause and will add a new result clause. The third person will change the new result clause to an unreal *if* clause and will add a new result clause. How long can you keep the chain going? See the example if you need help getting started.

Examples: Person 1—*If I had more time, I'd go to school full-time.*

Person 2—*If I went to school full-time, I would study architecture.*

Person 3—*If I studied architecture, I could design my own house.*

Person 1—*If I designed my own house, I would . . .*

 Do Online Exercise 4.1. My score: _____ /10. _____ % correct.

EXERCISE 5. Unreal Conditions in the Present or Future

Terri and Ken, a married couple, are discussing whether Terry should accept a job promotion she was offered by her employer. Accepting the promotion means moving out of state. Fill in the blanks with the correct form of the verb to make unreal conditions or results. The first one has been done for you as an example.

Terri's Job Promotion:
Stay in Denver or Move to San Francisco?

Terri: I have to let the company know this week whether or not I'm going to accept the position of regional manager they offered me.

Ken: If there ❶ _____ (be, not) so many factors to consider, this ❷ _____ (be) easy!

Terri: I know. If we ❸ _____ (like, not) living here in Denver so much, I ❹ _____ (jump) at the chance to move to San Francisco.

Ken: Yes, and if your salary ❺ _____ (stay) the same, it ❻ _____ (be) easier to turn this job down, but they've offered you a big increase.

Terri: I've been talking to some people at work about it. One of them said, "Terri, if I ❼ _____ (be) you, I ❽ _____ (accept) that promotion in a heartbeat!"

Ken: I was thinking that if San Francisco ❾ _____ (be) closer, you ❿ _____ (commute) to work, but it's just too far for that.

Terri: Hmmm . . . How **11** _____ (you, feel) if I just

12 _____ (come) home on the weekends?

Ken: I **13** _____ (like, not) it if I only **14** _____

(see) you two days a week.

Terri: Well, if I **15** _____ (take) the promotion, you

16 _____ (have) to quit your job. How

17 _____ you _____ (feel) about that?

Ken: I **18** _____ (be) okay with quitting if it

19 _____ (mean) that we **20** _____ (have)

more time together.

Terri: Then I guess we've decided! It's the right decision, isn't it?

Ken: If it **21** _____ (be, not), you **22** _____

(have, not) that big smile on your face!

EXERCISE 6. Mini-Conversations

Circle the correct words in parentheses in these mini-conversations.

1. *Sue*:   What's wrong? You look really stressed out about something.

   Ben: It's this research paper I'm writing. The outline is due tomorrow, and I'm still working on it. If I don't finish it tonight, I (get, will get, would get) an F!

2. *Sue*:   Well, I can help you if you (need, will need, would need) it.

   Ben: Really? That would be great! I get off work at 4:30. Man, I feel better already.

3. *Lynn*:   Are you ready? Let's go. The movie starts in half an hour. We need to leave right now if we (want, wanted, will want, would want) to get there in time.

   Tim: I know, I know, but I can't find my wallet.

4. *Lynn:*   Can I do something to help you get ready?

   Tim: Well, if you helped me look for it instead of telling me what time it was, that (is, was, would be) a big help.

5. *Lynn*:   Okay. But let me say just one more thing: I'd keep my wallet in the same place every day if I (am, were, can be) you. That way I'd always know where it was.

ONE-MINUTE LESSON
The word **get** has many meanings. One very common meaning is "arrive," but the word *arrive* is more formal and less usual. Examples from conversation include: *What time did you get to the meeting? When did you get there?*

Grammar Lesson

KEY
15

Unreal Conditions in the Past

Unreal Past Condition or *If* Clause	Result or Main Clause	Meaning
If we **had saved** more money, **past perfect tense**	we **could have taken** a longer vacation. **would/could/might + have + past participle**	We didn't save money, so we were not able to take a longer vacation.
If you **had been** on time, **past perfect tense**	we **would** not **have missed** the plane. **would/could/might + have + past participle**	We weren't on time, so we missed the plane.
If it **hadn't rained** so hard, **past perfect**	it **would have been** a perfect day. **would/could/might + have + past participle**	It rained hard, so it was not a perfect day.
If she **had bought** her ticket last spring, **past perfect**	she **might** not **have had** to pay so much. **would/could/might + have + past participle**	She did not buy her ticket last spring, so she had to pay a lot for it later.

<u>Rule 1</u>. Unreal conditions in the past express situations that did not happen. Consequently, it is impossible for the results of the situations to happen. Unreal conditions in the past are often used to express a regret about the situation.

<u>Rule 2</u>. Unreal conditions in the past use the past perfect form in the **if** clause and **would have, could have**, or **might have** plus the past participle of the verb in the result clause.

Sentences	Meaning
I **could have gotten** the job if I **had sent** in my resume on time.	I didn't get the job because I didn't send my resume in on time.
If they **hadn't read** the book, the ending of the movie **would have been** a surprise.	They read the book, so the ending of the movie was not a surprise.
He **might have won** the tournament if he **had trained** harder and more often.	He didn't win the tournament because he didn't train hard or often.

BE CAREFUL!

Common Learner Errors	Explanation
1. If I ~~studied~~ **had studied** more last night, I could have done better on this morning's test.	The conditional sentence is talking about an unreal past event. Do not use simple past tense. Instead, you must use past perfect tense.
2. If he'd **had** more time, he'd **have taken up** a new sport. he'd had = he **had had** he'd have taken up = he **would have taken up**	Do not get confused by the contracted 'd form used with conditionals. The 'd can be either **had** or **would**.

EXERCISE 7. Past Unreal Conditions in Context

Read the passages about famous explorers. Fill in the blanks with the correct form of the verb to make unreal conditions or results in the past.

Two Famous Explorers

Throughout history, we have benefited from the courageous explorers whose daring adventures opened new frontiers to us. Whether they set out to sail the seas, cross unexplored lands, or take to the skies in flight, they changed our perception of the world.

Vasco da Gama is one such explorer. He was the first European to sail from Europe (Portugal) around Africa to India and back. In 1497, with four ships, he made the trip to India in 23 days. The return trip, however, took almost four and a half months because of the monsoon winds. If he ❶ (listen) _____ to the advice of the local people and waited, he ❷ (lose/not) _____ more than half of his crew. He returned with only two of the four ships. If he ❸ (wait) _____ a while before returning to Portugal, maybe all four ships ❹ (return) _____ with him. Da Gama was a true adventurer, and his discovery brought the spice trade to Portugal.

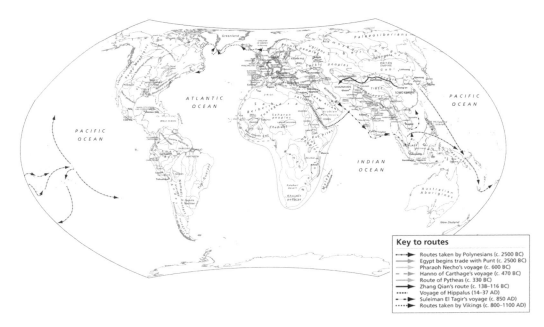

Key to routes

	Routes taken by Polynesians (c. 2500 BC)
	Egypt begins trade with Punt (c. 2500 BC)
	Pharaoh Necho's voyage (c. 600 BC)
	Hanno of Carthage's voyage (c. 470 BC)
	Route of Pytheas (c. 330 BC)
	Zhang Qian's route (c. 138–116 BC)
	Voyage of Hippalus (14–37 AD)
	Suleiman El Tagir's voyage (c. 850 AD)
	Routes taken by Vikings (c. 800–1100 AD)

Charles Lindbergh was an explorer of the skies who made the first solo flight across the Atlantic Ocean. As a young man, Lindbergh's interest was in aviation. He dropped out of college to travel around the country performing airplane stunts for audiences at county fairs. In 1924, he joined the Army and received pilot training. Later, he was hired to fly mail between St. Louis and Chicago. If Lindbergh ❺ (stay) _____ in school and ❻ (study) _____ engineering, he probably ❼ (become/never) _____ a pilot. In 1927, Lindbergh set a goal to be the first person to fly non-stop from New York to Paris and win a $25,000 prize for doing so. On May 20, 1927, Lindbergh took off in his plane, the *Spirit of St. Louis,* and flew almost 4,000 miles across the Atlantic in 33.5 hours. After this historic feat, Lindbergh continued to promote aviation and even wrote a book about his transatlantic flight. If Lindbergh ❽ (travel/not) _____ around the country on a post-flight tour, ❾ people (consider/not) _____ aviation as a means of travel.

 Do Online Exercise 4.2. My score: _____/10. _____% correct.

EXERCISE 8. Stories from History and Unreal Conditions

These sentences express actual situations from history. Write the unreal condition for each situation. Remember to use **would, could**, or **might** in the result clause. The first one has been done for you as an example. To help you, underline the main verb in each clause in the given sentences. (*Hint:* It is awkward to have the date between the word **if** and the subject, so move the dates to the end of the original clause.)

Asking What If Questions about History

1. In 1969, Commander Neil Armstrong <u>was</u> the first man to walk on the moon, so Pilot Buzz Aldrin <u>was</u> not.

   If Commander Neil Armstrong had not been the first man to walk on the moon

   in 1969, Pilot Buzz Aldrin would have been.

2. In 1769, Daniel Boone explored the frontier of Kentucky and was captured by the Indians there several times.

   _____

   _____

3. In 1978, Sally Ride was one of 8,000 applicants to be accepted into the astronaut training program, and in 1983 she became the first woman to orbit Earth.

   _____

   _____

4. Robert Peary valued Matthew Henson's knowledge about travel and Eskimo ways, so Peary chose Henson to accompany him on his quest to become the first man to reach the North Pole.

   _____

   _____

5. Jonas Salk discovered a cure for polio in 1952, and millions of people have been spared from this crippling disease.

   _____

   _____

EXERCISE 9. Speaking Practice: Applying Grammar to Your Own Examples of Facts and Unreal Conditions

Based on the last exercise, write two true situations of your own. Make sure each situation has two related events. Give your sentences to a classmate who will write an unreal condition for each sentence.

1. (my statement) _____

_____

(unreal condition) _____

_____

2. (my statement) _____

_____

(unreal condition) _____

_____

Grammar Lesson

KEY
15

Inverted Conditionals

It is possible to make unreal conditional statements about the present, future, or past without using **if**. These conditional statements, used only with **to be, should,** and **past perfect tense,** are called **inverted conditionals** because the subject and verb are inverted. Notice that **if** is omitted in these inverted conditionals.

Without *If*	With *If*
Were he here, he **would lead** the discussion skillfully.	If he **were** he here, he **would lead** the discussion skillfully. (present)
Had they **known** about the fundraiser, they **would have made** a donation.	If they **had known** about the fundraiser, they **would have made** a donation. (past)
Had I not **played** so badly, I could have won that match this afternoon!	If I **had** not **played** so badly, I could have won that match this afternoon! (past)

BE CAREFUL!

Common Learner Errors	Explanation
1. ~~If had I studied~~ **Had I studied** more, OR **If I had studied** more, I would have gotten a higher score on the test.	If you invert the subject and verb, you must omit **if**.
2. ~~Worked I~~ **If I worked** at two jobs, I'd have a much better salary.	Use the inversion structure only with **to be**, **should**, or **past perfect**.

EXERCISE 10. Inverted Conditionals Practice

Read the sentences. Where possible, omit the word **if**, and invert the subject and verb to form an inverted conditional sentence. If inverting is not possible, write an X on the line.

Buying a New House

1. They would have bought the house if they had been able to afford it.

   _____

2. If you skip the open house, you'll miss the chance to meet the realtor.

   _____

3. If you liked houses with small yards, I'd invite you to look at houses in my area.

   _____

4. If you had offered them $15,000 more, they'd have taken it and you'd have a house!

   _____

   _____

5. Jill and Sam would have known what repairs the house needed if they had arranged for an inspection.

   _____

   _____

 **Grammar Lesson**

Progressive Forms and Mixed Time Conditionals

It is possible to use progressive tenses as well with conditionals. To learn this grammar well, many students memorize simple formulas such as **if** + present, then **will** (*If you study, you will pass the test*). These formulas are very helpful when both clauses are talking about events happening at the same time (have the same tense, such as present and present or past and past). However, it is possible to have a condition in one time and a result in a different time. In this case, you have a mixed time conditional sentence.

Condition or *If* Clause	Result or Main Clause	Meaning
If I **weren't working** on my report right now, **past progressive tense**	I **would be looking** at vacation websites. **would/could/might** + **be** + base form of the verb + −ing	an unreal condition in present and result in present
If we **were driving** a convertible in this rainstorm, **past progressive tense**	we **would be getting** soaked! **would/could/might** + **be** + base form of the verb + −ing	an unreal condition in present and result in present
If you **had been waiting** where we agreed to meet, **past perfect progressive tense**	we **could be enjoying** a great meal right now. **would/could/might** + **be** + base form of the verb + −ing	an unreal condition in past and result in present
If she **had watched** the news last night, **past perfect tense**	she **would know** what happened. **would/could/might** + base form of the verb	an unreal condition in past and result in present
If he **weren't** away on business, **simple past tense**	he **would have joined** us. **would/could/might** + **have** + past participle	an unreal condition in present and result in past

<u>Rule 1</u>. It is possible for conditional sentences to use the progressive forms of the verb.

<u>Rule 2.</u> It is also possible for conditional sentences to have different tenses in each clause.

<u>Rule 3.</u> The verb forms in the clauses change depending on two things: (1) whether the condition is real or unreal, and (2) whether the condition and result are in the present, past, or future.

EXERCISE 11. Progressive Forms and Mixed Time Conditions

Fill in the blanks with the correct verbs to form progressive and mixed conditional sentences. Use the tenses indicated in parentheses. You may need negative forms.

Comforting a Sick Friend

1. If you _____ (feeling/not) so sick, I _____ (invite) you to go to a movie. (present/present)

2. If you _____ (coughing) less, you _____ (stop) taking the medicine that makes you sleepy. (present/present)

3. If you _____ (eating) right, your immune system _____ (be) stronger. (past/present)

4. If you _____ (blowing/not) your nose so much, it _____ (get/not) so red. (past/past)

5. If I _____ (be/not) your true friend, I _____ (give/not) you a hug. (present/past)

6. If you _____ (call/not) me, you _____ (enjoying/not) my homemade chicken soup right now. (past/present)

ONE-MINUTE LESSON
noun + noun combinations. *Chicken soup* is a **noun + noun combination** that means that the second noun (*soup*) is made of the first noun (*chicken*). Similar items are *chocolate cake* and *potato salad*. Different items, however, are *pizza sauce*, which is not sauce that is made of pizza, and *cookie dough*, which is not dough that is made of cookies.

Do Online Exercise 4.3. My score: ____ /10. ____ % correct.

Grammar Lesson

Wishes in the Present, Future, or Past

Using the verb **wish** plus a clause about the wish is a very common construction in English, especially in spoken language. The verb after **wish** is one tense before the actual time. In other words, if you want to wish for the present time, use past tense. If you want to wish for the past time, use past perfect tense. If you want to wish for the future time, use **would**.

Wish	Meaning
I **wish** that I **had** today off. *wish* + subject + past tense form	I am working today.
I **wish** I **were lying** on a warm sunny beach right now. *wish* + subject + *be* + base form of verb + –ing	I am not lying on a beach.
He **wishes** she **would let** him have a week off. *wish* + subject + *would/could* + base form of verb	She will not let him have a week off.
They **wish** that they **hadn't spent** $500. *wish* + subject + *had* + past participle	They spent $500.
She **wishes** she **could have stayed** in Orlando one more day. *wish* + subject + *could/would* + *have* + past participle	She was not able to stay in Orlando an extra day.

Rule 1. Sentences with **wish** are similar in meaning to unreal conditions in the present, future, or past. The situation is imaginary, does not exist, or did not happen.

Rule 2. Using **wish** expresses the fact that you want the opposite of the real situation to be true.

Rule 3. The use of **that** between **wish** and the following clause is optional.

 BE CAREFUL!

Common Learner Errors	Explanation
1. I wish I ~~can~~ **could** play rugby better.	To make a wish about the present time, use the past tense. Don't use the present tense after wish.
2. We got home from vacation last night. We really wish we ~~had~~ **had had** more vacation time.	To make a wish about the past time, **use the past perfect tense**. Don't use the past tense for past time.

EXERCISE 12. Practicing *Wish* in Context

Circle the correct form of the verb in this conversation.

Summer Study Abroad

Brad: I'm not really looking forward to taking classes this summer, but it's something that I have to do. I wish I ❶ (can, could) travel instead. That's what I did last summer: I traveled around Spain for two months.

Alan: Where would you want to go this summer? Around the U.S.?

Brad: No, I really wish I ❷ (have, had) the money to go overseas again. In fact, I wish I ❸ (could, could have) spend an entire year overseas.

Alan: An entire year?

Brad: Yeah, don't you wish you ❹ (can, could) do something like that, too? You know, just take a break from school and do something else?

Alan: No, not really. I'm happy studying here. But I sure wish I ❺ (took, were taking) a heavier load so I could finish school sooner. I need to start making some money.

Brad: Not me. I'm happy taking just 12 credits every semester. My only wish is that I ❻ (didn't wait, hadn't waited) so long to start college after high school. It took me a while to figure out what I wanted to do.

Alan: You know what? I just remembered something, and it just might be what you're looking for. I wish I ❼ (knew, had known) where I saw it. It was a poster about studying abroad. You go overseas and get credit for it.

Brad: That sounds perfect! I wish I ❽ (got, could have gotten) credit for the time I spent in Spain last summer. I went to so many places and learned so much about the history and culture of Spain.

Alan: Maybe you still can if you take a test or write a paper. Hey, I remember now . . . . I saw the poster near the International Center. It was a Study Abroad poster. Why don't you stop by and check it out?

Brad: I will. I wish I ❾ (knew, had known) about this program earlier. It sounds perfect for me. Thanks, Alan. Don't you wish you ❿ (are, were) able to come with me?

Connecting Grammar and Vocabulary

It is possible to use hundreds of different verbs in the clause after *wish*. It is useful for you to learn some of the most common verbs used with *wish*.

Memorize these verb combinations so that you can write them or say them easily in English.

Top 5 Verbs after I wish I ____	Top 5 Verbs after I wish I could ____	Top 4 Verbs after I wish I had/'d ____
1. I wish I could	1. I wish I could have	1. I wish I had been
2. I wish I had OR I wish I'd	2. I wish I could say	2. I wish I had known
3. I wish I knew	3. I wish I could be	3. I wish I had done
4. I wish I were	4. I wish I could tell	4. I wish I had had
5. I wish I did	5. I wish I could do	

Source: Davies, Mark. (2011). Word frequency data from the Corpus of Contemporary American English (COCA). http://corpus2.byu.edu/coca/

EXERCISE 13. Editing: Is it Correct?

If the sentence is correct, write a check mark (✓) on the line. If it is not correct, write an X on the line and circle the mistake. Then make the change above the sentence. (*Hint:* There are eight sentences. Three are correct, but five have mistakes.)

Choosing the Right School

_____1. If you research your options, you will make the right choice.

_____2. You would need to choose an accredited school, if you thought about transferring.

_____3. If you had talked to an advisor, he or she could suggest possible scholarships to apply for.

_____4. If you had filled out your application sooner, you would heard from the Admissions Office earlier.

_____5. If a student was to go to a community college, he or she would save money in lower tuition costs.

_____6. Students often wish they had taken the SAT or ACT test earlier than they did.

_____7. If universities will get lots of applications, they select the best students for admission.

_____8. Josh had to pay out-of-state tuition during his first year of college here. Had he been a resident of the state, he could have been paid in-state tuition.

Do Online Exercise 4.4. My score: _____ /10. _____ % correct.

EXERCISE 14. Sentence Study for Critical Reading

Read the numbered sentences. Then read the answer choices and place a check mark (✓) in the yes or no boxes in front of each sentence to show if that answer is true based on the information in the original sentence. If there is not enough information to mark something as yes, then mark it as no. Remember that more than one true answer may be possible.

1. My job as a business analyst requires me to work long hours and make important financial decisions. If I am under a lot of stress and need to relax, I take a book and go to the park, where I find a quiet spot to read. This helps me keep things in perspective.

    ☐ yes ☐ no   a. I am under a lot of stress at work every day.

    ☐ yes ☐ no   b. I go to the park to relax whenever I feel stressed by my job.

    ☐ yes ☐ no   c. My job does not cause me to feel a lot of stress.

2. Brenda would give up her apartment and move overseas if she were able to find another job as a web designer in an Asian country.

    ☐ yes ☐ no   a. Brenda is planning to move to Asia to work as a web designer.

    ☐ yes ☐ no   b. Brenda lives in an apartment and works as a web designer.

    ☐ yes ☐ no   c. Brenda has found another job in Asia.

3. If Jacob had not sold his baseball card collection when he moved to a smaller house, he would have had something of value to display in his new home office.

    ☐ yes ☐ no   a. Jacob sold his valuable baseball card collection when he moved.

    ☐ yes ☐ no   b. Jacob did not sell his valuable baseball card collection when he moved.

    ☐ yes ☐ no   c. Jacob's baseball card collection is displayed in his new home office.

4. I'd be standing in line waiting to buy the newest cell phone if I hadn't signed a two-year contract for the phone I bought six months ago.

    ☐ yes ☐ no   a. I am not standing in line waiting to buy a new cell phone today.

    ☐ yes ☐ no   b. I signed a two-year contract for the phone I am currently using.

    ☐ yes ☐ no   c. I bought a phone six months ago and I am in line to buy another one.

5. More students would enroll in college full time if they received financial help.

☐ **yes** ☐ **no** a. Some students want to enroll in college full time but cannot.

☐ **yes** ☐ **no** b. Some students study part time because they cannot afford to study full time.

☐ **yes** ☐ **no** c. Some students enroll in college to study full time but want to study part time.

REVIEW **EXERCISE 15. Review Test 1: Multiple Choice**

Circle the letter of the correct answer.

1. If you park in a restricted area, you _____ a ticket on your windshield.

   a. would find   b. will find   c. found   d. could found

2. I get nervous if I _____ in front of a group.

   a. had to speak   b. spoke   c. have to speak   d. will speak

3. If today _____ Friday, we could sleep in tomorrow morning.

   a. is   b. were   c. will be   d. was

4. If you ____ more sleep, you _____ be so tired all of the time.

   a. get/would   c. got/wouldn't

   b. got/won't   d. don't get/aren't going to

5. She _____ $20 in finance charges if she _____ her bill by the due date.

   a. had saved/pays   c. could have saved/will pay

   b. could save/will pay   d. could have saved/had paid

6. They_____ such a big van _____ the price of gas would skyrocket.

   a. would have bought/if they knew

   b. wouldn't have bought/if had they known

   c. wouldn't have bought/had they known

   d. wouldn't have bought/had they knew

7. If I _____ so much in this class, I _____ here.

    a. wasn't learning/would be   c. weren't learning/wouldn't be

    b. am not learning/won't be   d. wasn't learning/wouldn't be

8. I wish I _____ myself better in English, but I _____.

    a. will express/won't   c. would express/won't

    b. could express/can't   d. can express/can't

 EXERCISE 16. Review Test 2: Production and Evaluation

Part 1.

Read these conditional sentences. Fill in the blanks with the correct verb form.

1. My grandmother always used to say, "If it rains, it _____ (pour)."

2. Do you believe that if you _____ (walk) under a ladder, you'll have bad luck?

3. Imagine—if money _____ (grow) on trees, we'd all be rich!

4. I don't understand the meaning of the proverb, "If wishes _____ (be) horses, beggars would ride."

5. If John Pemberton _____ (invent, not) Coca-Cola in 1886, we _____ (drink, not) it today.

6. If you _____ (live) in the U.S. in 1824, you _____ (be) one of the first Americans to taste pretzels.

7. Do you ever wish you _____ (be) someone famous?

8. _____ we _____ (study, not) inverted conditionals in this chapter, we _____ (know, not) the answer to this!

Part 2.

Read each sentence carefully. Look at the underlined verbs. If the underlined part is correct, circle the word *correct*. If it is wrong, circle the word *wrong*. Then write the correction above.

correct   wrong   1. If I get home before 10:00 PM, I usually <u>watch</u> the local news.

correct   wrong   2. She'll sell me her old car if the bank <u>approves</u> her loan for a new one.

correct   wrong   3. I <u>had volunteered</u> to work at the library a few hours a week if they needed help, but no one has asked me.

correct   wrong   4. Were he to ask, he <u>could receive</u> extra tutoring help after class.

correct   wrong   5. If we <u>would have bought</u> them online, we could have gotten our concert tickets for half-price.

correct   wrong   6. If I <u>had studied</u> this chapter more thoroughly, I wouldn't be so confused by this sentence.

EXERCISE 17. Reading Practice: Living Longer and Healthier

Read the information in this diet and health article. Then answer the comprehension questions that follow. The grammar from this unit is underlined for you.

Live a Longer and Healthier Life

Do you <u>wish you could live</u> to be 100 or older? Do you <u>wish you could be</u> in perfect health your entire life? Well, you might just be able to get what you wish for! Recent scientific research has shown that <u>if people practiced</u> just five simple behaviors, they could not only prolong their lives but make them healthier as well. <u>If you are willing</u> to commit to leading a longer, healthier life, read on.

First, eat the right foods in the right amounts. Three-fourths of your plate should be filled with fruits, vegetables, and whole grains. <u>If you cannot give up</u> eating meat, choose lean meats. Eat poultry, fish, beans, and foods that are low in saturated fats, trans fats, cholesterol, salt, and sugar. People who <u>wish they could more easily control</u> the amount they eat may find that using a smaller plate will help.

Next, exercise at least 30 minutes a day at least three days a week. <u>If you exercise</u> five or more days a week or at least 75 minutes each time, the results will be even better for you. Choose the type of exercise you enjoy. <u>If you don't have</u> 30 consecutive minutes, then you can break it into three 10-minute periods and get some of the same benefits. Exercise helps increase muscle, strengthen bones, and improve balance. <u>If you haven't exercised</u> in a while, you should see your doctor before you begin a program. Not only will exercise improve your physical health, it also relieves stress and fosters good mental health.

Third, find time to volunteer in your community. <u>If you volunteer</u> even just a few hours a month, you will still get the benefits that helping others gives you. People who volunteer suffer less from depression and are less likely to have heart disease than those who do not volunteer.

In addition, <u>if you want</u> to live longer and be healthier, be sure to get sufficient sleep. <u>If you are</u> over the age of 18, you probably need seven to nine hours of sleep each night. <u>If you cannot get</u> that much sleep, take a short nap of 20–30 minutes per day.

Finally, it's important to drink water. The body is between 55 percent and 75 percent water, and water helps it metabolize fat and maintain muscle tone. You can get water through fruits and vegetables, but <u>if you really want</u> to be good to your body, you could simply drink lots of water!

These five behaviors are the keys to living a longer and healthier life. Imagine, <u>if you had started</u> these behaviors years ago, you would be way ahead of the game!

1. What is the author's purpose for writing this article?

   _____

   _____

2. Who is the intended audience for this article?

   _____

   _____

3. What are the positive effects associated with volunteering?

   _____

   _____

4. What advice does the author give about beginning a new exercise program if you have not exercised in a while?

   _____

   _____

5. What are the five behaviors the author says will prolong a person's life?

   1. _____

   2. _____

   3. _____

   4. _____

   5. _____

EXERCISE 18. Vocabulary Practice: Word Knowledge

Circle the answer choice that is most closely related to the vocabulary on the left. Use a dictionary to check the meaning of words you do not know.

Vocabulary	Answer Choices	
1. commute to work	prepare to work	travel to work
2. sage	friendly	wise
3. consequently	the result of	the cause of
4. a feat	an amazing person	an amazing thing
5. a ladder	climb	destroy
6. call off	cancel	postpone
7. a down payment	the first payment	the last payment
8. be stressed out	be angry	be worried
9. a vet	for animals	for vehicles
10. a donation	money you earn	money you give
11. an expedition	a climate	a trip
12. a fee	you buy it	you pay it
13. soil	in a garden	in a race
14. design	plan	wonder
15. bald	no hair	no sun
16. to display	to manage	to show
17. courageous	angry	brave
18. tuition	for a hospital	for a school
19. outstanding	above average	below average
20. a factor	an element	a guess
21. issued	collected	distributed
22. an exit row	a plane	a supermarket
23. X is in dispute	we are not sure about X	we need to fix X
24. tough	difficult	easy
25. to range	to maintain	to vary
26. damage	after a storm	before a storm
27. on the other hand	however	therefore
28. look forward to X	we are afraid of X	we want X to happen
29. board a train	buy a train ticket	get on the train
30. weeds	a type of bad grass	a type of good grass

EXERCISE 19. Vocabulary Practice: Collocations

Fill in each blank with the answer on the right that most naturally completes the phrase on the left. If necessary, use a dictionary to check the meaning of words you do not know.

Vocabulary	Answer Choices	
1. a regional _____	manager	employee
2. _____ a doubt	within	without
3. the patient's physical _____	health	salary
4. _____ a goal	let	set
5. _____ an option	jump	explore
6. kidnap _____	someone	something
7. to be a resident _____ the city	of	for
8. a courageous _____	house	person
9. a _____ survey	satisfaction	satisfied
10. to suffer from mental _____	ill	illness
11. _____ a great deal of stress	below	under
12. keep something _____ perspective	in	of
13. devote a lot of _____ to X	luck	time
14. _____ a down payment	do	make
15. drop out _____ a club	about	of
16. many factors to _____	believe	consider
17. for the _____ being	present	time
18. _____ a suitcase	pack	try on
19. jump at the _____	chance	charge
20. _____ or negative	affirmative	optimistic
21. get _____ work at 4:30	off	on
22. _____ their website	check in	check out
23. _____ soil	delicious	rich
24. _____ damage	comfortable	severe
25. _____ to do something	eager	weak
26. to be away on _____	business	television
27. in _____ heartbeat	a	the
28. _____ a donation	do	make
29. a means of _____	money	travel
30. to orbit _____ the earth	around	finally
31. _____ from 92 to 100	dispute	range
32. an _____ feat	available	incredible
33. turn down a _____	job decision	job offer

EXERCISE 20. Writing Practice: Motivating People

Part 1. Editing Student Writing

Read these sentences about motivation and job satisfaction. Circle the 15 errors. Then write the number of the sentence with the error next to the type of error. (Some sentences have more than one error.)

_____ a. comma	_____ d. subject-verb agreement
_____ b. verb tense	_____ e. singular-plural of nouns
_____ c. word order	_____ f. *this, that, these, those*

Motivation in the Workplace
1. If employers want a successful business, their staff must consist of employees motivated.
2. If employees are not motivated this will result in the loss of many customer.
3. Today many employers wish, they know how to motivate their workers better.
4. There are several way to find out if your workers seems happy about their job conditions.
5. Having employees fill out worker satisfaction surveys is one way to obtain these information.
6. If a survey doesn't work you could try having informal meetings with the workers.
7. Sometimes this short meetings between the boss and a worker can solve many issues.
8. Many workers mention salary as one of the most important issue, but more money does not always lead to more satisfaction with the job.
9. For instance, if you had given your workers a raise last week, will they be happier today?
10. Some reports have shown that allowing workers to have some say in their work schedules are more effective in the long run.
11. In addition, allowing employees to make suggestions on how to improve the business often work.
12. You had attended my motivation seminar last week, you would now know exactly what to do!

Part 2. Original Student Writing

Imagine that the employees at the company where you work are not very motivated. You have some ideas on how to change that, and your supervisor has asked you to put your ideas in writing. Write a short report listing and explaining 5 to 10 of your ideas. After each suggestion, add a sentence explaining the benefit that might result. Be sure to use conditional sentences in your report. Underline the grammar points that you have used so the teacher can see what you are trying to practice.

Example:

If people had a more flexible schedule, they could come in later and leave later. This would reduce tardiness.

Then

Now

Unit **5**

Adverb Clauses

Discover the Grammar

Read the passage about cars, and then answer the questions that follow.

Line	
1	Cars have come a long way since Henry Ford invented his first "horseless
2	carriage" in the late 1890s. Think of today's modern cars, and compare them
3	with those of the early years of production. One interesting difference is in
4	what is considered an "extra" when buying a car. In the 1900s, for example,
5	buyers had to purchase tires, a windshield, headlights, and even a top for wet
6	weather as extras. In contrast, extras today include leather seating, computer
7	technology, and satellite radio.
8	When Ford introduced the Model T in 1908, this cutting-edge vehicle
9	could reach an amazing top speed of approximately 45 miles per hour.
10	Although the first cars were expensive, Henry Ford was determined to make his
11	machines accessible so that everyone could afford one. Eventually, he was able
12	to sell his vehicles for less because his factory production techniques made it
13	faster to produce cars. In fact, the price eventually dropped as low as $260
14	(without extras) even though it had started at $850.

15 Without any doubt, the invention of the car has revolutionized our lives. To
16 some people, the car is the greatest invention of all time because of all the
17 improvements it has made to our lives. While the car certainly has brought
18 many positive changes to our lives, there have also been unforeseen conse-
19 quences, with two of the most serious of these effects being air pollution and
20 highway accidents. Automobiles were not the first source of pollution, but the
21 automobile has massively increased air pollution. In particular, large cities such
22 as Mexico City, Los Angeles, Ankara, and Beijing face mounting air pollution
23 exacerbated by the number of cars in each city. Another serious consequence of
24 the rise in car use is the number of deaths in automobile accidents. More than
25 one million people die each year in car accidents. Some recent figures from the
26 World Health Organization reported the highest fatalities from China
27 (220,783), India (196,455), Nigeria (47,865), and the U.S. (42,642).

28 After people started driving cars, the world changed in dramatic ways.
29 Although pollution and traffic deaths are realities, most people would agree that
30 the benefits of having automobiles in our lives outweigh the drawbacks. Henry
31 Ford would certainly be proud if he could see the impact that his invention has
32 had on people's lives around the world.

1. Words such as *because, although,* and *while* are commonly used to connect two parts of a sentence. These words that introduce adverb clauses are called **subordinating conjuctions.** Find these connector words in the lines indicated. Copy the subject, verb, and the rest of the clause that follows each connector. The first one has been done for you as an example.

Line	Connector	Subject	Verb	Rest of the Clause
1–2	since	Henry Ford	invented	his first "horseless carriage" in the late 1890s
8	When			
10	Although			
12–13	because			
14	even though			
17–18	While			
28	After			
29	Although			
31–32	if			

2. In the first question, you identified 9 adverb clauses. How many of these are followed by a comma? _____ How many of these clauses are preceded by a comma? _____ Can you figure out when you need to use a comma with adverb clauses?

_____

_____

3. In Lines 1–2, *since* is a subordinating conjunction because it introduces an adverb clause. However, *since* can also be a preposition when it introduces a noun as the object of the preposition. Identify the part of speech of *since* in these sentences.

_____ a. Since the business lost so much money last year, it had to close down.

_____ b. Since last year, the business has not been open.

_____ c. Since the closing of the business last year, I have been unemployed.

_____ d. Since the business closed last year, I have been unemployed.

4. The subordinating conjunction *because* introduces adverb clauses. Its preposition cousin is *because of*. Fill in the blanks with *because* or *because of*.

a. _____ the hard rain, the coach called off the football game.

b. _____ it was raining so hard, the coach called off the football game.

c. The coach called off the football game _____ the hard rain.

d. The coach called off the football game _____ it was raining so hard.

5. What questions do you have about adverb clauses?

_____

_____

_____

_____

Grammar Lesson

9 Types of Adverb Clauses

An adverb clause consists of a connector word (subordinating conjunction) followed by a subject and a verb. This unit introduces nine different kinds of adverb clauses according to the function of the clause. In general, the kind of adverb clause depends on the question that the adverb clause answers, such as *When? Where? Why? How?* Adverb clauses function the same way that adverbs function.

Adverb Clause,	Main Clause
When the students finished the exam, **subordinator + subject + verb**	the teacher collected their papers. **subject + verb**

Rule 1. It is possible to reverse the order of most adverb clauses without changing the meaning of the sentence.

Main Clause	Adverb Clause
The teacher collected their papers **subject + verb**	when the students finished the exam. **subordinator + subject + verb**

Rule 2. Notice how the punctuation changes depending on the order of the clauses:

Adverb clause , main clause .   vs.   Main clause adverb clause .

If it rains tonight, I will stay home.   I will stay home **if it rains tonight.**

When she called, I was asleep.   I was asleep **when she called.**

BE CAREFUL!

Common Learner Errors	Explanation
1. As soon as I arrive in ~~Paris I~~ **Paris, I** will call you.	Always use a comma after an opening adverb clause.
2. Several of the shipping companies went ~~bankrupt, because~~ **bankrupt because** the steep price of oil cut deeply into their profits.	Do not use a comma between an independent clause and an adverb clause.
3. ~~The war ended,~~ **By the time the war ended,** half a million people had died.	Be sure to **use a connector (subordinating conjunction)** to introduce an adverb clause.

EXERCISE 1. Punctuation for Adverb Clauses

Each of these sentences contains an adverb clause, which has been underlined. Add a comma if it is necessary.

Why I Love Popcorn

1. <u>Whenever I have the munchies</u> I like to make popcorn.

2. Popcorn is my first choice for a snack <u>because it is easy to make</u>.

3. <u>Because it is so easy to make</u> even young children can pop popcorn.

4. Popcorn is also a good snack food <u>because it can be a healthy food to eat</u>.

5. <u>As long as you don't drench your popcorn in butter</u> popcorn is low in calories.

 Do Online Exercise 5.1. My score: ____ /10. ____ % correct.

Grammar Lesson

Adverb Clause 1: Time

Common Subordinating Conjunctions that Introduce Adverb Clauses of Time	
after	Most of the students were happy **after they heard the exam results.**
before	**Before the rain started,** Brenda and I played two sets of tennis.
as long as	She has been my best friend **as long as I can remember.**
once	**Once I took the medicine,** I felt much better.
whenever	**Whenever it gets too cold,** we have to cover the plants with sheets.
since	The company has grown by leaps and bounds **since he started here.**
as soon as	**As soon as you arrive home,** please call me to tell me you're OK.
as	The audience stood up **as the singers returned to the stage.**
by the time (that)	They had eaten almost all of the cookies **by the time that I arrived.**
when	Lyndon Johnson became president **when Kennedy died in 1963.**
while	**While they were watching TV,** I was cleaning the kitchen cabinets.
until	**Until I checked my email,** I didn't know Jack had gotten a new job.

 BE CAREFUL!

Common Learner Errors	Explanation
1. As soon as I ~~will arrive~~ arrive in Paris, I will call you.	When you want to express a future action of a sentence that has an adverb clause, **use future tense in the main clause only,** not in the adverb clause of time.
2. By the time that the war ended, half a million people ~~died~~ had died.	With the subordinating conjunction **by the time,** the verb in the main clause should be in past perfect for a past action and in future perfect for a future action.

EXERCISE 2. Time Connectors

Underline the correct subordinating conjunction. Consult your dictionary about any time words you do not understand.

One Teacher's Story

1. I have been teaching English to non-native speakers (when, since) I graduated in 2000.

2. (Whenever, While) I was a student, I often wondered if I would ever be able to find a good teaching job.

3. (As soon as, Until) I graduated, I landed a really good job teaching English in an intensive program for adults.

4. I was very interested in teaching English overseas, but I knew that I needed some classroom experience (before, as) I could teach in another country.

5. I taught in the U.S. (once, until) I felt that I had enough experience to venture on to another country.

6. (After, Whenever) I had taught in the U.S. for five years, I decided that it was time to go overseas.

7. I applied for a job in Saudi Arabia, and (once, by the time) I got the job, I started taking Arabic lessons to help me prepare for my new life.

8. (As soon as, By the time) I landed in Saudi Arabia, I had learned the alphabet as well as some simple grammar and vocabulary.

9. I learned a great deal about teaching English outside an English-speaking country and about Saudi Arabia (while, before) I was living there.

10. Although I taught in Saudi Arabia a long time ago, I can still remember so much of my life there (whenever, until) I think of it.

Grammar Lesson

Adverb Clause 2: Reason

Common Subordinating Conjunctions that Introduce Adverb Clauses of Reason	
since*	**Since Joe got sick,** we decided not to attend the party.
because	The price of car insurance has gone up **because car theft is on the rise.**
as	**As the term paper is due tomorrow,** we need to stay home tonight to do it.
so that	We enrolled in a Spanish course **so that we could improve our Spanish.**
given that	She had to take the course again **given that she did not pass the final.**
now that	**Now that the stores are having their annual clearance sales,** today is the perfect day to go shopping.

*_since_ as a subordinating conjunction is very common in spoken English.

BE CAREFUL!

Common Learner Error	Explanation
Since I arrived in Brazil, I ~~saw~~ **have seen** many of my old friends.	Be careful with the two meanings of **since.** When **since** means "because," various verb tenses are possible. When **since** means "from the starting time of," the most common verb tense is present perfect.

EXERCISE 3. Adverb Clauses of Reason

Read the short passage and complete the sentences. For some answers, you will have to use your imagination.

Mr. and Mrs. Vickers are in a pet store with their twin seven-year-old daughters Mandy and Misty, who want to get a pet. Mr. Vickers is not crazy about the idea because his daughters may not take good care of the animal. Mrs. Vickers is allergic to cats. Mandy likes dogs, but Misty would like to have a cat. Three of them do not want a bird, and nobody wants a snake.

1. The twins want a pet because _____

2. Given that Mrs. Vickers is allergic to cats, _____

   _____

3. They do not want a bird since _____

   _____

4. Mr. and Mrs. Vickers want their girls to have a pet so that _____

   _____

5. In the end, they decided to get a dog since _____

   _____

EXERCISE 4. Sentence Study for Critical Reading

Read the numbered sentences. Then read the answer choices and put a check mark (✓) in the yes or no boxes in front of each sentence to show if that answer is true based on the information in the original sentence. If there is not enough information to mark something as yes, then mark it as no. Remember that more than one true answer may be possible.

1. While I was driving to the airport last Friday, I was listening to the radio. Suddenly, I saw a bolt of lightning and heard a loud clap of thunder. Then my radio went silent.

   ☐ yes ☐ no   a. I was doing two things at the same time.

   ☐ yes ☐ no   b. I heard a clap of lightning.

   ☐ yes ☐ no   c. I turned off the radio.

2. Since the teacher saw Harvey squinting, she moved his seat to the front of the room. Harvey thanked her because he could see much better.

   ☐ yes ☐ no   a. The teacher moved Harvey's seat because he asked her to.

   ☐ yes ☐ no   b. Harvey is probably nearsighted.

   ☐ yes ☐ no   c. Harvey was polite.

3. After chicks hatch, the mother bird leaves the nest in search of worms or other food for her hatchlings.

   ☐ yes ☐ no   a. Hatchlings are baby birds.

   ☐ yes ☐ no   b. Chicks are baby birds.

   ☐ yes ☐ no   c. The mother bird only looks for worms.

4. By the time computers came into wide use, the adding machine and the slide rule had become obsolete. Accountants and engineers easily adapted to the new tools.

   ☐ yes ☐ no   a. Computers took the place of adding machines and slide rules.

   ☐ yes ☐ no   b. The adding machine was invented before the slide rule.

   ☐ yes ☐ no   c. Slide rules made computers obsolete.

5. As soon as Ella walked in the door, she sensed something was wrong. All of the lights in the house were turned on. There were dirty dishes on the table, and the back door was open.

   ☐ yes ☐ no   a. When Ella walked in the door, she turned on the light.

   ☐ yes ☐ no   b. Ella washed the dishes.

   ☐ yes ☐ no   c. Ella saw that the back door was open.

Grammar Lesson

Adverb Clause 3: Opposition

Common Subordinating Conjunctions that Introduce Adverb Clauses of Opposition	
although	**Although they worked very hard,** they didn't finish on time.
even though	These cars cost less **even though they are larger than those.**
though	**Though I called him up several times,** no one answered.
despite the fact that	She decided to travel to Cuba **despite the fact that this was prohibited by the State Department.**
in spite of the fact that	**In spite of the fact that this dictionary has more words in it,** the other dictionary seems to have better information.

 BE CAREFUL!

Common Learner Errors	Explanation
1. Although we planned the trip carefully, ~~but we~~ we encountered many problems.	Do not use **but** and **although** in the same sentence. Choose one or the other, not both.
2. ~~In spite~~ In spite of the fact that it was cold, we drove to the ocean.	Use the preposition **of** with **in spite**.
3. ~~Despite of~~ Despite the fact that it was cold, we drove to the ocean.	Do not use an additional preposition with **despite**.

 ONE-MINUTE LESSON
In natural conversation, **though** occurs at the end of an utterance:
I wasn't very hungry, though. Some people misunderstand **though** because they do not expect this connector to come at the end of an utterance.

EXERCISE 5. Editing: Is It Correct?

If the sentence is correct, write a check mark (✔) on the line. If it is not correct, write X on the line and circle the mistake. Then change the sentence to make it correct. Write the change above the sentence. (*Hint:* There are six sentences. Two are correct, but four have mistakes.)

My Neighbor

_____ 1. I'm going to write about my neighbor because she the most interesting person that I know.

_____ 2. She is ninety-seven years old.

_____ 3. In spite the fact that she is ninety-seven years old, she lives alone.

_____ 4. Even though she is quite old, she still does a great many things by herself. For example, she is frequently outside watering or even weeding her lawn.

_____ 5. Her companion is a fourteen-year-old cat named Cocoa. Despite the fact that Cocoa is not brown. Her name is Cocoa.

_____ 6. Although she will turn one hundred in a few years, but my neighbor is full of energy.

Do Online Exercise 5.2. My score: _____ /10. _____ % correct.

 **Grammar Lesson**

Adverb Clause 4: Direct Contrast

Common Subordinating Conjunctions that Introduce Adverb Clauses of Direct Contrast	
while	**While Chile has a long coast,** its neighbor Bolivia does not.
whereas	The Aztecs lived in the central part of Mexico, **whereas the Incas lived in the southern part of the country.**

<u>Rule 1</u>. With adverbs of direct contrast, it is good to use a comma even if the adverb clause comes second.

> According to the police report regarding yesterday's thunderstorm, the wind did a great deal of damage, **whereas the water did not.**

<u>Rule 2</u>. The conjunction **while** has two meanings. When it means "during the time that," the verb tense is often present progressive or past progressive. When it means "contrast," various verb tenses are possible.

> **While I was cleaning the kitchen,** she was washing the car. (= time)
>
> **While this TV has a great picture,** the price is too high for me. (= contrast)

<u>Rule 3</u>. The conjunction **whereas** is not at all common in conversation. It is used in formal and legal language. Do not try to use this is in your daily speech.

> strange: *Jack*: **"I ate eggs for breakfast, whereas my wife only had toast."**
>
> natural: *Jack*: **"I ate eggs for breakfast, but my wife only had toast."**

EXERCISE 6. Sentence Completion

Write complete sentences to contrast the food items.

1. Whereas pizza is high in calories, _____.

2. While pizza and tacos _____.

3. Though James likes pizza, _____.

4. Whereas some of the ingredients in pizza _____

   _____.

5. For meat lovers, pizzas and tacos can be a dream come true, while _____

   _____.

 # Grammar Lesson

Adverb Clause 5: Condition

Common Subordinating Conjunctions that Introduce Adverb Clauses of Condition	
if	**If the weather is nice tomorrow,** I think we will go to the beach.
only if	We will go to the beach **only if the weather is nice tomorrow.**
even if	**Even if the weather is nice tomorrow,** we will not go to the beach.
whether or not	We will go to the beach tomorrow **whether or not the weather is nice.**
unless	**Unless the weather is nice,** we will not go to the beach tomorrow.
provided that	We will go to the beach tomorrow **provided that the weather is nice.**
in case	**In case the weather is not nice tomorrow,** the school will cancel the trip.
in the event that	The school trip will be canceled **in the event that the weather is bad tomorrow.**

EXERCISE 7. Editing: Is It Correct?

If the sentence is correct, write a check mark (✓) on the line. If it is not correct, write X on the line and circle the mistake. Then change the sentence to make it correct. Write the change above the mistake. (*Hint:* There are twelve sentences. Four are correct, but eight have mistakes.)

What to Do in a Thunderstorm

_____ 1. If is lightning, what should you do?

_____ 2. Whether or no you have taken lightning seriously in the past, it is important to take several precautions during a lightning storm.

_____ 3. If you are outdoors, do not seek shelter under a tree as lightning might strike the tree.

_____ 4. Even it is raining really hard, do not be tempted to wait out the lightning storm under the tree.

_____ 5. If you are outdoors, you should avoid water, high ground, and open spaces.

_____ 6. Provided that you can maintain a minimum of fifteen feet between you and someone else it is safe to wait out the storm with another person. Thus, it is best not to wait out the storm in a small group.

_____ 7. In an event that the storm is really severe, crouch down and cover your ears with your hands to reduce any ear damage from the thunder.

_____ 8. You will be safe in a vehicle if only it is a fully enclosed metal vehicle and all the windows are shut. Thus, a convertible is not a safe option.

_____ 9. If are you indoors, avoid water and do not go near windows or doors.

_____ 10. Unless it is an emergency, do not use the telephone.

_____ 11. Finally, you should unplug all appliances in your house in a severe storm even you are not using them.

_____ 12. You can survive a thunderstorm provided that you follow these important precautions.

Grammar Lesson

Adverb Clause 6: Place

Common Subordinating Conjunctions that Introduce Adverb Clauses of Place	
where	Preston is located **where the Red River and the Elk River meet.**
wherever	**Wherever I have lived,** I have made new friends quite easily.
anywhere	It is important to drive more carefully **anywhere it has just rained.**
everywhere	**Everywhere I shop,** people tell me "Have a good day!"

EXERCISE 8. Adverb Clause Subordinators

Do an Internet search for the words *anywhere* and *everywhere*. Write 2 examples for each. Then work with a classmate to compare your examples. How are they different?

_____

_____

_____

_____

_____

_____

_____

_____

_____

_____

_____

_____

Do Online Exercise 5.3. My score: _____ /10. _____ % correct.

Grammar Lesson

Adverb Clause 7: Result

Common Subordinating Conjunctions that Introduce Adverb Clauses of Result	
so (adjective) that	It was **so** hot **that** you could fry an egg on the sidewalk!
such (adjective + noun) that	They were **such** delicious doughnuts **that** no one could eat just one.

Rule 1. In conversation or informal writing, the word **that** is often omitted with these two subordinating adverbs.

informal: It was such a good book **I recommended it to all my friends.**

formal: It was such a good book **that I recommended it to all my friends.**

Rule 2. Adverb clauses of result do not use commas.

The exam was so hard **that no one passed it.**

BE CAREFUL!

Common Learner Errors	Explanation
1. The exam was ~~such~~ so hard that no one passed it.	Do not use **such** with an adjective unless there is an accompanying noun.
2. It was ~~so~~ such bad weather that all flights were canceled.	Do not use **so** with a noun.

EXERCISE 9. Sentence Production

Change the sentences with **so** to sentences with **such** and those with **such** to **so**. Then make other changes as needed.

Basketball

1. Basketball is such an entertaining sport that many children want to learn to play it.

   _____

   _____

2. LeBron James is so good at playing basketball that spectators can't take their eyes off him.

   _____

   _____

3. Those are such expensive tickets that I don't know if I can afford to go to the game.

   _____

   _____

4. Playing basketball at the professional level is such a difficult thing that it takes years of practice.

   _____

   _____

5. He had such big hands that he could balance two basketballs in one hand.

   _____

   _____

6. The U.S. and Spanish Olympic basketball teams are so good that they have played in several Gold Medal games.

   _____

   _____

Grammar Lesson

Adverb Clause 8: Purpose

Common Subordinating Conjunctions that Introduce Adverb Clauses of Purpose	
so that	George added sugar to the coffee **so that it would be sweeter.**
in order that	**In order that we understand the lesson better,** the professor asked us to write a summary of each part of the unit.

<u>Rule 1</u>. With **so that** and **in order that,** the word **that** is optional. In conversation, **so** sounds more normal than **so that.**

<u>Rule 2</u>. Following **so that,** use a **modal + verb** in the adverb clause of purpose.

I need to go to the library **so that I can finish my report.**

 BE CAREFUL!

Common Learner Errors	Explanation
1. We got to the airport early ~~, so that~~ so that we would not be rushed during the check-in process.	Do not use a comma before **so that** or **in order that.**
2. There is a tax on gasoline purchases so we ~~have~~ **can have** (OR **might have**) better roads.	Do not use a verb after **so that.** Use a **modal + verb.**

EXERCISE 10. Matching Adverb Clauses of Purpose with Their Independent Clauses

Match the main clauses on the left with the best adverb clause on the right. Write the letter of the matching clause on the line in front of the number.

_____ 1. I'm going to study as much as I can tonight

_____ 2. He added more sugar to the cookie dough

_____ 3. Cats' whiskers are as wide as their bodies

_____ 4. I bought six extra bottles of juice

_____ 5. The gardener soaked the plants in the small pots

_____ 6. She saved up all her extra money for a year

_____ 7. We arrived at the airport three hours early

_____ 8. Animals often gain more weight just before winter

_____ 9. Some people have to wear glasses

_____ 10. I bought you a medium one

a. so they can see well.

b. so that we would not miss our flight.

c. so that they would have enough water for the rest of the week.

d. so that the cookies would be as sweet as possible.

e. so that she could buy herself a digital camera.

f. so we would be sure to have enough for everyone.

g. so that they will have enough nutrition for their bodies.

h. so that they can judge how wide an opening is before entering.

i. so that I won't have so much studying to do tomorrow night.

j. so it would fit you for sure.

ONE-MINUTE LESSON

as . . . as/the same . . . as. When we compare two things that are not so different, we use **as . . . as** with adjectives (*as wide as*) and **the same . . . as** with nouns (*the same width as*). The meanings are the same.

EXERCISE 11. Mini-Conversations

Circle the correct words in these mini-conversations.

1. *A.* Do you enjoy the water?

   B. Yes! Ever (when, since) I was a small child, I have loved going on my dad's boat.

2. *A.* Oh, isn't that dangerous for children to be on a boat?

   B. Not really. We always wore our life jackets (because, so that) we would be OK if we fell into the water.

3. *A.* Oh, that's good. (After, Although) I grew up near the water, I never wanted to get in it.

   B. Really? I didn't know that.

   A. Yes. (Since, If) we lived near a lake in Florida, my sisters would go swimming and tubing, but I was always afraid.

   B. You were afraid of the water?

4. *A.* Not exactly. I was afraid of the snakes and the alligators!

   B. I don't blame you! (While, Wherever) there is water, there is the possibility of water snakes and other animals. Luckily, I haven't seen any.

5. *A.* OK, well (since, when) you haven't seen any dangerous animals, maybe I can go with you on your dad's boat.

   B. That would be great! (While, As soon as) I talk to him again, I will mention it.

Grammar Lesson

Adverb Clause 9: Manner

Common Subordinating Conjunctions that Introduce Adverb Clauses of Manner	
as	He answered the phone **as any native speaker would.**
as if	He answered the phone **as if he were expecting an important call.**
as though	He looks **as though he were only a child.**
in that	The two tickets differ **in that the first one is business class.**

<u>Rule 1</u>. Adverb clauses of manner usually come after the main clause. They do not usually start a sentence.

<u>Rule 2</u>. The subordinators **as if** and **as though** introduce unreal situations. When the action after **as if** or **as though** is unreal, the verb must be in **subjunctive mood.** This resembles simple past tense for a present action and past perfect tense for a past action.

Joe likes to act **as if he were rich.** (use *were*, not *is*)

Joe looked **as though he had received some bad news.** (use *had received*, not *received*)

 ## BE CAREFUL!

Common Learner Errors	Explanation
1. ~~As if he were a native speaker, Joe answered the phone.~~ Joe answered the phone as if he were a native speaker.	Avoid beginning a sentence with an adverb clause of manner.
2. Joe likes to act as if he ~~was~~ were rich.	Use subjunctive mood for verbs describing unreal situations following **as if** and **as though**.

EXERCISE 12. Unreal Situations

Circle the correct verb form in parentheses.

1. Situation: Mary does not know Sue at all, but she always speaks very highly of her.

    Statement: It's as though Sue actually (knows, knew, had met) Mary.

2. Situation: Bill is 23 years old, but he still acts like a child sometimes.

    Statement: Bill sometimes behaves as though he (is, were, had, had been) 10 years old.

3. Situation: Kathy had a very hard day at work today. She is really tired.

    Statement: Kathy looks as if she (is, were, had been) exhausted.

4. Situation: Gregory is not an expert on plant care, but I have heard him give others some advice about their plants.

    Statement: Gregory talks as though he (knew, knows, had known) plants inside and out.

5. Situation: Mark and Lea do not know the flavor of the dessert. It does not have nuts in it, though.

    Statement: This dessert tastes as if it (has, had, had had) nuts in it.

Do Online Exercise 5.4. My score: _____ /10. _____ % correct.

EXERCISE 13. Review Test 1: Multiple Choice

Circle the letter of the correct answer.

1. I'm a tennis fanatic! _____ I am tired, I usually have enough energy to play tennis.

    a. Only if   b. Since   c. Even if   d. Now that

2. By the time Beethoven reached the young age of 10, he _____ several impressive musical works.

    a. already wrote   c. had already written

    b. already writes   d. will already write

3. _____ the assignment is due tomorrow, it is imperative that we finish it today.

    a. Unless   b. So that   c. Everywhere   d. As

4. I can't believe you are having trouble lifting that box. You are acting as if it _____ really heavy.

    a. is   b. had   c. had been   d. were

5. _____ singer left the stage after singing another incredibly beautiful song, but no one wanted to leave the auditorium.

    a. When the   b. In order that the   c. Although the   d. The

6. Given that _____, your grade for the class is an F.

    a. you worked so hard in this course

    b. your final exam in the course was so bad

    c. the book for this course was fairly easy

    d. you were not absent a single day in this course

7. She is an excellent teacher who has taught in four schools. _____ she has taught, she has received wonderful evaluations from her principal.

    a. Everywhere   c. Where

    b. Despite   d. In such good schools that

8. The bus driver waited at the stop for an extra minute so that the old woman _____ on the bus.

    a. could get   b. got   c. will get   d. had gotten

9. Although we tend to think that they are basically the same animal, dolphins, porpoises, and fish are not alike. Despite how similar they might seem, these three animals _____ dolphins and porpoises are mammals while fish are not.

   a. different in that   c. different so that

   b. differ in that   d. differ so that

10. As soon as I _____ at my apartment, I promise that I will call you to let you know that I have arrived safely.

    a. arrive   b. will arrive   c. arrived   d. arriving

EXERCISE 14. Review Test 2: Production and Evaluation

Part 1.
Read these sentences, and underline the correct adverb clause connector.

My Favorite Italian Restaurant

1. Last night my cousin and I went to an Italian restaurant (because, whereas, so that) we wanted to eat pasta.

2. Broadway Eatery has (so, such, such a) good food that we decided to spend 30 minutes driving there (even though, as if, in that) it's so far away.

3. (Whenever, Wherever, However) I go to Broadway Eatery, I order chicken parmesan. It is by far my favorite dish there!

4. The food took a little while, so my cousin and I sat telling jokes to each other (as soon as, until, while) we were waiting.

5. (Whereas, Though, In the event that) I had not eaten all day, I was doing OK (even though, provided that, because) I knew that my favorite dish would soon be in front of me.

6. (The, Although the, If the) food finally arrived, and we started eating!

7. One thing that I really like about this restaurant is that the food always comes covered with extra cheese (unless, in that, whether or not) you ask for it.

8. (Despite, In spite, Because) the fact that my plate was incredibly full, I managed to eat everything on my plate. What a great meal we had!

Part 2.

Read each sentence carefully. Look at the underlined part. If the underlined part is correct, circle the word *correct*. If it is wrong, circle the word *wrong*. Then write the correction above.

correct   wrong   1. <u>Whenever that I have</u> a headache, I take two aspirin with a large glass of water.

correct   wrong   2. The price of airline tickets is going to go up <u>as soon as the current summer season will end</u>.

correct   wrong   3. <u>Giving that her car had</u> more than 100,000 miles on it, Cecilia decided that is was probably time to sell it.

correct   wrong   4. The employees <u>got their paychecks, so they went</u> to the bank to cash them.

correct   wrong   5. I can't play golf tomorrow because I have to work all day. <u>Even the weather is perfect</u>, with sunny skies and no wind, I still can't play.

EXERCISE 15. Reading Practice: A Conversation

Read the conversation between Johnny and his parents. Then answer the questions. The grammar from this unit is underlined for you.

Johnny: Hi, Mom and Dad.

Dad: How's it going? Don't you have some important news for us?

Johnny: Well, <u>since</u> you already seem to know, yes, I do. We got our report cards today.

Mom: <u>Now that</u> you mention it, I do recall your math teacher telling us to expect them this week.

Johnny: Let me tell you how I did. My grade in art is very high <u>though</u> my math grade is really low. <u>Even though</u> I did really well in English, I didn't do so hot in history. I did well in music <u>although</u> I didn't do so well in science. <u>Now that</u> you know all about all my grades, can I go to Tommy's to play video games?

Dad: Just a minute, young man. Just <u>because</u> you told us your grades, it doesn't mean you are off the hook. <u>When</u> you get home from school, you will do your homework first. <u>After</u> you've finished, you will show it to your mother and fix whatever needs fixing. <u>As soon as</u> I get home, you will tell me what you did in school, what your homework was, and what you didn't understand. If there is any time left <u>before</u> you have to go to bed, you can read a book of your choice. Are we clear?

1. Were Mom and Dad expecting the report card as the news? _____
   _____

2. Did Johnny tell his parents the good news or the bad news first? _____
   Why do you think he did that? _____
   _____

3. What do you notice about the placement of the adverb clauses? _____
   _____

4. How did Dad emphasize the sequence of events that he expected Johnny to follow every day? _____
   _____

5. When do you think Johnny can play video games with Tommy from now on?
   _____

EXERCISE 16. Vocabulary Practice: Word Knowledge

Circle the answer choice on the right that is most closely related to the vocabulary on the left. Use a dictionary to check the meaning of words you do not know.

Vocabulary	Answer Choices	
1. reverse	go backward	go forward
2. audience	participants	spectators
3. off the hook	a lot of people	no longer needed
4. drench	add a little liquid	add a lot of liquid
5. a pouch	a fence	a pocket
6. intently	seriously	weakly
7. memorize	to become a member	to remember
8. undefeated	lose 100%	win 100%
9. nearsighted	only see things close by	only see things far away
10. fonts	pictures	writing
11. obsolete	modern	out-of-date
12. the manual	by hand	the instruction book
13. precautions	presenting a danger	preventing a danger
14. A.S.A.P.	probable	soon
15. exotic	fancy	foreign
16. seek	call off	look for
17. brainwashing	asking you for your opinion	telling you what to think
18. stuck in traffic	a traffic jam	a traffic schedule
19. revenues	monies	wide streets
20. idolize	admire	persuade
21. inseparable	cannot take apart	can take apart
22. to hatch	when eggs open	when rain falls
23. a lone person	a person with no friends	only one person
24. a nest	where baby birds live	where new vegetables grow
25. a fanatic	a person with many fans	a person with extreme enthusiasm
26. imperative	might	must

EXERCISE 17. Vocabulary Practice: Collocations

Fill in each blank with the answer on the right that most naturally completes the phrase on the left. If necessary, use a dictionary to check the meaning of words you do not know.

Vocabulary	Answer Choices	
1. determined _____ something	in doing	to do
2. _____ any doubt	with	without
3. _____ a hundred years ago	above	over
4. a _____ consequence	difficult	serious
5. it's _____ in calories	low	slow
6. the _____ speed it can reach	bottom	top
7. by leaps and _____	bounce	bounds
8. to _____ on	venture	adventure
9. annual _____ sale	clearing	clearance
10. learn something by _____	heart	mind
11. a _____ of lightning	bolt	bold
12. _____ rival	absolute	arch
13. _____ the munchies	get	set
14. _____ problems	call off	encounter
15. Let's _____ meatballs.	create	make
16. overhead _____	bins	boxes
17. we _____ ourselves	proud	pride
18. cookie _____	dough	munchies
19. _____ is getting short	our house	our time
20. a very _____ back person	went	laid
21. fall into _____	place	there
22. _____ three steps	make	take
23. right _____ to the bank	near	next
24. in _____	contrast	though
25. the sequence of _____	events	people

EXERCISE 18. Writing Practice: Comparing Now and Then

Part 1. Editing Student Writing

Read these sentences about one student's experiences while living near a beach. Circle the 15 errors. Then write the number of the sentence with the error next to the type of error. (Some sentences have more than one error.)

_____ a. missing article   _____ d. adverb clause punctuation

_____ b. wrong preposition   _____ e. subject-verb agreement

_____ c. verb tense   _____ f. singular-plural of nouns

Surfing
1. My friends say that I am one of the best surfer that they know. 
2. When I was young child, my family lives near from a beach.
3. During summer, I could go surfing, whenever I wanted to.
4. On some Saturday mornings, I used to get up before sunrise to get everything ready and then walk to beach with my surfboard.
5. Even at this early time of the day, a lot of surfer would already be at the beach.
6. I would see a lot of peoples who had come to our small town in California just so that they could go surfing.
7. This was surprising to me, because I never thought living near a beach was such special thing, but it is.
8. Being able to surf so much never seems very special to me until I moved to area where I did not have this opportunity to surf all the time.
9. However, now I truly appreciates the free surfing that I was having in my small hometown.
10. In hindsight, we was incredibly lucky because we grew up so close to a beach.

Part 2. Original Student Writing

Situation: Write a paragraph or short essay in which you compare or contrast two things or two people. Some possible topics include: two vacation destinations, two famous politicians, two languages, two typical dishes, two careers, and two fast-food restaurants.

Use at least three adverb clauses in your writing. Underline these adverb clauses and circle the initial connecting word so the teacher can see what you are trying to practice.

Unit 6

Noun Clauses

Discover the Grammar

Read the passage about a popular beverage. Each group of words in bold letters is a noun clause.
Then answer the questions that follow.

Line	
1	Some people believe **that a goat herder in Ethiopia discovered coffee**
2	**about 1,500 years ago.** According to legend, he had noticed **that his goats**
3	**became friskier after eating coffee berries.** He wondered **how the berries**
4	**might affect humans,** so he decided **that he would try some himself.** Conse-
5	quently, he was quite pleased **that he, too, became more energetic and alert.**
6	As the story goes, local monks soon heard about **what the goat herder**
7	**had experienced,** and they began to use the berries as a means of helping them
8	stay awake during long periods of prayers. At some point, although no one is
9	certain of **how it happened,** the monks began to make a stimulating beverage
10	from the berries by cooking them in hot water. As this information continued
11	to spread throughout the region of Ethiopia, traders from across the Red Sea
12	took coffee beans back to farmers in Yemen, who were hopeful **that the beans**

136

13	could be grown in the mountains there. Their cultivation was a success, and
14	that is why we have Arabica beans today.
15	Some stories say that the roasting of coffee beans began about 500
16	years after their discovery, yet no one is sure of where it first occurred.
17	Nevertheless, this roasting process is what gives us the dark color and intense
18	flavor of today's coffee.
19	Whether or not this legend is true remains unconfirmed. However, what
20	is evident is that this stimulating beverage is now enjoyed by millions of
21	people around the world.

1. A noun clause can be a subject of a sentence. Find the two noun clauses in the coffee story that function as **subjects**. Write them with their line numbers and corresponding main verbs here.

Line	Noun Clause as Subject	Main Verb

2. A noun clause can also be the object of a preposition. Find the two examples of a noun clause after a preposition. Write them here with their line numbers and preceding preposition.

Line	Preposition	Noun Clause as Object of a Preposition

3. Write what you consider to be the sentence that has the most complicated grammar.

Line	Sentence

In your opinion, what is difficult about the grammar of this sentence to you?

_____

4. What questions do you have about noun clauses?

_____

 # Grammar Lesson

Noun Clauses: Form and Function—Overview

A noun clause, like other clauses, has both a subject and a verb. A noun clause is a dependent clause and needs to be connected to an independent clause.

Independent Clause	Noun Clause
Our server said	that a **mocha latte** is made with chocolate syrup.

A noun clause has the same grammatical function as a noun in certain sentence positions. In other words, whatever a noun can do (subject, direct object, object of a preposition), a noun clause can do. Subordinators that begin noun clauses include **that, if, whether**, question words (**who, where**, etc.) and **–ever** (**whoever, whichever**, etc.)

Sentence Position	With Noun	With Noun Clause
Direct object of the verb	Our server said **his name**.	Our server said **that a mocha latte is made with chocolate syrup.**
Object of a preposition	I will think about **you**.	I will think about **what you said.**
Subject of the sentence	**The Nazca lines** remain a mystery.	**How the Nazca lines were made** remains a mystery.
Subject complement	A legend is **an unproven story from history.**	The legend is **that a goat herder discovered coffee.**
After **be** + adjective	The children are happy **campers**.	The children are happy **that summer vacation is near.**

EXERCISE 1. Recognizing Noun Clauses

Underline the noun clause in each sentence. Be sure to include the subordinator.

Study Abroad

1. *Miki:* For several years Fumiko has hoped that she could finish her education in the United States.

2. *Juri:* Do you know where she wants to study?

3. *Miki:* Where she wants to study is not the problem.

4. *Juri:* I guess that I misunderstood you.

5. *Miki:* The problem is whether or not she can save enough money to go.

 ## Grammar Lesson

Usage 1: Noun Clauses as Embedded Statements—*That* Clauses

Most people understand <u>that vitamin supplements are necessary</u>.
S   V   O

Rule 1. Noun clauses often appear in the object position within a sentence. This type of noun clause can begin with **that**.

Rule 2. In conversation, the word **that** may be omitted.

Most people understand that **vitamin supplements are necessary.**

Most people understand vitamin supplements are necessary.

Connecting Grammar and Vocabulary

Noun clauses follow verbs of mental activity. Some common verbs are listed.

believe	guess	know	understand
forget	hope	remember	wonder

EXERCISE 2. Recognizing Noun Clauses in a Conversation

Underline the noun clauses in the conversation. The first one has been done for you as an example.

Remembering a Previous Meeting

Patricia: Hi. My name is Patricia. I think <u>that we've met before</u>. Are you Carmella?

Carmella: Yes, my name is Carmella. I believe we met at the Petersons' house. They had a "Get to know your candidate" potluck* dinner.

Patricia: I think you sat next to me on the sofa.

Carmella: Yep. That get-together was a great idea. It was very informative, and I can't deny that I enjoyed the food a lot.

Patricia: I noticed that a lot of our neighbors asked the candidate about street repairs.

Carmella: Yes, there are some enormous potholes on West Central Street. I hope the candidate will address that issue in her speech next week.

Patricia: Can you imagine what it would cost to repair all the streets in town?

Carmella: I doubt that they'll all get fixed . . . probably just the most dangerous ones.

Patricia: I think you're right! Well, it was nice seeing you again.

Carmella: Same here. Take care.

*A *potluck* is an informal group dinner where people bring a dish to share with others.

EXERCISE 3. Creating Statements Using Noun Clauses

Use these facts to create noun clauses with **that.** The subject, verb, and verb tense for the main clause are in parentheses. The first one has been done for you as an example.

Talking about Volcanoes

1. Mt. Etna has erupted several times since July 2000. (Mario/know [present])

   Mario knows that Mt. Etna has erupted

   several times since July 2000.

2. It will erupt again. (He/be worried [present])

   _____

   _____

3. The lava on Mt. Etna flowed at a rate of 50 meters per hour in 2000. (Scientists/estimate [simple past])

   _____

   _____

4. Various gases can be expelled during an eruption. (It / be / a fact [present])

   _____

   _____

5. Volcanic eruptions can result in new islands. (Geologists/determine [present perfect])

   _____

   _____

ONE-MINUTE LESSON

When **result** is a noun, it is usually in the phrase *the result is* or *the result of (some-thing) is.* When **result** is a verb, it is usually followed by the preposition *in: The strong wind resulted __in__ several damaged houses on our block.*

Grammar Lesson

Usage 2: Noun Clauses as Embedded Questions— *Wh*– or Yes-No Clauses

> I don't know <u>where Pat and Jo are going for vacation</u>.
>   S   V   O
>
> Do you know <u>whether they're going to Costa Rica?</u>
>   S V   O

Using noun clauses as embedded questions can be an indirect way to ask for information, which is often considered more polite than asking directly, especially when talking to an unknown person.

Direct Question	Indirect Requests
What time is it?	Do you know what time it is? **(polite)** Can you tell me what time it is? **(more polite)** Could you tell me what time it is? **(even more polite)**

Rule 1. Statement word order (**subject + verb**) is always used in the embedded question (noun clause). The main clause can have either question word order or statement word order, but this has no effect on the noun clause, which always has the same word order.

Main clause as question: **Do you remember** what she said?

Main clause as statement: **I don't remember** what she said.

Rule 2. As a noun clause, an embedded question can function as any noun can. Three common functions include direct object, object of preposition, and subject.

direct object	I didn't hear **what she said**.
object of preposition	Did you pay attention to **what she said**?
subject	**What she said** confused all of us.

Rule 3. A yes-no question can become a noun clause using **if** or **whether**.

Direct question: **Is Mexico bigger than Colombia?**

Noun clause: **I wonder if Mexico is bigger than Colombia.**

BE CAREFUL!

Common Learner Errors	Explanation
1. Do you know **where** ~~are my keys~~ my keys are?	Remember to use statement word order (subject + verb) for embedded questions.
2. I didn't hear **what** ~~did she say~~ she said.	Do not use auxiliary verbs **do, did, does** in the embedded question.
3. Could you tell me what the time is~~.~~ ?	If the main clause uses question format, then you need to use a question mark (?).

EXERCISE 4. Identifying Embedded Questions in Context

Underline the embedded clauses in the following questions about volcanoes. Write S above the subjects of both the dependent and independent clauses. Write V above the verbs of both clauses. The first one has been done for you as an example.

Asking Questions about Volcanoes

1. Do you know <u>how many active volcanoes exist in the world today</u>?

2. Can you tell us what you know about volcanoes?

3. Can you remember if Mt. Etna is a dangerous volcano?

4. Have you forgotten where Mt. Etna is?

5. Would you please show us where it is on the globe?

6. Could you please explain what the different types of eruptions are?

7. Do you know how hot the lava can get?

8. Have you ever seen what happens to solidified lava?

EXERCISE 5. Speaking Practice: Trivia

Answer the questions using one of the four choices. Then practice speaking with a partner. Student A asks Student B Questions 2–4. Student B asks Student A Questions 5–7. When finished, compare your answers and discuss them.

Answer the trivia questions with these choices.

I don't know who / what / when / where / why / how many . . . .

I forgot who / what / when / where / why / how many . . . .

I think that . . . .

I'm pretty sure that . . . .

Remember that the main clause and the noun clause can have different tenses. The first one has been done for you as an example.

1. Who was Alfred Nobel?

   I forgot who Alfred Nobel was. (Or) I think that Alfred Nobel was a scientist.

2. What is a pothole?

   _____.

3. Where is Vanuatu?

   _____.

4. Who is on a U.S. five-dollar bill?

   _____.

5. How many continents do penguins live on?

   _____.

6. Why is the sky blue?

   _____.

7. What does the phrase *down-to-earth* mean?

   _____.

EXERCISE 6. Using Indirect Requests for Information

Change these direct questions into indirect requests. Be careful: both yes-no and *wh-* questions are asked. The first one has been done for you as an example.

Asking for Information Indirectly

1. What is a zeppelin?

   Can you tell me what a zeppelin is?

2. What is the difference between an alligator and a crocodile?

   _____

   _____.

3. Has there ever been a woman Secretary-General of the United Nations?

   _____.

4. What is a bear market?

   _____.

5. Does the bank open at 9:00 or 10:00?

   _____.

6. Was pizza invented in Italy or New York?

   _____.

7. How do I get to the post office from here?

   _____.

8. Excuse me, but what time is it now?

   _____.

 Do Online Exercise 6.1. My score: _____ /10. _____ % correct.

Grammar Lesson

Reducing *Wh-* Noun Clauses to Infinitives

If the modals **can, could,** or **should** are used in a **wh-** noun clause, it is possible to replace the subject and modal with an infinitive after the **wh- word**. The meaning is the same in both forms.

Vladimir forgot **where** *he* **can return** his books. →	Vladimir forgot **where** *to return* his books.
The teacher told *us* **how** *we* **should study.** →	The teacher told us **how** *to study*.

BE CAREFUL!

Common Learner Error	Explanation
I wonder ~~that~~ **why** grammar has to have so many rules.	The verb **wonder** must be followed by a **wh- word** or **if/whether.**

EXERCISE 7. Using Infinitives

Reduce the noun clause by using infinitives after the *wh-* words. Circle the infinitive in your answer. Make sure the subject is the same in both the main clause and the noun clause so that you do not change the meaning. The first one has been done for you as an example.

1. Kelly and Steve don't know where they should go for their vacation.

   Kelly and Steve don't know where (to go) for their vacation.

2. After I had wrecked my car, the insurance agent told me what I should do.

   _____.

3. Veronica doesn't know whether she should stay in Tampa or go back to Mexico.

   _____.

4. Do you know how you can find a new roommate?

   _____.

5. Penny and I don't know what we should wear to the graduation ceremony.

   _____.

6. I have tried everything to remove the stain from the carpet. I don't know what else I can try.

   _____.

 **Grammar Lesson**

Usage 3: Noun Clauses and Adjectives

Adjectives can be used to describe the idea or attitude in a noun clause that follows.

Positive attitude	The farmers are **relieved that** it will rain this week.
Negative attitude	It is **terrible that** she can't attend graduation.
Certainty	I am **confident that** Wei will pass the IELTS.
Negative certainty	Hyeon Ju is **doubtful that** Ruiji passed the TOEFL.

<u>Rule 1.</u> Some adjectives require a preposition when the noun clause starts with a **wh- word.** The noun clause will be the object of that preposition.

Positive attitude	The farmers are **relieved by** what the president said.
Negative attitude	I am **sorry for** what I said.

 EXERCISE 8. Speaking Practice: About Me

Step 1. Complete each of these sentences with a noun clause about yourself. The first one has been done for you as an example.

Step 2. Discuss your sentences with a partner or small group.

1. It is a fact <u>that I am studying English</u>   .

2. I am thankful for _____.

3. I am worried about _____.

4. I am not sure <u>if</u> _____.

5. I am excited about _____.

6. I am pleased with _____.

7. I am annoyed by _____.

8. It is too bad <u>that</u> _____.

9. I'm not clear about _____.

10. It's obvious <u>that</u> _____.

EXERCISE 9. Noun Clauses that Follow Adjectives

Read the dialogue between a host family and an exchange student. Underline the correct word in each set of parentheses to complete the sentences.

Meeting Your Host Family at the Airport

Mrs. Boyer: You must be Ariadne. I'm Mrs. Boyer, and we are your host family. This is Mr. Boyer; these are our daughters, Patty and Lori, and our sons, Rodney and Paul.

Ariadne: Hi. I'm pleased to meet you, all of you.

Mr. Boyer: We are so happy ❶ (what, that) you are staying with us this semester.

Ariadne: Thanks. I'm surprised to see that you have such a large family. Are you sure ❷ (that, if) it's okay?

Mrs. Boyer: Certainly. We have an extra bed in the girls' room because our oldest daughter is going to study in Panama City this semester.

Ariadne: Really? That's where I'm from. Do you know where she will be living?

Mrs. Boyer: Oh, she was very excited about that. I'm not ❸ (sure, doubtful) whether I remember the neighborhood, but it's near the beach. Bill, do you remember what it's called?

Mr. Boyer: I think it's called Coronado. Do you know anyone there, Ariadne?

Ariadne: Oh, yes. My Uncle Juan Carlos lives there. He and my Aunt Carmen are host parents, too. They sent me a text message yesterday to wish me good luck. They were disappointed ❹ (that/why) they didn't get to say good-bye at the airport. Anyway, they included a picture of their family with their new exchange student, Gina.

Mrs. Boyer: That's funny. That's our daughter Regina's nickname.

Ariadne: Really! Would you like to see the photo? I'm not certain ❺ (if, what) I can access my phone here, but let's see if I can. OK, here it is. It's remarkable ❻ (why, how much) your son Rodney looks like their student.

Mrs. Boyer: Oh my goodness! That's Gina! Oh, we are so relieved ❼ (that, why) she will be with such a nice family.

Ariadne: Yes. And my parents will be thankful ❽ (why, that) you are so kind.

Mrs. Boyer: What a small world!

Grammar Lesson

Usage 4: Noun Clauses as Subject of the Sentence

When you want to highlight the information in the noun clause, you can move it to the subject position of a sentence. In essence, you are causing the reader to pay attention to that information because it comes first.

<u>How the accident happened</u> was the main issue at today's meeting.
S   V

Rule 1. **Wh- words** and **that** can mark the beginning of a noun clause in the subject position.

Rule 2. **Whether,** but never **if,** can also begin a noun clause in the subject position.

Rule 3. **That** clauses in the subject position often begin with **the fact that.**

Rule 4. Whenever a noun clause is used as the subject, the verb in the main clause is singular.

Rule 5. Using a noun clause at the beginning of a sentence is more formal than using **it** (as the subject placeholder) to begin a sentence.

More Formal	Less Formal
How the fire started is not known.	**It is not known** how the fire started.
Whether or not Aspen has enough snow for skiing is not certain.	**It is not certain** whether or not Aspen has enough snow for skiing.

 # BE CAREFUL!

Common Learner Errors	Explanation
1. ~~If~~ **Whether** we can go swimming depends on the weather.	The words **if** and **whether** are usually interchangeable in a noun clause. However, do not use **if** to begin a noun clause that is used as the subject of the sentence.
2. What the organization does for senior citizens ~~are~~ **is** very helpful.	Whenever a noun clause is in the subject position, the verb that follows it must be singular in form. Don't be confused by other nouns within the noun clause.
3. How ~~did~~ the fire ~~start~~ started is unknown.	Do not use auxiliary question words **do, does, or did** in the noun clause.

EXERCISE 10. Formal Subject Clauses

Write these sentences so that the noun clause is the subject of the sentence. Circle the verb in the main clause. The first one has been done for you as an example.

Interesting Facts about Florida

1. It is still undetermined whether Florida will have a new rail system.

    Whether Florida will have a new rail system (is) still undetermined.

2. It has yet to be decided whether we will have time to visit all of the theme parks.

    _____

    _____

3. It is a fact that Florida has very competitive college football teams.

    _____

    _____

4. It is ironic that it rains nearly every day during the summer in the "Sunshine State."

    _____

    _____

5. It is a legend that the Fountain of Youth was discovered in Florida by Ponce de Leon in the 16th century.

    _____

    _____

Do Online Exercise 6.2. My score: _____ /10. _____ % correct.

Grammar Lesson

Usage 5: Noun Clauses to Stress Importance or Urgency (Subjunctive Mood)

> The doctor insisted that Shelly **go** to the hospital.
> It is important that Mr. and Mrs. Millburn **be** at my office at 8 o'clock tomorrow.
> That he **take** his medicine every day is critical to his improvement.

The **subjunctive mood** is created by using the base verb form within a noun clause to express urgency, to give advice, or to make a strong recommendation. It is used in formal writing or speech.

Verbs and Adjectives of Importance and Urgency that Require Subjunctive Mood	
Verbs	Adjectives
advise, demand, insist, order, prefer, require, recommend, suggest	critical, essential, imperative, important, necessary, urgent

<u>Rule 1</u>. When noun clauses appear with verbs or adjectives that express urgency or give advice, the verb in the noun clause is in the **base form**. This is called the subjunctive mood.

<u>Rule 2</u>. The subjunctive verbs are not affected by present, past, or future time, nor are they affected by a singular or plural subject.

It is important that I have the right information.

It is important that she have the right information.

<u>Rule 3</u>. A negative verb in the subjunctive is formed by **not + base form of verb**. Do not use helping verbs **do, does,** or **did**.

My parents prefer that I not buy a car now.

<u>Rule 4</u>. A passive verb in the subjunctive is formed by **be + PAST PARTICIPLE**.

It is necessary that all windows be closed at night.

BE CAREFUL!

Common Learner Errors	Explanation
1. It is necessary that you ~~are~~ **be** on time.	Remember to use the base form of the verb in noun clauses with certain expressions of urgency.
2. It is important that each student ~~has~~ **have** a computer for this activity.	Do not conjugate the verb in noun clauses after certain expressions of urgency.

EXERCISE 11. Identify Subjunctive Mood in Context

Read the sentences about an emergency phone call from a school nurse. Underline the verbs or adjectives that **express urgency** or **advice**. Write **S** above the subject and **V** above the verb in the noun clause. The first one has been done for you as an example.

An Emergency Phone Call

1. Mrs. Jonas, this is the nurse at your son Pierre's school. It is <u>urgent</u> that you call the school immediately.

2. Pierre had an accident on the playground, and it is important that you come to the school.

3. It's critical that he see a doctor right away.

4. If you prefer that he be taken by ambulance, please let us know immediately.

5. Since the hospital requires that permission forms be signed by a parent, you will have to meet us there.

6. The principal insisted that I ride in the ambulance with Pierre to comfort him.

7. Before we left, the principal recommended that you meet us in the emergency room.

8. I'm sure the doctor will insist that your son stay in bed for a few days.

EXERCISE 12. Using the Subjunctive

Complete these sentences with the correct verb forms. Use the subjunctive and passive where necessary. (Note: Not all verbs are subjunctive. Various tenses may be used.)

A Meeting with An Advisor

Advisor: Good Morning, Lisa. Please ❶ _____ (come) in.

Lisa: Good Morning, Dr. Canton.

Advisor: Please sit down.

Lisa: Because of the expenses, it is essential that I ❷ _____ (finish) my education as soon as possible.

Advisor: ❸ _____ (you, understand) what ❹ _____ (be) required for you to complete your degree?

Lisa: I think so.

Advisor: Well, if you ❺ _____ (want) a degree in aeronautical engineering, the department requires that each student successfully ❻ _____ (complete) a special course called Statics and Dynamics.

Lisa: And I need to take German, right? Because it is necessary that I ❼ _____ (take) German classes I plan to go to graduate school in Germany.

Advisor: OK, so it's imperative that your schedule ❽ _____ (be) revised to include German A.S.A.P.

Grammar Lesson

Usage 6: Noun Clauses in Reported Speech

Knowing how to use **reported, or indirect, speech** is useful when you need to tell someone what another person has said. It is also necessary to use both direct quotes and indirect speech when you are writing an academic report using other sources for your data.

Quoted Speech (direct)	Reported Speech (indirect)
At yesterday's meeting, the President said, "I have a new plan for creating more jobs."	At yesterday's meeting, the President **said that he had** a new plan for creating more jobs.

Rule 1. Quotation marks are used at the beginning and end of words that are written exactly as they were spoken or written in another book, journal, etc. This is also referred to as **quoted speech** or **direct quotes**.

> **"I have a dream today," Martin Luther King, Jr., said during his famous 1963 speech.**

Rule 2. Words that report what someone said do not require quotation marks when they become part of a noun clause that changes pronouns and time. This is also referred to as **reported speech** or **indirect speech**.

> **During his famous 1963 speech, Martin Luther King, Jr., said that he had a dream that day.**

Rule 3. Tense change: Notice the change in the verb tense from the example in Rule 1 to the example in Rule 2. The verb in the direct quotation is in the present tense (**have**). However, when the quotation is written as indirect **reported speech,** the verb is changed to past tense (**had**). This change is known as the rule of **sequence of tenses**. It applies to indirect or reported speech.

Rule 4. Pronoun and possessive adjective change: Also notice that the pronoun has changed in the example. In the quote, King says **I**, but when it is reported, the pronoun is changed to **he** to refer to King. Likewise, if a woman says, "My book is lost," you would change the possessive adjective: **She said her book was lost.**

Rule 5. Time expression change: In the quote, King says **today**. In the reported speech, it is changed to **that day** to refer to the day he gave the speech.

Rule 6. When you are reporting factual information, that is, information that does not change, you do not have to change the verb tense.

BE CAREFUL!

Common Learner Errors	Explanation
1. My sister ~~said me~~ said that this class is difficult.	The verb **say** is usually followed by a noun clause. It is never followed by an object pronoun. Remember that **that** may be omitted in informal speech.
2. Lynda ~~told that~~ told him that she would be home tonight.	The verb **tell** must be followed by an object pronoun, a name, or a noun.

Sequence of Tenses

In reported speech, what is being reported is something that was said earlier. Consequently, the main clause verb is usually past tense, such as **said.** This past tense verb acts to pull the noun clause verb back in time even further.

Quoted Speech	Reported Speech
Mike said, " . . . ."	
"I <u>am hungry</u>." **simple present**	Mike said that he **was** hungry. He said (that) he was . . . . **simple past**
"I <u>am eating</u> a pear <u>now</u>." **present continuous**	Mike said that he **was eating** a pear **then.** He said (that) he was eating . . . . **past continuous**
"I <u>have eaten</u> plums." **present perfect**	Mike said that he **had eaten** plums. He said (that) he had eaten plums. **past perfect**
"I <u>ate</u> a kiwi once." **simple past**	Mike said that he **had eaten** a kiwi once. He said (that) he had eaten . . . . **past perfect**
"I <u>was eating</u> at noon." **past progressive**	Mike said that he **had been eating** at noon. He said (that) he had been eating . . . . **past perfect progressive**
"I <u>will eat</u> a peach tomorrow." **simple future**	Mike said that he **would eat** a peach tomorrow. He said (that) he would eat . . . . **modal—past**

"I <u>may try</u> a mango." **modal**	Mike said that he **might try** a mango. He said (that) he might try . . . **modal—past**
"I <u>can't eat</u> gooseberries." **modal**	Mike said that he **couldn't eat** gooseberries. He said (that) he couldn't eat . . . **modal—past**
"I <u>must try</u> a papaya sometime." **modal**	Mike said that he **had to try** a papaya sometime. He said (that) he had to try . . . **modal equivalent—past**

EXERCISE 13. Using Reported Speech

Liz is telling Claudia what she missed in Professor Jones' science class yesterday. Explain why the underlined words have been or have not been changed.

Talking about Yesterday's Lecture

1. *Professor Jones:*   The blue whale is the largest mammal on Earth.

   Liz: <u>Professor Jones said</u> that the blue whale <u>is</u> the largest known mammal on Earth.

   _____.

2. *Professor Jones:*   In order to appreciate its size, you should think of a 10-story building.

   Liz: He said that in order to appreciate its size, <u>we</u> <u>should think</u> of a 10-story building.

   _____.

3. *Professor Jones:*   I am amazed that it has a heart nearly the size of a small car.

   Liz: He said that <u>he</u> <u>was</u> amazed that it <u>has</u> a heart nearly the size of a small car.

   _____.

4. *Professor Jones:*   In 1931, nearly 30,000 whales were killed for commercial purposes.

   Liz: He said that nearly 30,000 whales <u>had been killed</u> in 1931.

   _____.

5. *Professor Jones:*   Today only around 10,000 blue whales exist in all the world's oceans!

   Liz: He emphasized that only about 10,000 blue whales <u>exist</u> in the oceans today.

   _____.

6. *Professor Jones:*   In conclusion, I encourage you to take action to save the blue whale from extinction.

   Liz: He concluded by encouraging <u>us</u> to take action to save the blue whale from extinction.

   _____.

Connecting Grammar and Vocabulary

Noun clauses can be used only after certain verbs. This list contains verbs that are most frequently used in certain academic disciplines.

Discipline	Verbs and Frequency					
	Rank					
	1	2	3	4	5	6
Harder Sciences						
Biology	describe	find	report	show	suggest	observe
Physics	develop	report	study	find	expand	
Electrical Engineering	propose	use	describe	show	publish	develop
Mechanical Engineering	describe	show	report	discuss	give	develop
Epidemiology	find	describe	suggest	report	examine	show
Nursing	find	suggest	report	identify	indicate	show
Medicine	show	report	demonstrate	observe	find	suggest
Softer Sciences						
Marketing	suggest	argue	find	demonstrate	propose	show
Applied linguistics	suggest	argue	show	explain	find	point out
Psychology	find	show	suggest	report	demonstrate	focus
Sociology	argue	suggest	describe	note	analyze	discuss
Education	find	suggest	note	report	demonstrate	provide
Philosophy	say	suggest	argue	claim	point out	think

Source: Data for Biology, Physics, Electrical Engineering, Mechanical Engineering, Applied Linguistics, and Sociology from Hyland, K. Academic attribution: Citation and the construction of disciplinary knowledge, *Applied Linguistics* 20 (1999): 341–367. Other data thanks to Carson Maynard, University of Michigan English Language Institute.

EXERCISE 14. Reporting Information

A travel agent, Norm, gave you information and now you must report everything to a friend. Be careful to change the verb tenses and pronouns as needed.

Remembering the Contents of a Phone Call

1. Norm said, "A round-trip ticket to New York on a Saturday is $308."

   The agent said that _____.

2. Norm said, "It will cost $348 to travel midweek."

   He also said that _____.

3. Norm said, "Last month the price was $256 round trip."

   He told me that _____.

4. Norm said, "Your friend should make his reservation soon."

   He said that _____.

5. Norm said, "There have been some great prices on hotels, too."

   He told me that _____.

Grammar Lesson

Reported Questions and Requests as Noun Clauses

Quoted Question	Reported Question
Felipe asked, "Will we have a test next week?"	Felipe asked **whether we would have a** test next week.

Rule 1. For reported questions, use statement word order and **wh- words, if,** or **whether** noun clause markers.

Rule 2. Apply the sequence of tense rule and make any necessary changes in pronouns, possessive adjectives, and time expressions.

Rule 3. If you are writing a direct quotation that contains a question, be sure to use a **question mark** before the final quote mark. When you are writing a reported question, use a **period** at the end of the sentence.

Rule 4. Reported requests using **can, could,** or **would** are used with a noun clause the same way as reported questions, *or* they can be reported using the infinitive verb.

Kathy to Rod:	**"Would** you play my favorite song?"
with noun clause:	She asked him **if he would play** her favorite song.
with infinitive:	She asked him **to play** her favorite song.

 BE CAREFUL!

Common Learner Errors	Explanation
1. Sandy asked me what ~~did I buy~~ I bought at the mall.	When reporting a question, use statement word order. Do not use the auxiliary verbs **do, does,** or **did.**
2. Felipe asked ~~would we~~ if we would have a test next week.	When reporting a yes-no question, use the clause marker **if** or **whether.**
3. Tina asked where we were going for vacation~~?~~.	Do not use a question mark after a reported question.

 Do Online Exercise 6.3. My score: _____ /10. _____ % correct.

EXERCISE 15. Editing: Is It Correct?

If the sentence is correct, write a check mark (✔) on the line. If it is not correct, write X on the line and circle the mistake. Then change the sentence to make it correct. Write the change above the sentence. (*Hint*: There are ten sentences. Three are correct, but seven have mistakes.)

Making Valentines in Class

_____ 1. The teacher asked, "If the kindergarteners would like to make valentines?"

_____ 2. Yes, everyone exclaimed with delight.

_____ 3. Philip wondered should I pass out scissors?

_____ 4. Owen asked him do you want any help.

_____ 5. Madison wanted to know if she could pass out the red construction paper.

_____ 6. Can I give everyone some pink paper, too, Joshua asked.

_____ 7. The teacher suggested that Ethan, would you please pass out the glue sticks.

_____ 8. The teacher stated, "You have 40 minutes to work on your cards."

_____ 9. The kindergarteners wondered whether or not can we take them home today?

_____ 10. The teacher responded, "Yes, you can."

Do Online Exercise 6.4. My score: _____ /10. _____ % correct.

EXERCISE 16. Mini-Conversations

Pretend that you are reporting these conversations **the day after they were spoken**. Use the verbs in parentheses and pay attention to pronouns, time expressions, or punctuation that may need to be changed. The first part of one has been done for you as an example.

1. *Dave:*   "John, do you plan to go fishing?"

        (ask) Dave asked John if he planned to go fishing. _____

  John: "Do you want to go with me?"

        (wonder) _____.

2. *Jane:*   "I just got back from a trip to Colorado."

        (exclaim) _____.

  Carol: "Oh. What did you do while you were there?"

        (ask) _____.

  Jane: "I went skiing every day."

        (tell/Carol) _____.

  Carol: "How long were you there?"

        (want to know) _____.

3. *Student:*   "Can you explain reported speech to me?"

        (ask)_____.

  Teacher: "Can you come to my office at 4 o'clock?"

        (inquire)_____.

  Student: "Yes, I will be there."

        (say)_____.

4. This conversation took place in a hospital waiting room.

  The surgeon: "Your daughter is out of surgery and in the recovery room."

        (tell/ the parents) _____

        _____.

  The parents: "When will we know how well she is doing?"

        (ask) _____

        _____.

EXERCISE 17. Sentence Study for Critical Reading

Read the numbered sentences. Then read the answer choices and put a check mark (✓) in the yes or no boxes in front of each sentence to show if that answer is true based on the information in the original sentence. If there is not enough information to mark something as yes, then mark it as no. Remember that more than one true answer may be possible.

1. It's a fact that there are at least three professional football teams in Florida.

    ☐ yes ☐ no a. There are six professional football teams in Florida.

    ☐ yes ☐ no b. The exact number of teams is not stated in this sentence.

    ☐ yes ☐ no c. That there are at least three professional football teams in Florida is a fact.

2. Whether or not a passenger has a red boarding pass for the flight is irrelevant.

    ☐ yes ☐ no a. Most of the passengers have a red boarding pass.

    ☐ yes ☐ no b. Any color boarding pass is acceptable.

    ☐ yes ☐ no c. It does not matter whether or not a passenger has a red boarding pass.

3. The flight will be leaving soon, so it is crucial that we go to the gate now.

    ☐ yes ☐ no a. It will be a short flight.

    ☐ yes ☐ no b. It's not necessary to leave soon.

    ☐ yes ☐ no c. It's urgent that we go there now.

4. The doctor prefers that he be called before we leave for the hospital.

    ☐ yes ☐ no a. The doctor will call us before he gets to the hospital.

    ☐ yes ☐ no b. We should not disturb the doctor by calling him.

    ☐ yes ☐ no c. When we get to the hospital, the doctor will call us.

5. The President announced that he would support a tax cut.

    ☐ yes ☐ no a. The President is in favor of reduced taxes.

    ☐ yes ☐ no b. The President will sign a bill for fewer taxes.

    ☐ yes ☐ no c. Taxes will be cut out entirely.

ONE-MINUTE LESSON

verbs in time clauses. Even though the verb in a time (adverb) clause refers to the future, we usually use simple present tense: *When we get home tonight, we will call you.* We do not usually use future tense in that kind of time clause.

EXERCISE 18. Review Test 1: Multiple Choice

Circle the letter of the correct answer. Some are conversations.

1. "Have you ever heard of Andy Warhol?"
   "No, I haven't. Can you tell _____?"

   a. who is he   b. me who is he   c. who he is   d. me who he is

2. "Andy Warhol is an artist who is claimed _____ America's first pop artist."

   a. who he is   b. that is   c. to be   d. to be that

3. "His first art show was in 1962, and it consisted of paintings of Campbell's Soup cans."

   "Did people really like _____?"

   a. what he had done   c. that he had done

   b. what had he done   d. why he had done

4. "Not at first, but a gallery in Los Angeles bought 32 of his paintings for $100 each."

   "Do you know _____ now?"

   a. where are they   c. they are where

   b. where they are   d. that they are

5. "Look at this brochure! It _____, '*The Museum of Modern Art in New York acquired the collection for $15 million.*'"

   a. says   b. said   c. had said   d. did say

6. "There are thousands of other Warhol paintings in addition to the soup cans. _____ they are all authentic remains to be determined."

   a. If   b. Whether   c. That   d. When

7. "Thus, it is critical that a buyer _____ an art expert _____ the authenticity of the painting."

   a. have/determine   c. may have/determine

   b. has/determines   d. has/determine

8. "Were you aware _____ his art has influenced other design? You can find it in everything from skateboards to jeans."

   a. for what   b. of how   c. by how   d. about why

EXERCISE 19. Review Test 2: Production and Evaluation

Part 1.

Complete the conversation with the information provided in parentheses. Change the word order and verb tense or form as needed.

Gail: ❶ _____ (you/know) no person had ever been able to go

up the Salmon River until my grandfather made that trip in 1963?

Albert: Sure. Everyone was amazed ❷ _____ (when/he/do that).

Gail: He told me ❸ _____ (pioneers/be able/float) barges

down the river, but ❹ _____ (they/can never return)

through the fierce rapids.

Albert: That's right, and that is ❺ _____ (why/it/be called) the

River of No Return.

Part 2.

Read each sentence carefully. Look at the underlined part. If the underlined part is correct, circle the word *correct.* If it is wrong, circle the word *wrong.* Then write the correction above.

correct wrong 1. In his report to the committee, the Vice President said that the tax cut <u>was being</u> too extreme.

correct wrong 2. The judge concluded <u>whether</u> the evidence was not convincing enough to convict the woman.

correct wrong 3. The student <u>asked the teacher does not give</u> any homework over the weekend.

correct wrong 4. The instructor asked the student if he would prefer homework <u>or a quiz</u>.

correct wrong 5. The student replied, "<u>We would</u> prefer to have neither."

correct wrong 6. The history teacher questioned what <u>was their motive</u>.

EXERCISE 20. Reading Practice: An Unusual Fundraising Activity

Read the passage about the Polar Bear Plunge. Then answer the questions that follow. Write your answers in complete sentences. The grammar from this unit is underlined for you. Look carefully because some noun clauses have other clauses embedded within them.

The Polar Bear Plunge

Have you ever taken the Polar Bear Plunge? Well, I have! One winter, my brother Mike dared me to take a dip into the icy cold waters of the Atlantic Ocean with him. When he said <u>that it was for a good cause,</u> my ears perked up. Mike told me <u>that all the money we raised would benefit the Special Olympics.</u>

Helping others is a way of life in our small town. Whenever there is someone in need, we readily do all that we can. One example took place during the Great Blizzard of 1978. Approximately three feet of snow had accumulated in a very short time. Residents were told not <u>to drive for a week.</u> Snow-removal equipment was needed to clear the streets without the hindrance of traffic. Our neighbor Larry, an electric company worker, drove the repair truck home every night. Each day, Joan, Larry's wife, called all the neighbors for a list of groceries and supplies that were needed. She then called Larry with the list. He went shopping for all of us, returning home every night like a victorious warrior. Larry and Joan's son Bobby is mentally challenged. Bobby immediately came to mind when Mike mentioned the Special Olympics.

The Special Olympics is <u>where children and adults who are mentally challenged or have developmental disabilities can participate in competitive sports.</u> These competitions build confidence, self-esteem, and physical strengthen while fostering a greater understanding and acceptance between people with and without disabilities. How could I refuse such a good cause?

Mike explained <u>what to do before the plunge</u>. First, we had to register and sign a waiver. Then we solicited donations from everyone we knew. Uncle Eddie promised <u>he would pledge ten dollars for every inch of water we could tolerate.</u> He also suggested <u>that he drive us to and from the event.</u>

At first, I was worried about <u>what to wear.</u> I felt relieved when Mike told me he found a website with answers to our questions. <u>Why we should wear something on our feet</u> was not so obvious to me. In the cold water, our feet could become numb and not feel sharp objects. Mike was amused that it mentioned <u>that we should bring an extra set of dry clothing.</u> The website also suggested <u>that plungers not stay in the water more than fifteen minutes.</u>

On New Year's Day, January 1st, we were both nervous and excited at the same time. Uncle Eddie was all smiles when he arrived with the camera, hot chocolate, measuring tape, and checkbook. I couldn't believe <u>how many people there were</u>. We all lined up along the shore. The whistle blew. We started in first 1 inch in and then 2, 3, 4 inches in. Then all the way to 10 inches. Uncle Eddie caught our shocked expressions on film, opened the hot chocolate, and happily wrote out two checks for one hundred dollars each.

It took a few days to feel normal again. Uncle Eddie sent a copy of our picture to the local newspaper. Weeks later, Mike asked <u>if I wanted to do it again the next year.</u> I was surprised <u>that he seemed ready to do it again.</u>

1. How did the author and her brother specifically ask for money for the Special Olympics?

    _____

    _____

2. Why was the author particularly interested in helping to raise money for the Special Olympics?

    _____

    _____

3. What did Bobby's father do that left an impression on the author?

    _____

    _____

4. Why do you think Mike was amused that they were advised to bring an extra set of dry clothing?

    _____

    _____

5. Is the Polar Bear Plunge a direct part of the Special Olympics? Why or why not?

    _____

    _____

EXERCISE 21. Vocabulary Practice: Word Knowledge

Circle the answer choice that is most closely related to the vocabulary on the left. Use a dictionary to check the meaning of words you do not know.

Vocabulary	Answer Choices	
1. flow	heat	movement
2. pretend	imaginary	physical
3. demonstrate	conceal	show
4. determine	decide	put on hold
5. erupt	explode	trickle
6. expel	in	out
7. roast	cook in a fire	cook in oil
8. pledge	promise	purpose
9. confirm	check if correct	remove from a place
10. a potluck	a dinner	a restaurant
11. down-to-earth	a regular person	a special person
12. a victorious team	the team lost	the team won
13. a stain	from coffee	from money
14. wreck	destroy	maintain
15. remarkable	significant	written again
16. obvious	clear	not clear
17. a senator	a customer	a politician
18. relieved	a negative feeling	a positive feeling
19. annoyed	angry; bothered	hurt; injured
20. mentally challenged	a difficult book	difficulty with learning
21. your destiny	your future	your past
22. an ambulance	going to the airport	going to the hospital
23. exclaim	show enthusiasm	repeat the past
24. a species	an animal	a rock
25. trim	cut	fail
26. likelihood	possibility	probability
27. ultimate	final	initial
28. intense	strong	weak
29. entice	destroy	persuade
30. frisky	high energy	low energy
31. numb	no feeling	a very strong feeling
32. pass out things	give things	sell things
33. dormant	where students live	not active

EXERCISE 22. Vocabulary Practice: Collocations

Fill each blank with the answer on the right that most naturally completes the phrase on the left. If necessary, use a dictionary to check the meaning of words you do not know.

Vocabulary	Answer Choices	
1. _____ a beverage for each person	do	make
2. the emergency _____	office	room
3. a _____ of eggs	couple	dozen
4. _____ a degree	complete	end
5. a three-story _____	chapter	house
6. I'll go _____ a few weeks	after	in
7. he answered _____ great delight	with	without
8. _____ skiing	go	make
9. _____ Florida	in	on
10. the authenticity _____ an object	for	of
11. solicit _____	money	trees
12. my feet _____ numb	became	changed
13. _____ an impression on someone	give	leave
14. a dark _____	color	smell
15. _____ awake	find	stay
16. sit _____ the sofa	in	on
17. a foul _____	crash	odor
18. _____ cooperation	foster	wonder
19. a down-to-earth _____	house	person
20. _____ a stain	decrease	remove

EXERCISE 23. Writing Practice: *Chupacabra:* Fact or Fiction?

Part 1. Editing Student Writing

Read the sentences about a legendary animal. Circle the 15 errors. Then write the number of the sentence with the error next to the type of error. (Some sentences have more than one error.)

_____ a. noun clause marker   _____ d. article

_____ b. subject-verb agreement   _____ e. singular-plural of nouns

_____ c. verb tense   _____ f. preposition

Chupacabra: Fact or Fiction?
1. Whether a *Chupacabra* is a real animal or a myth has been a mystery since the first reports in 1990s.
2. These reports, which came from Puerto Rico, said that sheep, goats, and other farm animal were found with puncture wounds and the blood drained from them.
3. At first, the farmers didn't know what that caused these unusual deaths.
4. Then one day a woman spotted hairless animal about the size from a small bear with spikes protruding from its back to the end of its tail.
5. Soon, the name *Chupacabra* was given to this unknown animals. *Chupacabra* is a Spanish word that means "blood sucker."
6. Since these original sighting in Puerto Rico, reports had come from other Latin American countries, Texas, and even as far away as Maine.
7. In 2007, reports from a Colombian newspaper, *El Tiempo,* claimed if more than 300 sheep had been found dead and a specimen of a *Chupacabra* was captured.
8. Another animal, thought to be a *Chupacabra,* were found dead in a barn in Texas in 2009. CNN recorded close-up images of this unidentified animal and aired it on television.
9. The *Chupacabra* has been described in many report as a hairless animal with thick, grayish-green skin about the size of a dog. It is said to have fangs and spikes along its back. Some people have reported if they could smell a foul odor.
10. In the 2010, a University of Michigan biologist concluded that *Chupacabras* were coyotes with parasites that caused them to lose their hair and develop a strong, unpleasant odor.
11. However, other people are uncertain for what the biologist said. Whichever theory is correct are unimportant to those who continue the legend by writing and selling novels, movies, and even songs about the mysterious *Chupacabra.*

Part 2. Original Student Writing

Now write about an unsolved mystery. Use at least three noun clauses. Underline the noun clauses so that the teacher can see what you are trying to practice. You can search the Internet for information, but write original sentences. Do not copy. On the bottom of your paper, write the names/addresses of the websites where you found your information. Give some background information about the mystery (where, when, how, who, what it is). What do other people claim? Use reported speech. Finally, what do you believe?

Amelia Earhart's disappearance	the Bermuda Triangle
Easter Island	crop circles
Stonehenge	Atlantis
Black Holes	the curse of King Tut

You may choose another topic such as a legend from your culture or a report on a current article in a magazine or newspaper (attach the article).

Unit 7

Reduction of Adjective and Adverb Clauses, Including Appositives

Discover the Grammar

Read the passage, and then answer the questions that follow.

Line	
1	Studying abroad is a dream for many people and a reality for a lucky few.
2	People able to live and study in another country are changed by the experience.
3	Their worldview, once narrow, becomes broader. Their intercultural knowledge
4	expands as they meet people and form friendships. Opportunities for career
5	development increase as they advance academically and add to their knowledge,
6	skills, and abilities.
7	Let's consider one example of a person who studied abroad. Mohamed,
8	now living in Egypt, is one of those lucky few. Before going overseas to study,
9	he worked for an Internet news agency, writing and translating news stories
10	coming across his desk. His goal, however, was to be a broadcast journalist. He

11	soon realized that in order to get his dream job, he would need education
12	beyond his bachelor's degree.
13	He applied for and received a scholarship to study abroad. He quit his job,
14	left his family, and spent one year in the U.S. earning a certificate in broadcast
15	production. While he was studying in the program, his knowledge of English
16	and U.S. culture grew, as did his journalism skills and abilities.
17	After completing an internship at a television news station, he went back to
18	his home country and began his search for a job that would put him in front of
19	a television news camera. Having lived and studied overseas, he was able to
20	connect with an international news agency and get part-time work as a trans-
21	lator. Finally, a year after his return, he realized his dream.
22	A new television station, formed in the capital city of his country last spring,
23	began broadcasting news in early summer, and Mohamed was hired to join the
24	team. Today, he finally has the job that he dreamed about. The people with
25	whom he works are professional broadcast journalists, and the new station is
26	highly respected in his country. Being able to study abroad, Mohamed acquired
27	the additional skills he needed to land right where he was aiming: in front of a
28	TV news camera.

1. Many adjective and adverb clauses in the reading have been reduced to phrases. Find the phrases in the reading that correspond to the clauses below. Write the phrases and the line number.

a. *People who are able to live and study in another country*

Line ___: _____

b. *which was once narrow,*

Line ___: _____

c. *Before he went overseas to study,*

Line ___: _____

d. *that came across his desk*

Line ___: _____

e. *After he completed an internship at a television news station,*

Line ___: _____

2. Compare the full clauses and the phrases. Write the words in the full clauses that are not in the phrases.

a. _____

b. _____

c. _____

d. _____

e. _____

3. Study the five examples in Number 1 carefully. What is similar about a–c? What is similar about d–e?

_____

_____

_____

4. Reduced clauses can be a difficult area of English grammar. What questions do you have about reduced adjective and adverb clauses?

_____.

_____.

_____.

 **Grammar Lesson**

Reduction of Adjective Clauses

Adjective clauses can be reduced to phrases in at least six ways.

Reduction	Clause (C) → Phrase (P)
prepositional phrase	**C:** They are making her book **that is on the best-seller** list into a movie. **P:** They are making her book **on the best-seller list** into a movie.
adjective phrase	**C:** The student **who is absent the most from this class** is Jason. **P:** The student **absent the most from this class** is Jason.
passive voice	**C:** The laptop **that was stolen yesterday** belonged to my sister. **P:** The laptop **stolen yesterday** belonged to my sister.
–ing verb (from progressive tense)	**C:** The grammar structures **that are causing students the most trouble** are reduced clauses. **P:** The grammar structures **causing students the most trouble** are reduced clauses.
appositive	**C:** George Washington, **who was the first U.S. president**, died in 1799. **P:** George Washington, **the first U.S. president**, died in 1799.
–ing verb (from simple tense)	**C:** Most of the people **who live in this area** are farmers. **P:** Most of the people **living in this area** are farmers.

<u>Rule 1</u>. An adjective clause can be reduced by omitting the subject pronouns **who, that, which + be** when it is followed by a **prepositional phrase**.

<u>Rule 2</u>. An adjective clause can be reduced by omitting the subject pronouns **who, that, which + be** when **it** is followed by an **adjective**.

<u>Rule 3</u>. An adjective clause can be reduced by omitting the subject pronouns **who, that, which + be** when it is in **passive voice**.

<u>Rule 4</u>. An adjective clause can be reduced by omitting the subject pronouns **who, that, which + be** when it is in a **progressive tense**.

Rule 5. An adjective clause can be reduced by omitting the subject pronouns **who, that, which + be** when **be** is followed by a noun. The reduction that results is called an **appositive.** An appositive or its original adjective clause are always set off by commas.

Rule 6. An adjective clause can often be reduced by omitting the subject pronouns **who, that,** and **which** and changing the verb to **VERB + –ing.**

Rule 7. You can omit **that, which,** and **who(m)** when they serve as objects, but the result is still an adjective clause.

a. The car **that Sue bought** gets great gas mileage. b. The car —— **Sue bought** gets great gas mileage.	The relative pronoun **that** is optional here because it functions as the object of the verb. Both (a) and (b) include an adjective clause.

 BE CAREFUL!

Common Learner Errors	Explanation
1. ~~The book brought~~ The book that John brought is on the table.	Do not try to reduce a clause by omitting the subject.
2. ~~People living in that specific area of the city.~~ People living in that specific area of the city have poor mail service.	Do not think that the reduced verb form is the verb of the sentence. **Living** is the reduced verb form, and **have** is the main verb of the sentence. You must include a main verb **(have),** or you will write a sentence fragment.

EXERCISE 1. Adjective Clauses vs. Reduced Adjective Clauses

Underline the adjective clauses in these sentences. If these adjective clauses can be reduced, rewrite the resulting reduced clause on the lines. If they cannot be reduced, write *no change possible*.

The Construction of Paris's Most Famous Landmark

1. Perhaps the monument that is most frequently visited in Paris is the Eiffel Tower.

   _____

   _____

   _____

2. The number of tourists who visit this Parisian site each year is more than five million.

   _____

   _____

3. In fact, the number of tourists who have visited this site since it opened in 1889 is approximately two hundred million.

   _____

   _____

4. Construction of the Tower, which was begun in 1887, lasted for over two years.

   _____

   _____

5. Eiffel, which is the name that we most obviously associate with the tower, is actually the name of the owner of the construction company that built this landmark.

   _____

   _____

Do Online Exercise 7.1. My score: _____ /10. _____ % correct.

EXERCISE 2. Reducing Adjective Clauses to Create Appositives

Underline the adjective clause. Then create an appositive when possible. If no such reduction is possible, write *no appositive possible*.

Visiting Paris

1. My parents, who visited Paris for the first time in 2012, decided to make it an annual destination.

   _____

   _____

   _____

2. June and July, which are perhaps the most pleasant summer months to visit Paris, are peak months for tourism to the city.

   _____

   _____

   _____

3. The Latin Quarter, which is a popular area because of its many bistros, is near many of the city's institutions of higher learning.

   _____

   _____

   _____

4. The residents of Paris, who number over 2 million, make it one of the most culturally diverse cities in Europe.

   _____

   _____

   _____

5. Easy access to transportation, which includes air, rail, ship, and highway, makes Paris ideal for both tourists and residents alike.

   _____

   _____

   _____

EXERCISE 3. Recognizing and Punctuating Appositives

Underline the appositive in each of these sentences. Be sure to set off each appositive with the required punctuation.

Founding Father, Writer, Inventor

1. Thomas Jefferson the third U.S. president was born on April 13, 1743.

2. Monticello Jefferson's residence was located near Charlottesville, VA.

3. Thomas's father was Peter Jefferson a planter and surveyor.

4. Jefferson the third child of ten children had three brothers and six sisters.

5. Martha Wayles Skelton a 23-year-old widow became Jefferson's wife in 1752.

6. Jefferson was the primary writer of one of the most famous documents in history the Declaration of Independence.

7. Jefferson an accomplished but relatively unknown inventor is responsible for many items common in our lives today.

8. Jefferson the president of the United States for two terms retired from public life and returned to his home in Monticello.

Do Online Exercise 7.2. My score: _____ /10. _____% correct.

EXERCISE 4. Editing: Is It Correct?

If the sentence is correct, write a check mark (✔) on the line. If the sentence is not correct, write an X on the line and circle the mistake. Then change the sentence to make it correct. Write the change above the sentence. (*Hint:* There are ten sentences. Five sentences are correct, but five have mistakes.)

Collecting Stamps for a Hobby

_____ 1. The world's first postage stamp, issued in 1840, featured Britain's Queen Victoria on it.

_____ 2. Collecting stamps is a hobby pursued by children as well as by adults.

_____ 3. People who studying stamps are called philatelists.

_____ 4. Surprisingly, stamps that issued by some countries are done so primarily as a source of revenue for that nation.

_____ 5. Popular stamp themes found in collections include animals, flowers, people, and sports.

_____ 6. Printed in error, an American stamp of an upside-down airplane once sold for almost a million dollars.

_____ 7. According to collectors, the albums are used to display stamps are not so expensive.

_____ 8. Coveted by collectors, many rare stamps date back to the 1800s.

_____ 9. Stamp shows around the country.

_____ 10. Clubs are available for hobbyists to join number in the thousands.

ONE-MINUTE LESSON
When an action functions as a noun, we add **–ing** to that word as in *collecting*. This form is called a **gerund** and can be a subject (*Collecting stamps is fun*), a direct object (*I like collecting stamps*), or an object of a preposition (*I'm interested in collecting stamps*).

EXERCISE 5. Speaking Practice: Presentations on Your City

Form a small group. Imagine that a company has hired you to be a spokesperson for your home-town to promote tourism. Each student will have a different location. Take a few minutes to write out a very brief TV commercial in which you encourage tourists to come visit your special location. Try to use as many adjective clauses and reduced adjective clauses as you can in your mini-presentation. Keep in mind that a commercial is only 30 seconds long, so write about 6 to 10 sentences. Then take turns telling each other about your travel spots.

Example: One of my favorite vacation spots is Clearwater Beach, <u>located on the west coast of Florida</u>. The beach, <u>made up of fine white sand</u>, stretches for miles, so I can always find a quiet spot to relax. Cabanas, <u>available for rent</u>, are great for keeping out of the hot sun. The Gulf of Mexico, <u>warm and salty</u>, is great for swimming.

EXERCISE 6. Mini-Conversations

Circle the words correct in these mini-conversations. Sometimes more than one answer is possible.

1. A: Where is the report (wrote, you wrote, you written, which you wrote) yesterday?

   B: I sent it to you in an e-mail around noon yesterday. Didn't you get it?

2. A: What is a pomegranate?

   B: It's a delicious tropical fruit (that is full, is full, full) of small seeds.

3 A: We'd like to take a tour of Paris, but we have only an hour or so.

   B: That's impossible. Most of the tours (that schedule, scheduled, scheduling, which schedules) for today are at least three hours long.

4. A: What are relative pronouns?

   B: They're words (introduce, introduced, who introduce, that introduce) adjective clauses.

5. A: What is the longest flight (that you've, you've, which you've) been on?

   B: I think New York to Tokyo was fourteen hours.

6. A: The memo says that anyone (needs, needed, needing, who need) a visa must apply for one before the 15th.

   B: Yes, that's correct, but luckily, we have ours already.

7. A: What is your favorite proverb?

   B: People (who live, which live, that live, lived, living) in glass houses should never throw stones.

8. A: What is the name of the president (who, whom, whose, that, of which) last name starts with the letter R?

   B: Actually, there were several. Which one are you talking about?

Grammar Lesson

Reduction of Adverb Clauses

Adverb Clause	Adverb Phrase
When Lorena is at work, she dresses professionally.	**When at work**, Lorena dresses professionally.
When people are angry, they refuse to listen to reason.	**When angry**, people refuse to listen to reason.
While I am eating, I never answer the phone if it rings.	**While eating**, I never answer the phone if it rings.
While Derek was running on the beach, he fell and hurt his knee.	**While running on the beach**, Derek fell and hurt his knee.
When my laptop was stolen, it had valuable company information on it.	**When stolen**, my laptop had valuable company information on it.
After Ana left the company, she started her own business.	**After leaving the company**, Ana started her own business.
Before I registered for classes, I met with an advisor.	**Before registering for classes**, I met with an advisor.
Since I enrolled in this course last fall, I have made a lot of progress in my language skills.	**Since enrolling in this course last fall**, I have made a lot of progress in my language skills.
When Todd isn't working, he goes fishing.	**When not working**, Todd goes fishing.
Although I wasn't familiar with the topic, I found it interesting.	**Although not familiar with the topic**, I found it interesting.
While Jill was working in France, she learned to speak French well.	**Working in France**, Jill learned to speak French well.
While I was waiting for the elevator, I checked my phone messages.	**Waiting for the elevator**, I checked my phone messages.

Rule 1. An adverb clause can be reduced by omitting the **SUBJECT + be** when **be** is followed by a prepositional phrase, an adjective, a present progressive or past progressive verb, or when it is in passive voice.

Rule 2. An adverb clause that does not contain the verb **be** can be reduced by omitting the subject and changing the verb to **VERB + –ing.**

Rule 3. An adverb clause that is negative can be reduced by omitting the **SUBJECT + be** or by omitting the subject and changing the verb to **VERB + –ing** and then adding the word **not.**

Rule 4. Adverb clauses beginning with **while** sometimes omit **while** in the adverb phrase when the meaning is "at the same time."

NOTE: See Unit 5 for a review of adverb clauses.

 BE CAREFUL!

Common Learner Errors	Explanation
1. ~~After getting off the plane, the workers removed their bags.~~ After the passengers got off the plane, the workers removed their bags.	In order to reduce an adverb clause, the subjects of both the main clause and adverb clause must be the same. In the original sentence, the two subjects are different: *passengers* and *workers*.
2. ~~When flying economy class.~~ When flying economy class, passengers receive only a complimentary beverage.	The reduced verb form is a present (**–ing**) or past participle form (**–ed, –en, –ne,** etc.), not the main verb of the sentence. You still need to include a main verb.
3. ~~Because tired from the long trip, Josh fell asleep quickly.~~ Because he was tired from the long trip, Josh fell asleep quickly. **(no reduction)** Being tired from the long trip, Josh fell asleep quickly. **(omit SUBJECT, use being)** Tired from the long trip, Josh fell asleep quickly. **(omit SUBJECT + be)**	Do not use reduced adverb phrases with **because.** For clauses that have **because + SUBJECT + be,** a phrase with **being** is possible. It is also possible to omit the **SUBJECT + be** and use only an adjective

EXERCISE 7. Adverb Clauses vs. Reduced Adverb Clauses

Underline the adverb clauses in these sentences. If an adverb clause can be reduced, rewrite the sentence with the reduced phrase. If it cannot be reduced, write *no change possible*. The first one has been done for you as an example.

Taking a Cat on an International Flight

1. <u>When Maria flew from Paris to New York recently</u>, she traveled with her cat.

   <u>When flying from Paris to New York recently</u>, Maria traveled with her cat.

2. Before Maria entered the plane, her cat had to be put in its cage.

   _____

   _____

3. After the cat was put in its cage, it began to meow loudly.

   _____

   _____

4. Although Maria tried to calm the cat down, she was unsuccessful.

   _____

   _____

5. When Maria could not make the cat be quiet, a flight attendant helped her.

   _____

   _____

6. Once the cat was held by the flight attendant, it became amazingly quiet.

   _____

   _____

ONE-MINUTE LESSON

The verb **make** can be used to express the idea that Person A forces or persuades Person B to do something: *My dad made me find a job.* The grammar is SUBJECT + **make** + Person B + VERB. Note that the verb after **make** is the base or simple form.

EXERCISE 8. Editing: Is It Correct?

If the sentence is correct, write a check mark (✔) on the line. If it is not correct, write an X on the line and circle the mistake. Then change the sentence to make it correct. Write the change above the sentence. (*Hint*: There are six sentences. Three are correct, but three have mistakes.)

A Near Accident while Driving Home

_____ 1. While driving my car home from work one day last month, a squirrel ran right in front of me.

_____ 2. After slamming on the brakes, I honked the horn to scare the squirrel away.

_____ 3. Although unable to see anything from inside the car, the little bushy-tailed rodent had not been hit.

_____ 4. While sitting there feeling a surge of adrenaline, it scampered away.

_____ 5. After calming down a little, I continued on my way home.

_____ 6. Since almost hitting that little creature, I have started driving more slowly through that area of my neighborhood.

Do Online Exercise 7.3. My score: _____ /10. _____ % correct.

Grammar Lesson

Reducing Adverb Clauses to Prepositional Phrases

Adverb Connector	Preposition	Adverb Clause	Prepositional Phrase
because since	because of due to on account of	Because the weather was bad, the flight was canceled.	Because of bad weather, the flight was canceled. Due to bad weather, the flight was canceled. On account of bad weather, the flight was canceled.
although even though	in spite of despite	Although I paid a lot for the concert ticket, I had a bad seat. Even though I paid a lot for the concert ticket, I had a bad seat.	In spite of paying a lot for the concert ticket, I had a bad seat. Despite paying a lot for the concert ticket, I had a bad seat.
whether or not	regardless of	Whether or not we start on time, we will finish late.	Regardless of the start time, we will finish late.
when	during	When I had a coffee break, I checked my text messages.	During my coffee break, I checked my text messages.

Rule 1. Many adverb clauses can be reduced to prepositional phrases. The prepositions must have the same or similar meaning as the adverb clause connector.

Rule 2. The preposition must be accompanied by a noun.

EXERCISE 9. Adverb Clauses vs. Prepositional Phrases

Underline the adverb clauses in these sentences. Then change the adverb clause to a prepositional phrase. The first one has been done for you as an example.

My Evening Watching a Play

1. <u>Because there was a huge traffic jam</u>, I missed the chance to eat dinner before the opening act of the play.

   Due to the huge traffic jam, I missed the chance to eat dinner before the

   opening act of the play.

2. When it was intermission, I was able to get a light snack and something to drink.

   _____

   _____

3. The intermission bell rang, and I walked back to my seat even though I was still hungry.

   _____

   _____

4. When the curtain call came, I started to think about a good place to have dinner after the show.

   _____

   _____

5. Since there were many good restaurants in the area, I had no trouble finding one that was open and that served my favorite French cuisine.

   _____

   _____

6. I had a most enjoyable evening at the theater whether or not it started the way I had hoped it would.

   _____

   _____

 Do Online Exercise 7.4. My score: _____ /10. _____ % correct.

EXERCISE 10. Speaking Practice: Proverbs

Part A. Preparation for Speaking Activity

Read these proverbs. For each underlined part of the proverb, write **ADJC** if it is an adjective clause, **RADJ** if it is a reduced adjective clause, **ADVC** if it is an adverb clause, or **RADV** if it is a reduced adverb clause. Then, in your own words, write what you think the proverb means.

1. Don't attempt to close the barn door <u>after the horse runs away</u>. _____

    _____

    _____

2. <u>Justice delayed</u> is <u>justice denied</u>. _____   _____

    _____

    _____

3. Those <u>who cannot remember the past</u> are condemned to repeat it. _____

    _____

    _____

4. <u>Something well begun</u> is <u>something already half done</u>. _____   _____

    _____

    _____

5. <u>When in Rome</u>, do as the Romans do. _____

    _____

    _____

6. <u>While the cat's away</u>, the mice will play. _____

    _____

    _____

7. Let's cross that bridge <u>when we come to it</u>. _____

    _____

    _____

8. <u>A friend in need</u> is a friend indeed. _____

    _____

    _____

Part B. Speaking Activity

Work with a partner or in small groups. Take turns presenting your answers for the proverbs. Practice adjective and adverb clauses and reduced clauses in your discussion.

EXERCISE 11. Mini-Conversations

Circle the correct words in these mini-conversations.

1. A: Have you started your college application yet?

   B: No, not yet. (Looking, To look, I looked, I had looked) at the application online, I decided I needed some help filling it out. What about you?

2. A: Did the winners receive any money?

   B: Yes, they did. The top three contestants (choosing, to choose, chosen, were choosing, were chosen) by the judges earned $500.

3. A: How's your English now? You were taking courses at the local college, right?

   B: I think my English is better now. In fact, since (I am enrolling, enrolling, I enrolled, enroll, I have enrolled) in courses three years ago, many people have commented on how much better my English is.

4. A: After (you were leaving, left, to leave, leaving, you were left) Tokyo last year, what did you do?

   B: As soon as I got home, I got a job working with Japanese tourists in California.

5. A: My favorite proverb in English is about getting things done. "(Making, To make, You make, You have made) an omelet, you have to break a few eggs."

   B: OK, but what does that mean?

   A: It means you have to experience difficulties in order to achieve something great.

EXERCISE 12. Editing: Is It Correct?

If the sentence is correct, write a check mark (✓) on the line. If it is not correct, write an X on the line and circle the mistake. Then change the sentence to make it correct. Write the change above the sentence. (*Hint*: There are eight sentences. Three are correct, but five have mistakes.)

Different Types of Insurance

_____ 1. The cost of health insurance for people who smoke even a few cigarettes a day is higher than the cost for non-smokers.

_____ 2. Although am not a world traveler, travel insurance is a necessity for me.

_____ 3. Without a doubt, people living near an ocean pay more for home insurance.

_____ 4. When shopping for auto insurance, companies will charge higher premiums for sports cars.

_____ 5. I found a good deal on life insurance due to I am under 30 years of age.

_____ 6. My car, purchasing more than ten years ago, has affordable insurance premiums.

_____ 7. Before signing up for pet insurance, compare costs among different companies.

_____ 8. Some medicines selling in the United States are not covered by insurance.

EXERCISE 13. Speaking Activity: Individual Ways of Reducing Stress

Form a small group of three or four members. In the group, take turns discussing ways that you reduce stress in your life. For example, do you volunteer or exercise or spend time with friends in order to relieve stress? When you have finished telling the group your methods, your group members will ask you questions about your methods. Use adverb and adjective clauses and reduced forms in your discussion and in your questions.

EXERCISE 14. Sentence Study for Critical Reading

Read the numbered sentences. Then read the answer choices and place a check mark (✓) in the yes or no boxes in front of each sentence to show if that answer is true based on the information in the original sentence. If there is not enough information to mark something as yes, then mark it as no. Remember that more than one true answer may be possible.

1. Psychologists, studying behavior and mental processes, may specialize in one of many areas. Focusing on how people influence, and are influenced by, the environment in which they live, environmental psychologists may study the differences between people living in the city and those residing in the country, for example.

   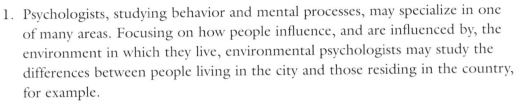

   ☐ yes ☐ no   a. Psychologists study behavior and mental processes in different settings.

   ☐ yes ☐ no   b. People are affected by environmental factors in the areas in which they live.

   ☐ yes ☐ no   c. Environmental psychologists might study how crowded cities influence people's behavior.

2. My cousin has acrophobia, a fear of heights. When climbing more than two flights of stairs, she starts to feel panicky and her palms begin to sweat. Unable to change a light bulb at home, she will not get a chair or stepladder to stand on. Instead, she will ask someone else to change it for her. Before going to a movie or attending a sports event, she makes sure she will not have to sit in the upper level of the theater or stadium.

   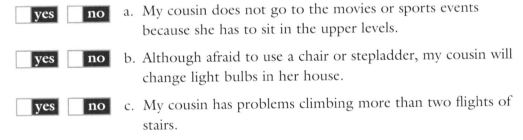

   ☐ yes ☐ no   a. My cousin does not go to the movies or sports events because she has to sit in the upper levels.

   ☐ yes ☐ no   b. Although afraid to use a chair or stepladder, my cousin will change light bulbs in her house.

   ☐ yes ☐ no   c. My cousin has problems climbing more than two flights of stairs.

3. There are numerous ways to change a person's behavior. One way, called positive reinforcement, is to offer the person praise for a behavior you want repeated. For example, if a child picks up toys scattered about the room and hears, "Good job," the child, experiencing pleasure from these words, will repeat the behavior in the future. Research conducted over the years shows that positive reinforcement is more powerful than negative reinforcement or punishment in changing behavior.

[ ] yes [ ] no   a. Research on how to change behavior has been conducted for years.

[ ] yes [ ] no   b. Changing a person's behavior is called positive reinforcement.

[ ] yes [ ] no   c. An example of positive reinforcement is when children who scatter toys about the room hear the praise, "Good job."

4. Despite going to bed at a reasonable hour every night, I suffer from sleep deprivation. When I am at work, I sometimes fall asleep at my desk. Because of this condition, I make poor decisions and sometimes miss deadlines. Before attending important meetings, I have a quick cup of coffee and take a short nap. Although helpful, they are not the solution to my problem.

[ ] yes [ ] no   a. Sleep deprivation causes me to make bad decisions.

[ ] yes [ ] no   b. I have sleep deprivation because I go to bed at a reasonable hour.

[ ] yes [ ] no   c. Coffee and naps are helpful solutions to the problem.

5. Volunteerism, also called community service, has become commonplace in many high schools and colleges. Community service, helping volunteers connect what they are learning in school to what is happening in the community, is hands-on learning. Volunteering raises students' awareness of what is causing specific social problems and helps them identify possible solutions. Volunteer activities, including picking up trash along the beach, feeding the homeless, or helping children learn to read, benefit volunteers and the community alike.

[ ] yes [ ] no   a. Volunteers learn while they are doing community service work.

[ ] yes [ ] no   b. Picking up trash on the beach is an example of community service.

[ ] yes [ ] no   c. Volunteerism helps volunteers feel connected to their community.

EXERCISE 15. Review Test 1: Multiple Choice

Circle the letter of the correct answer.

1. A friend _____ a friend indeed. (proverb)

   a. who in need is   c. is who is need

   b. is in need   d. in need is

2. The people _____ in the accident were taken to a nearby hospital emergency room for treatment.

   a. involved   c. involving

   b. who involved   d. who involving

3. Before entering its cage, _____.

   a. the cat began to meow loudly

   b. the owner had to give the cat some food

   c. the loud meow of the cat could be heard

   d. the food was given to the cat by the owner

4. Written in central Canada in the early part of the twentieth century, _____, depicts life in Manitoba.

   a. *The Midnight Sun* was Victor Frank's last novel

   b. Victor Frank's last novel *The Midnight Sun*

   c. which was Victor Frank's last novel, *The Midnight Sun*

   d. *The Midnight Sun*, which was Victor Frank's last novel

5. _____ lasted for over two years.

   a. Began in 1887, construction of the Tower

   b. Begun in 1887, construction of the Tower

   c. Construction of the Tower, began in 1887,

   d. Construction of the Tower, which begun in 1887,

6. Taken from a previously unknown plant found only in a remote part of the Amazon rainforest, _____.

   a. scientists may be able to develop a new cure for cancer from it

   b. it is possible that scientists may be able to develop a new cure for cancer from it

   c. a cure for cancer might come from this new medicine

   d. the new medicine might be a cure for cancer

7. _____ the meeting in Detroit lasted so long, I missed my connecting flight to Houston.

   a. Due to   c. Although

   b. Since   d. Despite

8. _____ all the taxes and additional fees that were added to the base price of the car, the final price tag was much higher than anyone expected it to be.

   a. Despite   c. Because of

   b. Regardless of   d. Because

 EXERCISE 16. Review Test 2: Production and Evaluation

Part 1.

Fill in the blanks using words from the word list. Do not use any word/phrase twice.

word list	because	in spite of	which
	despite	when	while
	even though	whether or not	who

1. Last night my cousin, _____ was in town for a conference, called me and invited me to go with him to a Japanese restaurant for sushi.

2. Miki's Sushi has such good food that we decided to spend 30 minutes driving there _____ it was so far away.

3. Whenever I go to Miki's Sushi, I order the spicy tuna roll, _____ is by far my favorite dish there!

4. The food took a little while, so my cousin and I sat telling jokes to each other _____ we were waiting.

5. _____ not having eaten all day, I was doing OK _____ I knew that my favorite dish would soon be in front of me.

6. _____ the food finally arrived, we stopped telling jokes and started eating!

7. One thing that I really like about this restaurant is that the food always comes with extra ginger _____ you ask for it.

8. _____ my plate being incredibly full, I managed to eat everything. What a great meal we had!

Part 2.

Read each sentence and look at the underlined part. If the underlined part is correct, circle the word *correct*. If it is wrong, circle the word *wrong*. Then write the correction above.

correct   wrong   1. <u>Before submitting my application</u>, I went over it once more to make sure I hadn't missed anything.

correct   wrong   2. The price of airline tickets, <u>going up again as soon as tourist season ends</u>, is becoming unaffordable for the average person.

correct   wrong   3. <u>Driving my sports car</u>, I was taking her motorcycle for a spin.

correct   wrong   4. The employees <u>which got their paychecks early</u> went to the bank to cash them.

correct   wrong   5. <u>Although saying the light bulb was the greatest invention of all time</u>, I say the printing press was.

correct   wrong   6. <u>After leaving her job as a corporate lawyer</u>, Theresa started a not-for-profit group to help homeless families.

EXERCISE 17. Reading Practice: Small Steps to Saving Earth

Read the information on how to help protect the environment. Then answer the comprehension questions that follow. The grammar from this unit is underlined for you.

What Can You Do To Help the Earth's Environment?

Earth's environmental alarm bell, <u>ringing for years</u>, continues to sound. Despite hearing the alarm, many people fail to act. Perhaps they think that saving the environment is too monumental a task for one person's actions to make much of a difference. Nothing could be further from the truth. If each person were to take a few small steps toward saving the environment, the results would be tremendous.

One of the easiest steps a person can take to help the planet is to recycle. Most communities have programs <u>promoting the recycling of plastic, paper, and glass</u>. To do your part, keep a large basket or a bin in the kitchen or outside the back door so that it's easier to toss that empty milk carton or yesterday's paper into the bin rather than into the trash can. Instead of using paper napkins and paper towels, <u>requiring the use of fossil fuels for production</u>, use cloth napkins at mealtime and clean up spills with a dishcloth. Instead of buying bottled water at the store, buy a reusable bottle and fill it with tap water from home.

Equally as important as recycling is conserving water. <u>Taking steps to conserve water</u> not only helps save this renewable resource, but also lowers your monthly water bill. Taking short showers and installing low-flow shower heads are effective ways to save water and money. Not letting the water run <u>while brushing your teeth</u> or <u>while rinsing dishes</u> is an additional way to help. Consider watering your flowers with rain water <u>caught in a rain barrel</u>. Run your dishwasher only when it's full.

Conserving water goes hand in hand with conserving energy. Turn off the lights <u>when leaving the room</u>. Open your blinds or curtains to let in the natural light. <u>During hot weather</u>, using ceiling fans will allow you to turn the air conditioner up two or three degrees and still stay cool, but remember to turn off the fans <u>when leaving the room</u>. Exchange incandescent bulbs for florescent ones; they may cost more to purchase, but florescent bulbs last longer and ultimately save both energy and money.

People <u>choosing to live more simply</u> are taking positive steps toward helping Planet Earth sustain itself for future generations. Once you are used to recycling and conserving energy and water, take another step. Start a garden, plant some trees, or ride a bike instead of driving a car. Mother Earth will thank you.

1. What is the author's purpose for writing this article?

   _____

   _____

2. Who is the intended audience for this article?

   _____

3. In your opinion, which suggestion is the easiest to implement? Why do you think so?

   _____

   _____

   _____

4. What steps mentioned in the article, if any, are you taking to help save Earth?

   _____

   _____

5. If you had to choose one way to help the planet, what would you choose?

   _____

   _____

EXERCISE 18. Vocabulary Practice: Word Knowledge

Circle the answer choice that is most closely related to the vocabulary on the left. Use a dictionary to check the meaning of words you do not know.

Vocabulary	Answer Choices	
1. X belongs to me	X is mine	X is yours
2. vehemently	loudly, seriously	playfully, jokingly
3. previously	subsequently	beforehand
4. diverse	all the same	many differences
5. acquire	get	lose
6. a residence	a business	a house
7. approximately 100	95-110	50 or 200
8. an intermission	a break	a work meeting
9. my peak day of the week	my busiest day	my slowest day
10. a surge	a decrease	an increase
11. implement a plan	make the plan happen	stop the plan in the middle
12. quit a job	begin a new job	end your old job
13. display my ID	you can see my ID	you cannot see my ID
14. refuse to do something	agree to do something	not agree to do something
15. a surge in the price of gold	the price went up a little	the price went up a lot
16. register for a class	drop a class	enroll in a class
17. a task	a strategy	an assignment
18. be involved in	participate	remember
19. expand	increase	limit
20. a frame	around a necklace	around a painting
21. throughout the hotel	in a few hotel rooms	in many hotel rooms
22. benefit	gain	lose
23. annual	every year	last year
24. reject	discard	accept
25. easy access to your money	it is easy to get your money	it is rarely easy to get your money

EXERCISE 19. Vocabulary Practice: Collocations

Fill in the blank with the answer on the right that most naturally completes the phrase on the left. If necessary, use a dictionary to check the meaning of words you do not know.

Vocabulary	Answer Choices	
1. to fly economy _____	class	section
2. conduct a lot of _____	research	researches
3. a link _____ the past	for	to
4. a complimentary _____	beverage	decision
5. the company is _____ in London	basing	based
6. _____ a corporate lawyer	attend	hire
7. _____ located near	has	is
8. to consider environmental _____	factor	factors
9. used in technical _____	writers	writing
10. pursue a _____	hobby	sport
11. have _____ access to something	easy	hard
12. despite _____ all day	to work	working
13. a renewable _____	origin	resource
14. a source of _____	people	revenue
15. _____ an awareness of	to have	to make
16. the construction _____ a new project	of	to
17. X corresponds _____ Y	to	without
18. an Academy _____	Reward	Award
19. a new theory _____ how the planet was formed	of	on
20. realize a _____	accident	dream
21. immigrated _____	to	from
22. his _____ of English	ability	knowledge
23. send a text message _____ someone	by	to
24. published _____ the newspaper	in	on
25. make a great deal of _____	progress	success

EXERCISE 20. Writing Practice: Do What You Love, Love What You Do

Part 1. Editing Student Writing

Read these sentences about choosing a career. Circle the 15 errors. Then write the number of the sentence with the error next to the type of error. (Some sentences have more than one error.)

_____ a. punctuation

_____ b. subject-verb agreement

_____ c. incorrect pronoun

_____ d. missing article

_____ e. wrong preposition

_____ f. missing –*ing*

1. Someone once said, "Choose job you love, and you will never have to work a day on your life."

2. Everyone wants a job what is exciting and fun and that pays well, but not everyone are lucky enough to find one.

3. Some people which do not know what they are interested in choose their careers based solely in how much money jobs in the field will pay.

4. After they begin working, the job is not as interesting as they thought it was go to be.

5. Spending long hours doing unpleasant jobs these people are miserable but sometimes refuse to acknowledge they are making a mistake.

6. In spite of get a big paycheck, they discover that their job brings them little or no happiness.

7. Other people choose jobs which follow an interest they have, even though their family and friends tell them there is no future in it because job pays very little.

8. Many college students graduate with a lot of debt, and these people who are new to the workforce is often more concerned with pay off their debt as quickly as possible.

9. Therefore, my advice are to follow your passion and find a job that you love, knowing that the money may eventually come.

10. As someone else once said, "Find a job is simple. It's just not easy." I agree completely with the person who said this.

Part 2. Original Student Writing

Write a paragraph or short essay in which you tell in your own words a well-known or popular folk tale or children's story. This kind of writing will naturally have many adjective and adverb clauses, but you should also try to include adjective and adverb phrases. Put one line under all the adjective and adverb clauses and two lines under the adjective and adverb phrases so that the teacher can see what you are trying to practice.

Unit 8

Past Modals

 Discover the Grammar

Three friends have made plans to see a movie together and agreed to meet inside the theater half an hour before the film begins. Read the conversation between two of them, and then answer the questions that follow.

Line	
1	*Amy:* Oh, no! Janet's late. Do you think she forgot we were going to meet at
2	7:30?
3	*Dave:* I don't know. She could have forgotten. I didn't call to remind her. Did
4	you?
5	*Amy:* No, I didn't either. Maybe I should have called, though. I just assumed
6	she'd remember.
7	*Dave:* She's usually on time, so maybe she just had to work late. She's been
8	working a few hours overtime at least two or three nights a week lately.
9	*Amy:* I know. I suppose she might have been asked to stay late to help with
10	the company's new marketing campaign. She told me last week that her
11	boss was supposed to submit a new proposal by the end of this week.

12	*Dave:* Don't you think she would have called to let us know she was going to
13	be late?
14	*Amy:* Yeah—in the past, she always used to let us know whenever she was
15	running late. In fact, she would call to say she was going to be on time,
16	too.
17	*Dave:* Do you think I should call her?
18	*Amy:* Don't bother! Look—there she is!
19	*Dave:* Great! I'm glad she was able to make it, but now I wonder why she
20	wasn't able to call us.
21	*Amy:* Let's get our popcorn. The movie is going to start soon.

1. Use the chart to study the phrases from the conversation. Match them with their meanings found in the column on the right. If you need extra help, refer to the line numbers of the conversation where the phrases can be found.

Phrase	Meaning
_____ 1. she used to let us know (Line 14)	a. a past necessity
_____ 2. she might have been asked (Line 9)	b. a past regret
_____ 3. she had to work (Line 7)	c. a planned and expected action
_____ 4. I should have called (Line 5)	d. the possibility existed
_____ 5. her boss was supposed to submit (Line 11)	e. habitual past

2. Underline the four phrases in the conversation that have the form modal + *have* + past participle. Write the line number, the subject, and the phrase.

Line	Subject	Modal Phrase

3. Compare the phrases from the conversation. Decide whether each modal or modal phrase is talking about the present or the past. Write the word *present* or *past* on the line next to each phrase.

a. _____ *She could have forgotten.* (Line 3)

b. _____ I'm glad *she was able to make it.* (Line 18)

c. _____ Do you think *I should call her?* (Line 16)

d. _____ *Maybe I should have called, though.* (Line 5)

e. _____ *she might have been asked to stay late.* . . . (Line 9)

f. _____ . . . *her boss was supposed to submit a new proposal.* . . . (Line 11)

g. _____ Don't you think *she would have called* . . . ? (Line 12)

h. _____ *In fact, she would call to say she was going to be on time.* (Line 15)

4. What questions do you have about using the modals in the past tense?

_____

_____

_____

Grammar Lesson

Past Modals and Phrasal Modals

Modal	Meaning
He **may have left** a voicemail message. He **might have left** a voicemail message.	possibility in the past; less certain
Yukiko **could swim** before she was five. Yukiko **was able to swim** before she was five.	ability in the past
They **could have brought** a gift to the party, but they didn't. .... They **could have forgotten** about the party.	suggestion about past possibilities .... a slight possibility something happened
As a child, I **would visit** my grandparents during the summer. As a child, I **used to visit** my grandparents during the summer.	repeated action in the past
We **would have gone** to St. Thomas on vacation if we had known there were such cheap flights available.	unreal condition in the past
You **should have paid** your rent instead of buying a new smartphone. You **ought to have paid** your rent instead of buying a new smartphone. .... You **should have received** my email by now. You **ought to have received** my email by now.	advice, suggestion, or obligation about something in the past that was not done .... expectation that something occurred
She **had to take** her car in for repairs.	necessity or obligation in the past
He **must have had** a lot of courage to do that. He **had to have had** a lot of courage to do that.	strong certainty; conclusion that something occurred
They **were supposed to arrive** at 6:30 today. .... They **were going to arrive** at 6:30 today.	expectation that something was going to occur .... past intention

<u>**Rule 1**</u>. Past tense modals generally have meanings that are different from the present tense modals. Some past modals have more than one meaning.

<u>**Rule 2**</u>. Most past modals are formed by using the **modal + have + PAST PARTICIPLE**. To form a negative sentence using a past modal with **have**, insert **not** between the modal and **have**.

He **should not have used** his phone in class.

Questions are formed by moving the modal to the front.

Should I **have bought** a new dictionary?

<u>**Rule 3**</u>. The past modals **could** and **would** do not always require **have** and a past participle. To form negative sentences, add **not** before the verb:

I **would not eat** vegetables when I was a child.

Questions are formed by moving the modal to the front.

Could she **swim** when she was a child?

<u>**Rule 4**</u>. The past modals **ought to have** and **had better have** are not used in questions. The negative forms are **ought not to have** and **had better not have**.

<u>**Rule 5**</u>. With the past phrasal modal **had to**, add **did not** before **have to** in order to form questions.

Didn't you **have to** work last night?

<u>**Rule 6**</u>. To form negatives with the past phrasal modals **be able to, be supposed to,** and **be going to**, use **wasn't/weren't** in place of **be**. To form questions, use **was/were** in place of **be**.

<u>**Rule 7**</u>. Past modals can also be used in the progressive form. Use the **modal + be + verb + –ing** or **modal + have + been + verb + –ing**.

At our summer family reunions, the adults **would be telling** stories, and the children **would be sitting** at their feet, listening to them.

The kids **must have been having** a wonderful time because they didn't want to leave.

EXERCISE 1. Identifying Past Modals

Underline the past modals or phrasal modals in each paragraph, and write them in the left column. In the right column, write their meanings.

1. Over the years, as CEO of Watson Imports-Exports, John Watson used to make major decisions on a regular basis. He would approve million-dollar contracts to buy goods from overseas manufacturers and would implement marketing concepts to sell domestic products to dozens of nations around the world.

Past or Phrasal Modal	Meaning

2. Watson and his VP for marketing were going to travel to Asia next summer. They had already decided which countries and cities they were going to target and had made their plane reservations in advance of the trip. They were supposed to make their hotel reservations this week, but suddenly everything changed. After several banks refused to commit to lending Watson Imports-Exports money to grow its business, Watson and his associate decided to cancel their travel plans.

Past or Phrasal Modal	Meaning

3. The news hit the townspeople of Riverview, home of Watson Exports-Imports, hard. Word spread that the company had to get more funding in order to stay in business. Other communities might have given up and accepted impending layoffs as unavoidable, but not Riverview. Instead, the community assessed the problem and then recruited investors willing to take a chance on the company's future. With a large infusion of cash, Watson's business continued to operate. Watson, his employees, and the townspeople all must have breathed a collective sigh of relief at the news.

Past or Phrasal Modal	Meaning

Grammar Lesson

May Have **and** *Might Have*

| Affirmative | I **may have brought** some money with me. Let me check. | I **might have brought** some money with me. Let me check. |
| Negative | He **may not have gotten** the job. He'll find out tomorrow. | He **might not have gotten** the job. He'll find out tomorrow. |

<u>Rule 1</u>. **May have** and **might have** + PAST PARTICIPLE are used to express the possibility that something occurred in the past. Whether it actually occurred is uncertain. Note that **may have** and **might have** can be used interchangeably.

<u>Rule 2</u>. The contracted form of **may not have** is not used; the contracted form **mightn't have** is possible but not commonly used.

<u>Rule 3</u>. Questions with **may have** and **might have** are not commonly used.

⚠ BE CAREFUL!

Common Learner Errors	Explanation
1. He **may** ~~to~~ **have** gone home already.	Do not put **to** between the modal and **have**.
2. He ~~mayn't~~ **may not have** paid his bill on time.	Do not use a contracted form for **may**.
3. He **may not** ~~of~~ **have** left us a message.	Do not use **of** to replace **have**.

EXERCISE 2. Mini-Conversations with *may have* and *might have*

Use **may have + past participle** to complete B's sentences in the conversations. Use **might have + past participle** for A's response. The first one has been done for you as an example.

1. *A:* Your neighbor Judd just quit his job.

   B: He _may have won_____ (win) the lottery.

   A: __He might have found a better job that pays more.____

2. *A:* I'm looking for Ivan. Is he still here? I don't see him anywhere.

   B: He _____ already _____ (go) home.

   A: _____ .

3. *A:* Bev is waiting to find out if she got the job she interviewed for.

   B: Has she checked her answering machine? They _____ (leave) her a message.

   A: _____ .

4. *A:* I can't believe you've agreed to take on more responsibility at work.

   B: I know. I _____ (bite) off more than I can chew!

   A: _____ .

5. *A:* I tried calling Sami last night, but her line was busy for over an hour.

   B: She _____ (talk) to her sister in Chile.

   A: _____ .

Grammar Lesson

Could, Be Able To, and Could Have

Affirmative	As a doctor, my mother **could treat** us at home.	As a doctor, my mother **was able to treat** us at home.	As a doctor, my mother **could have treated** us at home. However, she didn't.
Negative	I **couldn't find** my car keys this morning, so I had to take a cab.	I **wasn't able to find** my car keys this morning, so I had to take a cab.	I don't know where my car keys are. I **couldn't have lost** them at the mall because I remember putting them on the counter when I came home last night.

<u>Rule 1</u>. **Could + VERB** and **be able to + VERB** are used to express past ability. Both **could** and **be able to** are used for a repeated action or for an action that happened over a period of time in the past.

<u>Rule 2</u>. Only **be able to** is used in the affirmative to express a single action or event that occurred in the past.

> Last night, I **was able to finish** the 600-page book I've been reading.

<u>Rule 3</u>. Both **could** and **be able to** can be used in the negative to express a single action or event that occurred in the past.

> Last night, I **couldn't finish** the 600-page book I've been reading.

> Last night, I **wasn't able to finish** the 600-page book I've been reading.

<u>Rule 4</u>. **Could have + PAST PARTICIPLE** is used to offer suggestions about what was possible in the past but that didn't happen and is often used in conditional sentences. **Could have + PAST PARTICIPLE** is also used to express a slight chance or small possibility that something happened.

> We **could have had** eggs for breakfast, but we didn't. (was possible)

> If I had known you were going to the concert, we **could have gone** together. (was possible)

> I'm pretty sure I turned off the iron, but I **could have left** it on. (slight chance)

Rule 5. Couldn't have + PAST PARTICIPLE is used to express the belief that it was impossible for an action or event in the past to have happened or to indicate the strong possibility that a situation didn't occur.

> He **couldn't have taken** the car. I was driving it! (impossible)

> That **couldn't have been** Ali in the library. He told me he had to work till 10:00 tonight, and it's only 7:30. (strong possibility it didn't happen)

For some situations, usually related to the present or recent past, **can't have** and **couldn't have** are used interchangeably to indicate emphasis.

> I **can't have lost** my passport. I just had it a minute ago!

> You **couldn't have misplaced** your house keys. I saw you put them on the counter when you walked in.

Rule 6. As with **might have, could have** is sometimes used to express a complaint.

> This project is due tomorrow. I was counting on getting your help with it.

> You **could have told** me last week that you wouldn't have time to help me.

 ## BE CAREFUL!

Common Learner Errors	Explanation
Last night I ~~could finish~~ **was able to finish** the 600-page book I've been reading. OR Last night I ~~could finish~~ **finished** the 600-page book I've been reading.	**Be able to** is used in the affirmative to express a single action or event that occurred in the past.

Do Online Exercise 8.1. My score: _____ /10. _____ % correct.

EXERCISE 3. *could* or *be able to?*

Read each sentence carefully. Look at the underlined part. If the underlined part is correct, circle the word *correct*. If it is wrong, circle the word *wrong*. Then write the correction above.

correct   wrong   1. Three years ago, I <u>could run</u> a marathon without any trouble.

correct   wrong   2. Six years ago, I <u>could run</u> a mile in seven minutes.

correct   wrong   3. This morning I <u>was able to run</u> a mile in ten minutes.

correct   wrong   4. Yesterday morning I <u>couldn't run</u> a mile in nine minutes.

correct   wrong   5. This morning I <u>could run</u> a mile in ten minutes.

correct   wrong   6. Yesterday morning I <u>wasn't able to run</u> a mile in nine minutes.

correct   wrong   7. Nowadays, I <u>couldn't run</u> a marathon even if I wanted to.

correct   wrong   8. This morning I <u>could run</u> faster than you.

EXERCISE 4. Practicing *could have*

Change the underlined part of the sentence to **could have + the past participle** of the verb. Then complete the sentence using **but**.

1. I <u>chose not to take</u> the job in Savannah.

   I could have taken the job in Savannah, but I chose not to.

2. My friends <u>didn't encourage</u> me to accept it.

   _____

3. My family <u>didn't get involved</u> in my decision.

   _____

4. They <u>refused to tell</u> me what to do. They said it was up to me.

   _____

5. The big increase in pay <u>didn't make</u> the decision any easier.

   _____

6. Making up my mind <u>didn't take</u> more than a few days. I came to the conclusion that I love my life here in Santa Fe.

   _____

7. Therefore, in the end, I <u>decided to stay</u> in New Mexico.

   _____

ONE-MINUTE LESSON
When a verb follows another verb, the second verb is usually an **infinitive**: I *chose* not *to take* the job, they *refused* *to tell* me, I *decided* *to stay*. A few verbs such as *enjoy* are followed by a gerund: I *enjoy* *reading*. Modal verbs are followed by the base form of the verb: I *can go*, you *must rest*, she *should help*.

EXERCISE 5. Practicing Modals for Past Possibility

Read the conversation. Fill in the blanks with **could have, couldn't have,** or **can't have + past participle** of the verb given.

1. *A:* What's wrong? You look panic-stricken!

   B: I can't find my homework assignment—the one that's due in 15 minutes.
   I _____ (lose) it. I had it just a few minutes ago.

2. *A:* _____ you _____ (leave) it in your car?

   B: No, I _____ (do) that. It was in my hand on the way into
   the building. I remember that.

3. *A:* Well, it didn't walk away on its own! It has to be around here somewhere.

   B: Before I came into the room, I decided to clean out my backpack. I
   _____ (throw) it in the recycling bin by mistake.

4. *A:* Let's go look.

   B: Oh no—the bin's empty!

   A: The maintenance people _____ (get) too far. Let's go find
   them.

   B: Wait a minute. Look! Here it is—it was inside my *Clear Grammar 4*
   textbook.

5. *A:* You are <u>so</u> lucky. You _____ (spend) hours looking
   through those recycling bins and never have found it.

   B: Or I _____ (tell) my instructor I had done the assignment
   and thrown it away by mistake and then hoped for the best!

EXERCISE 6. Mini-Conversations

Circle the correct words in these mini-conversations.

1. A: Did your team win the championship?

   B: Unfortunately, we did not. I think we (must, must not, could, could not) have won if our top two starters had not been injured.

2. A: I think Norah wrote this note.

   B: Norah's handwriting is different. She (might, might not, could, could not) have written that.

3. A: This soup tastes good, but it's spicy.

   B: Sorry about that. I (could add, couldn't add, might have added, might not have added) too much pepper.

4. A: Did you hear that I made 98 on my chemistry final?

   B: Wow, congrats! You (could, may, must, should) have studied a lot.

5. A: I'm in trouble now because my rent is late.

   B: I thought you were going to pay it yesterday.

   A: I spent most of it on a new phone.

   B: You (couldn't, shouldn't, must not, may not, might not) have done that.

Do Online Exercise 8.2. My score: _____ /10. _____ % correct.

Grammar Lesson

Would, Used To, and *Would Have*

Affirmative	As a teenager, I **would spend** hours listening to music.	As a teenager, I **used to spend** hours listening to music.	As a teenager, I **would have spent** hours listening to music if my parents had let me.
Negative	As a student, I **wouldn't watch** much TV during the week.	As a student, I **didn't use to watch** much TV during the week.	I **wouldn't have watched** much TV during the week even if my parents had said it was okay.
Question	**Would you ever study** on weekends?	**Did you use to study** on weekends?	**Would you have studied** on weekends if your parents hadn't been home?

<u>Rule 1</u>. **Would + VERB** and **used to + VERB** are both used to express repeated actions in the past. **Used to** is often used to introduce the past actions or to begin a story, and **would** is used for the follow-up sentences. When used to express repeated actions in the past, **would** and **used to** have the same meaning. They may be used in the negative and in questions.

<u>Rule 2</u>. **Used to** is also used to express a situation in the past that no longer exists. In this case, **would** is **not** used.

> They **used to** vacation in Utah, but now they go to Arizona.

<u>Rule 3</u>. **Would have + PAST PARTICIPLE** is used to express an unreal condition in the past.

> If we had known you were coming, we **would have met** you at the airport.

BE CAREFUL!

Common Learner Errors	Explanation
1. He ~~would live~~ **used to live** in Milwaukee, but he moved to Chicago in 2006.	Only **used to** is used to express a situation in the past that has changed or is no longer true. **Would** and **used to** can both be used to express repeated actions in the past.
2. He ~~use to live~~ **used to live** in Milwaukee, but he moved to Chicago in 2006.	Remember the expression is **used to** with the letter **d**.

EXERCISE 7. Using *would* and *used to* in Context

Fill in the blanks with **would** or **used to** and the correct form of the verb. More than one answer may be possible for some sentences.

Memories from When I Was a Child

Here's a story my mother ❶ _____ (tell) me whenever I

❷ _____ (complain) about my life: "When I was a young girl, about

10 years old, I ❸ _____ (get) up early, before dawn, in order to catch

the bus to school. My brothers and sisters and I ❹ _____ (wait) at the

corner for the bus to come. The ride ❺ _____ (take, not) more than

20 minutes, but it seemed like hours during the winter. After I got home from

school, I ❻ _____ (take) care of my baby sister while my mother

❼ _____ (make) supper. My brothers ❽ _____ (help, not)

with the dishes, so I ❾ _____ (do) them by myself after supper.

Then I ❿ _____ (sit) at our big kitchen table and do my homework.

Sometimes my father ⓫ _____ (help) me with math. I

⓬ _____ (go) to bed about 9:00."

EXERCISE 8. Using Modals to Past Events and Situations

Study the four groups of sentences. Identify the sentences that contain the wrong modal or modal phrase and correct them.

1A. I used to feed my cat every day after work.

1C. My cat wouldn't eat canned cat food. It would only eat fresh food.

1C. I would own a Siamese cat. I would have owned two if my parents had allowed me to.

2A. I would live near the west coast of Florida.

2B. It would rain there every afternoon, but it wouldn't cool off.

2C. It used to get unbearably hot and humid during the summer months. It would have been nice to go north to a cooler place for the summer.

3A. My grandfather used to tell me stories when I visited him.

3B. "Life is hard," he used to say to me.

3C. He would work in a machine repair shop before he retired. He wouldn't have retired if his health had been better.

4A. Steven would drive a Corvette years ago. He would never have sold it if he hadn't gotten married. His wife wouldn't ride with him because he drove so fast.

4B. He would always drive at least 15 miles over the speed limit.

4C. He used to get speeding tickets regularly, but he wouldn't always pay them.

EXERCISE 9. Speaking Practice: Making a Presentation about the Past

Plan a short (two to three minutes) presentation that describes (1) a special memory you had as a child or young adult or (2) how a holiday or special day is celebrated in your home culture. Try to include as many past modals as you can: **may have, might have, could, be able to, could have, would, used to,** and **would have.** Make your presentation to a small group of three or four of your classmates.

 **Grammar Lesson**

Had To, Must Have, and *Has To Have*

Affirmative	They **had to turn in** their assignments before noon today.	I heard you were in a car accident. That **must have been** scary.	I heard you were in a car accident. That **has to have been** scary.
Negative	They **didn't have to turn in** their assignments before noon today, but many of them did.	I saw you on campus yesterday, but you **must not have seen** me because you didn't wave back.	
Question	**Did they have to turn in** their assignments before noon today?		

<u>Rule 1</u>. The past tense form of the modal **must** is **had to,** which in the affirmative or questions is used to express obligation or necessity. The negative of **had to, didn't have to,** however, implies there is a choice, and thus expresses a lack of obligation or necessity.

Scott **had to start** his new job right away.

Did he **have to** start right away? Yes, he did. He had no choice. He left his old job on Friday and started the new one on the following Monday.

Scott **didn't have to start** his new job right away.

He had a choice. He could take time off in between his old job and his new one.

<u>Rule 2</u>. Must have + PAST PARTICIPLE and has to have + PAST PARTICIPLE are used to express strong certainty about an action or event that happened in the past. The evidence for believing the action occurred is very strong. **Must have** is more commonly used than **has to have.** Both are used in the affirmative, but only **must have** is used in the negative. Neither form is commonly used to make questions.

There are dirty dishes in the sink. The kids **must have made** themselves a snack.

The butler **has to have been** the killer. His fingerprints were on the weapon.

She ate hardly anything. She **must not have been** very hungry.

EXERCISE 10. Using Past Modals in Context

Circle the correct form in each sentence.

Johanna's Barbeque

A: I'm sorry I couldn't go to your barbeque, Johanna. I ❶ (had to, didn't have to) work late.

B: Don't apologize for not coming. It was a spur-of-the-moment thing. You ❷ (had to, didn't have to) come.

A: Well, I'm sorry I missed it. Knowing you, it ❸ (must have been, didn't have to be) a lot of fun.

B: Why do you say that? What makes you think it ❹ (has to have been, had to be) fun?

A: Every single time I've come to your house for a barbeque, it's been a success. This one certainly ❺ (must have been, didn't have to be) the same.

B: I appreciate the compliment, but if my barbeque was a success, it ❻ (must be, has to have been) due to the right combination of people who came!

EXERCISE 11. Practicing Past Modals to Discuss an Event

A group of neighbors is standing outside a home in their neighborhood. The homeowners, Oscar and Nadia Holmes, have just returned from their vacation and discovered that while they were enjoying the beaches of the Bahamas, burglars entered their house and made off with jewelry, electronics, and artwork worth thousands of dollars. Read each neighbor's speculations and comments on the recent robbery and complete what each said. Use the correct form of **should have, ought to have, had to, must have,** or **has to + the verb** in parentheses.

Oh, No! We've Been Robbed!

Bert English: Well, we know the thieves ❶ _____ (get) in and out quickly so no one in the neighborhood would see them. They ❷ _____ (come) during the day when we were all working. Maybe they came in a lawn maintenance truck.

Greg Sanders: It doesn't matter how they did it. I think we ❸ _____ (be) paying more attention to the house since we knew Oscar and Nadia were on vacation. Of course, they probably ❹ _____ (notify) their security alarm company that they were going out of town for two weeks. I don't know why they didn't. I always do.

Molly Sanders: Since the burglars targeted only their house, they ❺ _____ (know) Oscar and Nadia were out of town. I wonder why the alarm didn't go off. They ❻ _____ (put) up a camera to record any goings on while they were away. We have one.

Do Online Exercise 8.3. My score: _____ /10. _____% correct.

Connecting Grammar and Vocabulary

Here are 18 frequently used past modal phrases. In theory, any past participle could occur with these past modals, but note that the three most commonly used past participles are **been**, **done**, and **had**.

18 Frequent Verbs with Past Modals	
could have	**should have**
1. could have been 2. could have done 3. could have had 4. could have said 5. could have made	1. should have been 2. should have done 3. should have had 4. should have read 5. should have mentioned
might have	**must have**
1. might have been 2. might have had 3. might have seen 4. might have done	1. must have been 2. must have come 3. must have used 4. must have done

Source: Based on information in the Michigan Corpus of Academic Spoken English, www.elicorpora.info/

Grammar Lesson

KEY 12

Be Supposed To and *Be Going To*

Affirmative	You **were supposed to stop** at the grocery store on your way home. Did you forget?	I **was going to stop** at the grocery store on my home, but I decided not to.
Negative	I **wasn't supposed to work** today, but my boss called me and asked me to come in.	My neighbors **weren't going to go** on vacation this year, but they changed their minds.
Question	**Was** Anne **supposed to be** at the meeting this afternoon? I didn't see her there.	**Was** Tom **going to apply** for the job in Toronto? I know he was very interested in it.

<u>Rule 1.</u> Be supposed to + VERB is used to express an obligation or expectation in the past which was not fulfilled or did not happen. It can be used in affirmative and negative sentences and in questions.

<u>Rule 2.</u> Be going to + VERB is used to express a plan or intention for the future that was made in the past but that was not fulfilled or carried out. It can be used in affirmative and negative sentences and in questions.

EXERCISE 12. Practicing *be supposed to* and *be going to* in Context

Fill in the blanks with the correct form of **be supposed to** or **be going to**. Be sure to use **be supposed to** for actions that express or imply obligation.

The Best-Laid Plans

I should have stayed in bed today! Nothing seemed to go right. First of all, I

❶ _____ get up at 5:30 this morning

to exercise for half an hour. Unfortunately,

my alarm didn't go off, so I overslept. I

didn't wake up till almost 7:00, and I

❷ _____ be at work for an important

meeting at 8:00. I ❸ _____ take a quick shower, get dressed, and head

out the door, but I skipped the shower to save time and headed straight for the

office. To save even more time, I ❹ _____ take the expressway to work,

but then I figured rush hour would be in full swing so I took the side streets.

Wouldn't you know? The route I chose, which ❺ _____ be quicker,

took longer than the expressway would have. I finally got to work—with about

five minutes to spare! Just as I ❻ _____ walk into the conference room

for the meeting, my boss reminded me to bring the final draft of the handouts

I ❼ _____ distribute at the meeting. Handouts? Oh yes, the handouts I

❽ _____ copy when I got to work early this morning. The meeting,

which ❾ _____ start at 8:00 sharp, started 20 minutes late because of

me. I knew then that things ❿ _____ go as planned for the rest of the

day either. And they didn't. . . .

EXERCISE 13. Using Past Modals to Explain Good Intentions

Part 1.

Write three sentences listing things you were expected or obligated to do at home or work or in class but that you didn't do. Use **be supposed to.**

1. _____

2. _____

3. _____

Part 2.

Write three sentences listing things you were planning or intending to do but didn't. Use **be going to.** When you finish, share your sentences from Parts 1 and 2 with a classmate.

4. _____

5. _____

6. _____

ONE-MINUTE LESSON

The word **just** can be used as an intensifier: *just before noon, just as I opened the door, just now.* This adverb functions similarly to **right** (*right here*) or **very** (*very hot*).

Do Online Exercise 8.4. My score: ____ /10. ____ % correct.

EXERCISE 14. Sentence Study for Critical Reading

Read the numbered sentences. Then read the answer choices and put a check mark (✓) in the yes or no boxes in front of each sentence to show if that answer is true based on the information in the original sentence. If there is not enough information to mark something as yes, then mark it as no. Remember that more than one true answer may be possible.

1. Amani and her girlfriends went shopping at the mall. Her friends weren't supposed to leave the mall without her.

   ☐ yes ☐ no a. Amani's friends didn't leave Amani alone at the mall.

   ☐ yes ☐ no b. Amani's friends left the mall without Amani.

   ☐ yes ☐ no c. Amani is still at the mall with her friends.

2. The babysitter just texted me. She's locked out of the house, and the security code isn't working. The kids could have changed the security code.

   ☐ yes ☐ no a. The parent thinks it's a good idea for the kids to change the security code.

   ☐ yes ☐ no b. The parent thinks there is a chance that the kids changed the security code.

   ☐ yes ☐ no c. There may be another reason the security code is not working.

3. I might have seen that movie. Is that the one where the guy robs a bank and then ends up donating all the money to charity? Or is that the one where the guy is working as an informant and pretends to be in on the bank robbery just to catch the thieves?

   ☐ yes ☐ no a. It is possible that the speaker saw the movie.

   ☐ yes ☐ no b. The speaker clearly remembers having seen the movie.

   ☐ yes ☐ no c. The speaker isn't very sure about having seen the movie.

4. I should have been studying for this exam instead of chatting online.

   ☐ yes ☐ no a. I shouldn't have spent my study time chatting online.

   ☐ yes ☐ no b. I definitely studied for the exam after I finished chatting.

   ☐ yes ☐ no c. The time I spent on the computer was time I was supposed to be studying.

5. Tam, what a surprise to see you! Weren't you going to take the summer off and travel abroad?

   ☐ yes ☐ no a. Tam changed her summer plans and decided not to travel abroad.

   ☐ yes ☐ no b. The speaker was surprised because Tam had planned to travel overseas.

   ☐ yes ☐ no c. Tam was supposed to be spending the summer traveling abroad.

Grammar Lesson

Passive Modals

Modal +	*have been*	+ PAST PARTICIPLE
I **may/might**		**awarded** a sports scholarship.
You **could**		**hurt** in the accident.
They **would**	**have been**	**told** the news immediately.
He **should/ought to**		**elected** club president.
She **must/has to**		**hired** for the director's position.
We **were supposed to**		**seated** in first class.

<u>Rule 1</u>. The passive form of modals and modal expressions is **modal + have been +** PAST PARTICIPLE.

<u>Rule 2</u>. Passive modals may be used in negative sentences and in questions.

He **should not have been elected** club president.

Were we **supposed to have been seated** in first class?

 EXERCISE 15. Editing: Is It Correct?

If the sentence is correct, write a check mark (✓) on the line. If it is not correct, write an X on the line and circle the mistake. Then change the sentence to make it correct. Write the change above the sentence. (*Hint*: There are eight sentences. Three are correct, but five have mistakes.)

Ways to Spend a Vacation

_____ 1. On my last vacation, the kitchen must have been painted, so that's what I did.

_____ 2. Sam could have spent his vacation skiing in Tahoe, but he went to Vermont instead.

_____ 3. Did you had to even go away to be on vacation? Why didn't you just stay home?

_____ 4. My neighbors must not enjoy their vacation. They came back home the next day!

_____ 5. I should have been enjoying a relaxing time at the beach, but my entire vacation was spent writing a research paper.

_____ 6. My family and I were supposed to go camping in Canada, but my kids are afraid of bears and I hate mosquitoes, so we stayed in a hotel.

_____ 7. Davis could spend his entire vacation last week on a cruise to Alaska.

_____ 8. Alicia thinks I might not have gone to Las Vegas on vacation because I came home broke.

EXERCISE 16. Speaking Practice: Talking about a Date

Choose a partner. After reading the following situation, discuss with your partner what you think happened. Create a story about what happened to present to your classmates. Use as many of the past modal forms from this unit as you can: **may have, might have, could have, should have, ought to have, had to, must have, was/were supposed to,** and **was/were going to.**

Situation: A man and a woman are sitting across from one another at a table in a very nice restaurant. The tables are covered with white linen tablecloths, and fresh flowers decorate each table as well. The man and woman are talking quietly, but they are not smiling or laughing. Suddenly, the woman gets up from her chair, puts on her coat, and walks out of the restaurant. The man remains seated at the table for a moment, calls the waiter over, pays the bill, puts on his coat, and then leaves the restaurant.

EXERCISE 17. Review Test 1: Multiple Choice

Circle the letter of the correct answer.

1. A: Have you ever seen the movie *Always?*

   B: I'm not sure. I _____ it on TV last summer.
   - a. was going to see
   - b. might have seen
   - c. would have seen
   - d. used to see

2. I'm so tired I can hardly stay awake today. I guess I _____ that espresso at 10:30 last night and stayed up so late.
   - a. should have had
   - b. must not have had
   - c. shouldn't have had
   - d. could have had

3. You're such a wonderful dancer. You _____ lessons from an expert!
   - a. would have taken
   - b. ought to have taken
   - c. must have taken
   - d. shouldn't have taken

4. This scale has to be wrong. I _____ that much weight in only two months!
   - a. might not have gained
   - b. would have gained
   - c. couldn't have gained
   - d. can't have gained

5. At the last place Gary worked, they _____ an annual company picnic. All the employees _____ their families along and spend the day at a nearby park. It was great.
   - a. has to have / had to bring
   - b. would have / didn't have to bring
   - c. used to have / couldn't bring
   - d. used to have / would bring

6. My in-laws _____ New Year's on a cruise ship, but they changed their minds.
   - a. shouldn't have celebrated
   - b. can't have celebrated
   - c. were going to celebrate
   - d. had to celebrate

7. Leslie's upset. She invited about 20 people to her house for a party and then no one showed up. The least they _____ was to call to say they _____.
   - a. might have done / were going to come
   - b. could have done / weren't going to come
   - c. might have done / weren't supposed to come
   - d. should have done / were going to come

8. It _____ that one day she would run for public office. She's always hated speaking in public.
   - a. must not have been predicted
   - b. can have been predicted
   - c. might have predicted
   - d. couldn't have been predicted

EXERCISE 18. Review Test 2: Production and Evaluation

Part 1.

Read the passage. Fill in the blanks with the past modal and the correct form of the verb in parentheses. More than one answer may be possible for some sentences.

Dear Personnel Advisor:

I'm writing to ask your advice about a work situation. I probably

❶ _____ (should/write) to you months ago, but I didn't.

I hope it's not too late for your help.

When I was hired at my current company last year, I ❷ _____

(should/have) a review after six months. Well, it's now been a year, and I still

haven't had a job review. If I had had a review, I ❸ _____

(might/get) a raise.

In my previous job, my supervisors ❹ _____ (used to/

schedule) my review. We ❺ _____ (would/discuss) my

performance and set goals. But so far, at my new job, nothing has happened. My

supervisor ❻ _____ (must/forget) to schedule my review. My

dilemma is that if I remind my supervisor, she may think I'm implying she's not

doing her job well.

This ❼ _____ (could/happen/negative) at a worse time.

The company is laying people off, and I don't want to come across as a

complainer. I only want what I ❽ _____ (should/receive) six

months ago. What should I do now?

Sincerely,

Afraid to Ask

Part 2.

Read each sentence carefully. Look at the underlined part. If the underlined part is correct, circle the word *correct*. If it is wrong, circle the word *wrong*. Then write the correction above.

correct   wrong   1. I <u>would live</u> in Berlin, Germany, and study at the university.

correct   wrong   2. Where are the kids? They <u>should have been</u> here by now, but they're not.

correct   wrong   3. He <u>must to cancel</u> all his credit cards when his wallet was stolen.

correct   wrong   4. Whenever my dad sings to my mom, "You <u>must have been a</u> beautiful baby, 'cause, baby, look at you now," she laughs.

correct   wrong   5. They <u>weren't going to drive</u> to Florida for the winter, but they changed their minds after the first snowstorm.

correct   wrong   6. You <u>shouldn't have shaved</u> off your mustache. Why did you do it?

correct   wrong   7. It was the most wonderful wedding I've ever attended. The bride <u>could have looked</u> more beautiful!

correct   wrong   8. As children, my sister and I <u>would set</u> up a lemonade stand in front of our house at least once every summer.

EXERCISE 19. Reading Practice: Sensing Change

Read the information in this article on the five senses and how they change as you age. Then answer the comprehension questions that follow. The grammar from this unit is underlined for you.

Our Five Senses

Your five senses—sight, taste, smell, hearing, and touch—are your connection to the world around you. Although you may not give your working senses much thought, a change in any one of them can immediately affect your daily life. Whether you realize it or not, as you age, your senses change. Some of these changes can happen in your 20s and 30s.

Sight: You <u>might have noticed</u> that your eyes have started to feel dry or scratchy. Small print you <u>could have read</u> a year ago may now appear a little fuzzy or blurry. It <u>may have become</u> more difficult to read small fonts. In the past, you <u>were able to</u> read everything, but now it's hard to see the print in some documents. These changes in vision are easily correctible with eye drops or eyeglasses.

Taste and smell: These senses contribute to your enjoyment of food and even tell you if the food you are about to eat is safe. As you age, your taste buds become less sensitive. Tastes you <u>were easily able to discern</u> in the past may no longer register on your taste buds. Before, you <u>used to rattle off</u> all the herbs and spices in a bowl of soup served to you, but now you pronounce the same soup bland and tasteless. A younger you <u>could recognize</u> the differences among 10,000 smells. To deal with these diminished senses, add spices, not salt, to your food.

Hearing: As you get older, you will find that you can no longer hear some sounds you <u>could hear</u> when you were younger. Although some hearing loss is normal, some <u>could have been prevented</u>. Perhaps as a teenager, you <u>would listen</u> to loud music on your car radio or through earbuds on a personal audio device. Being exposed to loud noises for years led you to discover that one day you <u>had to turn up</u> the TV volume or <u>had to ask</u> someone to repeat what was said. You <u>should have guarded</u> your ears from loud sounds years ago. That advice still holds today.

Touch: As you grow older, your skin becomes drier, thinner, and less elastic. At a younger age, you <u>would not have been greatly affected</u> by temperature fluctuations. However, as you grow older, you may find it difficult to stay warm in cool temperatures and to stay cool in warm temperatures. Interestingly, the sense of touch is the sense least affected by age. You <u>must have heard</u> the advice for dealing with your skin hundreds of times: moisturize your skin with lotion, stay away from hot baths or showers, and dress according to the weather forecast. That advice hasn't changed.

Depending on your age, many of these sensory changes <u>could not have been prevented</u>, but perhaps some of them <u>would have occurred</u> more gradually if you had taken specific measures: had your eyes checked, turned down the volume, taken care of your skin. Why wait until it's too late to realize you <u>should have taken</u> these measures? Remember that appointment you <u>were going to make</u> with the eye doctor and the one you were <u>supposed to schedule</u> with your physician? Make them and keep them.

1. What is the author's purpose for writing this article?

   _____

2. Who is the intended audience for this article?

   _____

3. "The manufacturers of personal audio devices should have educated consumers about possible hearing loss from use of their products when these products first came on the market." Do you agree or disagree with this statement? Why?

   _____

   _____

   _____

4. If you had to identify one sense as the most important, which one would you choose and why? _____

   _____

   _____

   _____

5. What would you have done differently if you had read this article five years ago?

   _____

   _____

   _____

EXERCISE 20. Vocabulary Practice: Word Knowledge

Circle the answer choice that is most closely related to the vocabulary on the left. Use a dictionary to check the meaning of words you do not know.

Vocabulary	Answer Choices	
1. assume	prevent	suppose
2. distribute	hand out	turn in
3. give up	stop trying	try harder
4. an export	you sell it here	you sell it abroad
5. respond	answer	ignore
6. investors	people	rules
7. normal	odd	usual
8. refuse	say no	say yes
9. funding	emotional support	financial support
10. imply	directly state	indirectly state
11. chase	a dog runs after a cat	a person on a bike
12. adequate	insufficient	sufficient
13. make off with something	reduce the price	steal something
14. be aware of something	know	write
15. labeled	identified	unidentified
16. predict	about the future	about the past
17. a draft	the first version	the original idea
18. an assignment	behavior	homework
19. editing	revise	compose
20. an expert	a skilled person	an unskilled person
21. a route	an idea to think about	a way to go
22. overdraft	at a bank	at a hospital
23. insert	add	subtract
24. definitely	with doubt	without doubt
25. a policy	a way a company operates regarding a certain matter	a group of police officers who work together

EXERCISE 21. Vocabulary Practice: Collocations

Fill in each blank with the answer on the right that most naturally completes the phrase on the left. If necessary, use a dictionary to check the meaning of words you do not know.

Vocabulary	Answer Choices	
1. by _____	mistake	problem
2. the _____ limit	speed	travel
3. via _____	college	train
4. _____ major decisions	make	operate
5. I'm _____ late today	filling	running
6. ideas _____ from A to Z	assuming	ranging
7. _____ 8 hours of sleep	get	take
8. an overdraft _____	fee	tax
9. over a period _____ time	in	of
10. to be _____ to new ideas	exposed	exported
11. _____ your temper	find	lose
12. to have a _____ time	relaxed	relaxing
13. to experience changes _____	in vision	on vision
14. you should call _____	ahead	behind
15. unbearably _____	hot	important
16. I'm overloaded _____ work	for	with
17. _____ the volume up	make	turn
18. to comment _____ an idea	on	for
19. I couldn't stop _____	laughing	to laugh
20. be committed to _____ money	lent	lending
21. a diminished sense _____	of success	to succeed
22. _____ for doing something	apologize	succeed
23. _____ a conclusion	come to	hand out
24. _____ one item from many	pick	run
25. the changes occurred _____	gradually	precisely

EXERCISE 22. Writing Practice: The Choices We Make

Part 1.

Read these sentences about a student's decision to quit school. Circle the 15 errors. Then write the number of the sentence with the error next to the type of error. (Some sentences have more than one error.)

_____ a. wrong modal   _____ d. preposition

_____ b. incorrect verb form _____ e. subject-verb agreement

_____ c. missing *a/an*   _____ f. singular-plural of nouns

One Student's Tough Decision
1. I think Victor might have make the wrong decision when he decided to quit college at the end of the semester.
2. He had another options: He would have chosen to go to school part-time instead of quitting school altogether.
3. When I was part-time college student, I used to spending a couple of hours a day after class studying in the library and then head out to my job.
4. As a result, even though it took me longer to get my degree, I ended up getting good grade every semester, and I think I learned more.
5. If Victor had asked his family or friends or advisor for some advices, he probably would not have be in such a hurry to drop out of school.
6. He must not have taken so many difficult classes this semester, but he wouldn't listen to me when I talked to him for it.
7. He said he had to choosing between working full time and going to school full time.
8. Since he needed job to support himself, he chose to work.
9. He must have been under a lot of stress this semester to make him think in quitting school.
10. According to the last news that I heard, Victor were going to finish his degree at end of the school year and then look a better-paying job.

Part 2. Original Student Writing

We all make choices during our lives, including choosing where we work, live, and study. Write a paragraph about some of the choices you have made in your life. Start with what you had planned or were expected to do, and then tell what you actually did. End by telling some of the things you could have, might have, or would have done or been able to do if you had made different choices. Underline the past modals in your life story so your teacher can see what you are trying to practice.

Unit 9

Review of Verb Tenses

Discover the Grammar

Jane is describing how she improved her Spanish. Read her story, and answer the questions that follow.

Line	
1	Jane's Spanish is improving. Many of her company's clients are from Latin
2	America, and she really struggles to communicate with them. Jane has studied
3	Spanish off and on since she was in high school, but her vocabulary is very
4	limited and she doesn't know the verb tenses. During her one semester of high
5	school Spanish, she wasn't very motivated. However, when she was in college,
6	she chose to take part in an exciting four-week program in Costa Rica. She
7	earned college credits in Spanish while she was living in a new country. Jane
8	had never lived in a foreign country and would have been lost without
9	her school's help.
10	The college arranged for Jane to stay with a Costa Rican family, the
11	Calderons. Every day she rode the bus to and from the language school.
12	The lessons were intense, and she had to use Spanish everywhere she went.
13	One evening Jane was telling Mrs. Calderon about her adventures when

240

14 Mrs. Calderon suddenly said, "Jane! Do you realize how much your Spanish
15 has improved?"

16   "Thank you. I am trying," Jane answered. "The school has been good, but
17 you have helped me, too."

18   "Are you going to study Spanish after you get back to the U.S.?" Mrs.
19 Calderon asked.

20   "I'm going to take the next Spanish course, but I don't think I'll take any
21 more than that. I need just that one class so I can graduate."

22   A few years after Jane finished college, she took a job at a bank in Seattle.
23 One day she had a customer from Mexico who didn't speak English, but he
24 had a translator with him. She really wanted to speak to him in Spanish, but she
25 couldn't. "Wow, I've already forgotten everything I learned in Costa Rica," she
26 thought to herself.

27   The next day, she called the local library. "I'm looking for Spanish classes.
28 Do you have night classes?"

29   "Yes, we do," the woman answered. "We have a free, open-enrollment class
30 on Tuesday and Thursday evenings, but it has all levels in it, from beginning to
31 advanced."

32   "That's all right. What time does it meet?" Jane asked.

33   "It's from 6:00 to 7:00."

34   "Great. I'll be there Thursday night!"

35   "Oh, don't forget to bring your driver's license. We need to verify that you
36 are a resident of Seattle," the woman told her.

37   "I won't forget," Jane replied.

38   After a few weeks of classes, Jane started to remember some Spanish from
39 her old lessons, and she made great progress. Eventually, her Spanish was good
40 enough to allow her to help some of her customers who don't speak English.

1. Find the five examples of present perfect tense. Write the examples and their line numbers.

	Line Number	*has/have*	Past Participle
a.			
b.			
c.			
d.			
e.			

2. Is it possible to use the simple past tense instead of the present perfect in the examples from Question 1? Explain each answer.

	Line Number	Past Tense Possible?	Reason
a.			
b.			
c.			
d.			
e.			

3. Find the two examples of past progressive tense. Write the examples and their line numbers.

	Line Number	*was/were*	Verb + *–ing*
a.			
b.			

4. Is it possible to use the simple past tense instead of the past progressive in the two examples? Explain each answer.

	Line Number	Past Tense Possible?	Reason
a.			
b.			

5. Find an example of each of these verb tenses or expressions in the passage. Write the examples and their line numbers.

Verb Tense	Line Number	Example
simple present		
simple past		
present progressive		
simple future (*will*)		
be going to		
past perfect		

6. What questions do you have about these or any other verb tenses?

_____

_____

_____

 **Grammar Lesson**

Simple Present Tense

Past   *Now*   *Future*

usage	Use the simple present tense for facts, habits, routines, or customs.	
common time words	*every _____ (every day), always, frequently, usually, often, sometimes, occasionally, rarely, never*	
affirmative	I, you, we, they + VERB I **wash** my hands *frequently*.	he, she, it + VERB + –s It **looks** cloudy today.
negative	I, you, we, they + do not + VERB They **don't produce** cars there.	he, she, it + does not + VERB He **does not rely** on anyone for money.
question	Do + I, you, we, they + VERB **Do** you **initiate** all the contracts?	Does + he, she, it + VERB **Does** the contract **specify** the cost?

<u>Rule 1</u>. In the simple present tense, a verb has only two forms: VERB or VERB + –s.

<u>Rule 2</u>. SPELLING: For verbs that end in consonant + –y, change the –y to –i and then add –es: *study* → *studies*. However, if the verb ends in **vowel** + –y, only add –s: *play* → *plays*. For verbs that end in –o, –sh, –ch, –s, –z, and –x, add –es: *do* → *does*.

<u>Rule 3</u>. To make a negative statement, add **do not** OR **does not** before the base (simple) form of the verb. It is also possible to use contractions in informal English: **do not** = **don't**; **does not** = **doesn't**.

<u>Rule 4</u>. To make a question with a verb, add **do** OR **does** before the subject. Be sure to use only the base form of the verb.

BE CAREFUL!

Common Learner Errors	Explanation
1. Kathy ~~prepare~~ **prepares** oatmeal for breakfast every day.	Remember to use **VERB + –s** when the subject is **he, she,** or **it.**
2. (a.) The boxes that are on the bottom shelf ~~needs~~ **need** new lids. (b.) The box on those magazines ~~need~~ **needs** a new lid.	In sentences with prepositional phrases or relative clauses, be sure to locate the subject that belongs with the verb.
3. That color ~~doesn't looks~~ **doesn't look** good on me.	When using **does,** use the base verb form (no –s). You need only one **–s** for **he/she/it.**
4. Does your wife ~~speaks~~ **speak** English?	Use only the base (simple) form of the main verb. If the question begins with **does,** the verb doesn't have **–s.**

EXERCISE 1. Questions and Answers Using Simple Present Tense

Write the correct form of the questions and answers for this conversation. Use the information in the parentheses. Remember to use **do/does** in question forms and in affirmative short answers. Use **don't/doesn't** in negative forms. Some answers will be full form and others will be short form. Pay attention to the details and punctuation in the sentences.

Friends, Family . . . and Sushi!

Gustavo: (you, like) _____ ethnic food?

Jose: Yes, (my friends and I, often go) _____ to Japanese restaurants. What about you?

Gustavo: Actually, (I, like, not) _____ Japanese food, but (my sister, go) _____ to a Japanese restaurant with her friends every weekend. (I, prefer) _____ Chinese food.

Jose: (you, eat) _____ Chinese food frequently?

Gustavo: Yes, (I, order) _____ it whenever I have to pull an all-nighter.

Jose: Oh. I see. (your sister, like) _____ sushi?

Gustavo: Yes, (she, do) _____.

Jose: Hmmm. (you, think) _____ your sister and her friends would go out with my friends and me for sushi one night?

Gustavo: (I, know, not) _____. (you, want) _____ me to ask her?

Grammar Lesson

Simple Past Tense

usage	Use the simple past tense for actions or events that are finished.	
common time words	*yesterday, last _____ (last month), _____ ago (2 days ago)*	
affirmative	regular verbs: **subject + VERB + –ed** I **washed** my hands before dinner. wash → **washed**	irregular verbs: **subject + IRREGULAR VERB** We **found** a great restaurant. find → **found**
negative	**subject + did not + VERB** Our teacher **did not** pick up our homework.	
question	**Did + subject + VERB** **Did** you **identify** the problem with your car?	

<u>Rule 1</u>. In the simple past tense, a **regular** verb has one form: **VERB + –ed. An irregular form varies: go → went, take → took, begin → began.** (See Appendix C.)

<u>Rule 2</u>. For **one-syllable** verbs that end in consonant + vowel + consonant (**CVC**), **double the final consonant: stop → stopped** and **plan → planned.** However, do not double final letters for verbs that end in –w (**snowed**), –x (**taxed**), or –y (**played**)

<u>Rule 3</u>. For **two-syllable** verbs that end in CVC and have stress on the **second** syllable, double the final consonant: *ocCUR* → **occurred**, and *perMIT* → **permitted.** However, if the stress is on the **first** syllable, just add *-ed*: *HAPpen* → **happened**; and *LISten* → **listened.**

<u>Rule 4</u>. To make a negative statement, add **did not** before the base (simple) form of the verb. In informal speaking or writing, it is possible to use a contraction: **did not → didn't.** Contractions are not used in formal academic English.

<u>Rule 5</u>. To make a question with a past tense verb (not **be**), add **did** before the subject. Be sure to use only the **base** (simple) form of the main verb.

BE CAREFUL!

Common Learner Errors	Explanation
1. My uncle Juan Carlos ~~lives~~ lived in Chicago 20 years ago.	Remember to use simple past tense. Don't use **VERB** or **VERB + −s** for a simple past affirmative action.
3. The meeting ~~didn't started~~ didn't start on time.	If you have the auxiliary verb **did, did not,** or **didn't,** then don't use **−ed** with the verb.
4. Did you ~~installed~~ install a new lock on your door?	Do not use **−ed** or the irregular past form of the verb in yes-no questions. Use only the base (simple) form of the verb. **Did** is past, and you only need a past tense form once.

EXERCISE 2. Conversations Using Regular and Irregular Simple Past Tense

In these conversations, circle the correct word(s) in each set of parentheses. This exercise uses both simple present and simple past. You may need to go back and review the rules.

1. *Anne:* I ❶ (heared, heard) that you ❷ (growed, grew) 150 pounds of

   tomatoes this summer. That's an incredible amount! I'm sure you

   ❸ (didn't ate, didn't eat) all of them.

   Grace: No way! We ❹ (give, gave) most of them to the food bank for

   low-income families.

2. *Paul:* When I was a child, I ❶ (taked, took) the train from Portland to Seattle

   about once a month to see my grandparents.

   Rose: ❷ (Did you traveled, Did you travel) alone, or ❸ (was, were) your

   parents with you?

3. *Ina*:   Can you help me? I **ⓐ** (have, has) a problem, and I **ⓑ** (need, needed)

some help for a couple of hours.

Irene: Sure, I **ⓒ** (have, had) some time. What **ⓓ** (do you need, you do need)?

Ina: The director of the dance team **ⓔ** (asked, asks) me to make 45

sandwiches for their practice tonight.

4. *Shelly*:   Good morning! **ⓐ** (Was all of you practice, Did all of you practice) your

music this week?

Larry: Yes, I did, but I **ⓑ** (upsetted, upset) my neighbors because I **ⓒ** (played,

plaied) my guitar until 2 AM every night.

5. *Gale*:   **ⓐ** (Do you remember, You do remember) my cousin Cindy?

Pat: Isn't she the one who **ⓑ** (has, have) horses, chickens, goats, dogs, and cats?

Gale: Well, she **ⓒ** (doesn't have, don't have) chickens anymore. Anyway, last

week a physical therapist **ⓓ** (used, uses) her dogs in animal-assisted

therapy for stroke patients. The patients **ⓔ** (spent, spended) time

handling the animals. Many doctors now **ⓕ** (believe, believed) it's

very beneficial.

ONE-MINUTE LESSON
To indicate the duration of an activity, we can use **spend** + time + a gerund:
We spent an hour searching for the car keys.

EXERCISE 3. Asking Questions with Simple Past Tense

Write past tense questions for the bold words in each answer. There are both *wh*– questions and yes-no questions. Remember to use a **?** at the end of the question. Some pronouns may need to be changed. The first one has been done for you as an example.

1. Q: *When did you begin to study English?* _____

    A: I began to study English **in the 9th grade**.

2. Q: _____

    A: I went to bed **at 10:00 PM** last night.

3. Q: _____

    A: **Mr. Jenkins** taught grammar last year.

4. Q: _____

    A: **Yes**. I finished my homework.

5. Q: _____

    A: Prince William married **Kate Middleton**.

6. Q: _____

    A: I **played tennis, did my laundry,** and **studied** over the weekend.

Grammar Lesson

Present Progressive

usage	1. Use the present progressive tense for actions happening now. 2. It is also possible to use present progressive tense for future actions, especially when a future time word is used.
common time words	*now, right now, today, tonight, this _____ (this month), currently, these days, at this moment/minute*
affirmative	**I am, you/we/they are, he/she/it is + VERB + –ing** It is **raining** really hard right now.
negative	**I am, you/we/they are, he/she/it is + not + VERB –ing** It snowed a lot yesterday, but at least today it is **not snowing.**
question	**Am I, Are you/we/they, Is he/she/it + VERB + –ing** **Am I sitting** in your chair? I'm sorry.

<u>Rule 1</u>. In present progressive tense, a verb has three forms: **am VERB + –ing; is VERB + –ing;** and **are VERB + –ing.**

<u>Rule 2</u>. Do not use this tense with non-action verbs. Four kinds of verbs that typically do not occur in present progressive tense are: **senses** (*hear, see, smell, feel, sound*), **emotions** (*like, love, need, prefer, want*), **mental states** (*believe, forget, remember, seem*), and **possession** (*belong, have, own, possess*).

> <u>Exception 1</u>: You can say *I'm having a good time* or *We're having a test* because **have** is an action in these two examples. You cannot say *I'm having a new car* or *She's having a pencil* because in these examples, **have** shows possession and not action.

> <u>Exception 2</u>: You can also use **think** in the progressive if you are indicating it is a progressive action. You can say, *I am thinking about moving to a new apartment.* However you would not express your opinion by saying *I am thinking that car looks nice.*

<u>Rule 3</u>. Use the word **not** to make a negative sentence with the verb **be** in present progressive tense: **am not, is not, are not.**

<u>Rule 4.</u> To ask a question using present progressive tense, invert the subject and the **be** verb.

BE CAREFUL!

Common Learner Errors	Explanation
1. The earth ~~is taking~~ takes one year to go around the sun.	Don't use present progressive for actions that happen every day or all the time.
2. ~~eatting~~ eating, ~~colorring~~ coloring, ~~takeing~~ taking, ~~openning~~ opening, ~~cuting~~ cutting, ~~listenning~~ listening	Be careful with the spelling of –ing verbs.
3. Why ~~are walking Petra and Melissa~~ are Petra and Melissa walking home?	Put the subject between am, is, or are and the –ing verb.

EXERCISE 4. Present Progressive Sentence Completion

Fill in the blanks with the correct form of the simple present or present progressive—affirmative or negative. Use verbs from the word list. Use all of the words.

word list	cry	hug	stand	write
	fix	look	take	work

1. A: It _____ a long time for our lunch to arrive. Should I say

   something?

   B: Sure. They _____ very hard, but we're the only customers.

2. A: It has been a long time since we've talked, Patti. What's new?

   B: I _____ for a new job and _____ my

   thesis.

3. [phone rings] A: Hi. Can I speak to Paolo?

   B: Sorry, but he's in the garage. He _____ a car.

4. A: I wonder if that little boy is lost. He _____ all alone.

   B: Wait. That looks like his father who _____ him now, and

   the boy _____ any more.

EXERCISE 5. Speaking Activity: Charades

Work in pairs. Create a list of activities that you can act out without speaking. You can act alone, or you and your partner can act together. The rest of the class will guess what you are doing by asking yes-no questions (for example, *Are you cooking?*). You are only allowed to answer yes or no to continue guiding the class to guess the correct answer. If you answered no to this question, continue acting using specific gestures until the class guesses correctly. The second guess might be, *Are you baking a cake?* If that is what you have written, say, *That's correct.* The turn then passes to the next team.

A Few Ideas for Charades	
playing soccer	cutting someone's hair
cooking scrambled eggs	riding on a bus
feeding cereal to a baby	raking leaves and bagging them

Grammar Lesson

Be Going To **for Future Time**

KEY
4

We commonly use **be + going to + VERB** to talk about the future.

Affirmative: I **am**, You/We/They **are**, He/She/It **is** + **going to** (**VERB**)

Question: **Am** I, **Are** you/we/they, **Is** he/she/it + **going to** (**VERB**)

Be + going to + VERB for the future and **will + VERB** for the future have similar meanings, and sometimes they seem interchangeable. However, the reasons we use one more than the other depend on the situation at the time of speaking or the information that the speaker knows.

1. **Future plans** (arranged prior to when you talk about them)

2. **Predictions** (based on current evidence)

	Examples
Affirmative form	**A**: "I'm **going to see** my cousins in two more days." **Plan:** They talked about it on the phone weeks ago, and the plane tickets are bought. **B**: "If he doesn't hurry, he is **going to miss** his flight." **Prediction:** The evidence is the clock time.
Negative	**C**: "You're **not going to spend** a lot of money, are you, June?" **Plan:** June is going shopping. Del is asking about her intentions. **D**: "According to the weather forecast, it **is not going be** below freezing tonight." **Prediction with evidence**—Weather forecasters use scientific instruments.
Yes-No question	**E**: "**Are** you **going to buy** a new car next year?" Asking about your future **plans** **F**: "**Pat, is** that tree **going to fall?**" Asking Pat to make a **prediction** based on Pat seeing the tree.
Wh– question	**G**: "*When* **are** they **going to be** here?" Referring to the situation in G: this is a question about **plans** made before the question was asked. **H**: "*How many* people **are going to attend** the Super Bowl?" Asking the listener to make a **prediction**. The evidence is the size of the stadium and last year's attendance.

Rule 1. Use **be + going to + VERB** to talk about future plans that have been **arranged in advance**: A: "I am **going to make** a presentation tomorrow." B: "What time?"
A: "At 1:30."

Rule 2. Use **be + going to + VERB** to talk about predictions based on **current evidence**: A: "Oh, the sky is really dark." B: "Yes, **it's going to rain** soon."

Rule 3. In spoken language, **going to** before VERB often sounds like **gonna.** This is OK in informal spoken language, but we never use **gonna** in academic writing.

BE CAREFUL!

Common Learner Errors	Explanation
1. If you don't go to bed now, you're ~~going be~~ **going to be** tired in the morning.	Don't forget the word **to**. It is part of the infinitive VERB that follows.
2. Your application for a new credit card is **going to** ~~taking~~ **take** four to six weeks.	The verb after **be going to** is the base (simple) form. Don't use **–s** or **–ed** or **–ing** with the verb after **to**.
3. Written language example: Many economists think these new policies are ~~gonna~~ **going to** help the average person.	We often pronounce **going to** as *gonna*, but don't write *gonna*. It is not a written word.
4. Spoken language example: I really think it's ~~gonna to~~ **gonna rain** OR **going to** rain soon.	If you want to say *gonna*, don't say *gonna to*. The pronunciation of *gonna* means "going to," so the error *gonna to* really means "going to to."

EXERCISE 6. Information Questions with *be going to*

Complete the questions and answers in these conversations. Use the correct form of the future tense with **be going to**.

1. A: (finish) _____ your project this week?

    B: I (work) _____ on it the next two nights.

2. A: (purchase) _____ fireworks for the next celebration?

    B: Yes I am.

3. A: When (she, take) _____ diving lessons?

    B: Just before we leave for the Bahamas.

4. A: What (happen) _____ when the big suspension bridge is taken down next year?

    B: The Governor has already allocated emergency funds to build a bypass.

5. A: How much (they, practice) _____ next week?

    B: They have scheduled five hours on Tuesday and Thursday.

6. A: I need to take the dog to the groomer tomorrow.

    B: (we, meet, not) _____ for lunch?

    A: Yes. I can drop off Coco in the morning and then meet you at noon.

 EXERCISE 7. Editing: Is It Correct?

If the sentence is correct, write a check mark (✔) on the line. If it is not correct, write X on the line and circle the mistake. Then change the sentence to make it correct. Write the change above the sentence. (*Hint*: There are eight sentences. Two are correct, but six have mistakes.)

Global Forecasts

_____ 1. There is going to be a hot wind blowing off the Sahara after sunrise tomorrow.

_____ 2. The seas around Tahiti is going to have warm currents and light winds tomorrow.

_____ 3. The winds in the mountains of Ethiopia going to get cold after sunset tonight.

_____ 4. The Amazon River basin in Brazil goes to have heavy rain showers late in the morning.

_____ 5. There is going to variable fog and snow the next two days in Germany.

_____ 6. The cold weather in Alaska is going to include ice storms in the mountains until tomorrow afternoon.

_____ 7. In Egypt, the people living near the Great Pyramid going to need extra protection from sandstorms tomorrow.

_____ 8. It's going to clear and hot all along the Great Barrier Reef of Australia during the next two days.

 Do Online Exercise 9.1. My score: _____ /10. _____ % correct.

Grammar Lesson

Will for Future Time

Will + VERB has the same grammar forms as other modals that you have learned.

Affirmative Form: I/you/he/she/it/we/they **will** + **VERB.**

Negative Form: I/you/he/she/it/we/they **won't (will not) + VERB**

The form is easy to learn, but the uses and meanings take time to acquire.

1. future plans that are made **at or near the moment of speaking**

2. predictions that are less certain **(evidence is not required)**

3. promises (**with** *I*)

4. offers to help / requests for help

5. formal announcements

	Examples
Affirmative form	I/you/he/she/it/we/they **will call** you later. I'll **call** you later. (casual way of ending a conversation) I'll **call** you tomorrow. (promise, because of *I*) She'll **call** you tomorrow. (prediction) Sign on door: The bank **will be** closed tomorrow (formal announcement)
Negative form	I **will not** call you tomorrow. (formal or possibly angry) I **won't** call you tomorrow. (plan made at moment of speaking)
Yes-No question	**Will** you **call** me tomorrow? (request)
***Wh–* question**	**When will** you **call** me? (wanting a prediction) **Where will** you **be** tomorrow? (wanting a prediction)
Short answers	Speaker 1: What are you going to wear to the party Friday night? Speaker 2: I'm going to wear black pants. Speaker 1: OK. **I will**, too. (plan made at moment of speaking)
	(a woman is at a store with a baby in her arms and she is trying to open a door) Speaker 3: Can someone get the door for me? Speaker 4: Yes, **I'll help**. (offer to help) (Also possible: Can I help you?)

<u>Rule 1.</u> You cannot use **will** for future intentions that you have already planned. We ask, **What are you going to do tomorrow?** not **What will you do tomorrow?**

<u>Rule 2.</u> You can use **will** for a last-minute change in plans. For example, if your friend has planned to play golf tomorrow, we can ask, **What will you do if it rains tomorrow?** In other words, if Plan A is to play golf, then we are asking about Plan B.

<u>Rule 3.</u> The contraction for **will not** is **won't** and in conversation we usually use **won't** instead of **will not**.

EXERCISE 8. Mini-Conversations

Circle the correct words in these mini-conversations. Sometimes both answers may be possible.

1. *A:* Are you having trouble tying your shoes, Jimmy?

   B: Daddy, (will you, are you going to) help me?

2. *A:* See you tomorrow, right?

   B: No, because I read in the school paper that there (will be, are going to be) no classes tomorrow because it's Veterans Day.

3. *A:* Oh, I just dropped a glass on the floor, and it broke into a million pieces.

   B: Don't worry. I (will get, am going to get) it.

4. *A:* It's really cold, and I'm concerned about my flowers.

   B: I heard the weather report. Tonight it (will be, is going to be) in the low 30s, so I think you need to cover them.

5. *A:* Can you believe this headline: "The moon (will explode, is going to explode) in 2035"?

   B: That's just another sensational headline. They're just trying to scare us.

🔑 Grammar Lesson

Present Perfect Tense

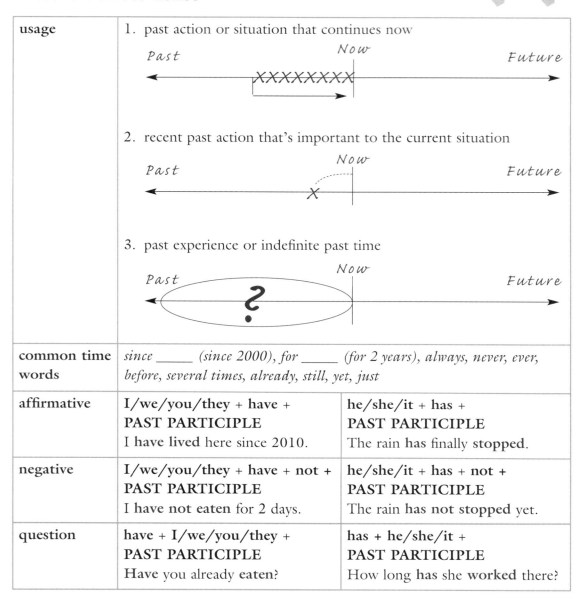

usage	1. past action or situation that continues now *Past* Now *Future* XXXXXXXX 2. recent past action that's important to the current situation *Past* Now *Future* X 3. past experience or indefinite past time *Past* Now *Future* **?**	
common time words	*since _____ (since 2000), for _____ (for 2 years), always, never, ever, before, several times, already, still, yet, just*	
affirmative	I/we/you/they + have + PAST PARTICIPLE **I have lived** here since 2010.	he/she/it + has + PAST PARTICIPLE The rain **has** finally **stopped**.
negative	I/we/you/they + have + not + PAST PARTICIPLE **I have not eaten** for 2 days.	he/she/it + has + not + PAST PARTICIPLE The rain **has not stopped** yet.
question	have + I/we/you/they + PAST PARTICIPLE **Have** you already **eaten**?	has + he/she/it + PAST PARTICIPLE How long **has** she **worked** there?

<u>Rule 1</u>. Use **have** for **I/you/we/they**. Use **has** for **he/she/it**.

<u>Rule 2</u>. The **PAST PARTICIPLE** is the second part of the present perfect tense. You can find a list of past participle forms in Appendix C.

<u>Rule 3</u>. The negative of present perfect is **have not** (**haven't**) or **has not** (**hasn't**).

<u>Rule 4</u>. To make a question with present perfect tense, move **have** or **has** before the subject: **Have you ever eaten sushi? OR, How long has Maria lived in China?**

<u>Rule 5</u>. **Ever** and **yet** are used with questions (about indefinite time) and negative answers (about an action that has not happened so far).

BE CAREFUL!

Common Learner Errors	Explanation
1. I ~~play~~ **have played** the piano since I was 10 years old.	Don't use simple present tense for an action that began in the past and still continues.
2. In 2010, I ~~have lived~~ **lived** in Bogota, Colombia.	Don't use present perfect tense for a specific past time (in 2010).

 EXERCISE 9. Editing Present Perfect Tense: Is It Correct?

If the sentence is correct, write a check mark (✔) on the line. If it is not correct, write X on the line and circle the mistake. Then change the sentence to make it correct. Write the change above the sentence. (*Hint*: There are ten sentences. Four are correct, but six have mistakes.)

A New Weight-Loss Shake Diet

_____ 1. How long have you being on the Lose Lots of Weight program?

_____ 2. I have used the program for a little more than a year.

_____ 3. Do you ever had such good weight loss results before?

_____ 4. I have never been able to keep my weight down long enough to buy smaller sizes of clothes.

_____ 5. I have already gave my old clothes away, and I'm looking for new ones.

_____ 6. Have you gotten a lot of compliments?

_____ 7. I haven't saw you look so physically fit since our last diving trip.

_____ 8. The manufacturer has just send me several free weight-loss shake samples.

_____ 9. My brother and I toured the shake production facility last month.

_____ 10. We know a lot about the company because they has given us five or six pamphlets with a lot of information about the weight-loss program.

EXERCISE 10. Understanding Present Perfect Time

Read each example of the present perfect. Determine which time is being expressed. Put a check mark (✓) in the appropriate column.

Examples with Present Perfect	Continues to Now	Recent Past	Indefinite Past
1. Tommy has played the clarinet since he was 12 years old.			
2. Have you ever been to Italy?			
3. I have gone to Busch Gardens ever summer since 2003.			
4. We have just returned from Africa and need malaria pills.			
5. They have shown their gem collection at several shows.			
6. I have already shown my ticket and want my boarding pass now.			
7. Paul hasn't worked on his project for about two weeks.			
8. Have you called the President recently?			
9. Trina has just finished dinner and wants to take a walk.			
10. We have taken diving lessons since 2003.			

Do Online Exercise 9.2. My score: _____ /10. _____ % correct.

Grammar Lesson

Present Perfect Progressive Tense

Past   *Now*   *Future*

usage	The present perfect progressive tense is used to express an action that began in the past and is continuing now with emphasis on the fact that it is still happening.	
common time words	*since* _____ *(since 2000), for* _____ *(for 2 years), all* _____ *(all year)*	
affirmative	I/we/you/they + have + been + VERB + –ing I have been living here since 2010.	he/she/it + has + been + VERB + –ing The meat has been cooking all night.
negative	I/we/you/they + have + not + been + VERB + –ing I have not been sleeping well recently.	he/she/it + has + not + been + VERB + –ing That door has not been squeaking for a long time.
question	have + I/we/you/they + been + VERB + –ing Have you been waiting for a long time?	has + he/she/it + been + VERB + –ing How long has she been working there?

<u>Rule 1</u>. Use **have/has + been + VERB + –ing** to form the present perfect progressive.

<u>Rule 2</u>. Negatives are formed by adding **not** or **n't** after **have/has.**

<u>Rule 3</u>. Questions are formed by moving **have/has** in front of the subject: **Has she been studying all day?**

EXERCISE 11. Practicing Present Perfect Progressive Tense

Re-write each sentence by changing the verb to present perfect progressive tense. In some cases, you can use the time words from the original sentences, but in many cases, you will need to change the time words or add your own.

1. I have worked here for 10 years.

   _____

2. We lived in Puerto Rico in 2005.

   _____

3. It is raining now.

   _____

4. They shop at Marco's Foods.

   _____

5. Fatimah started to work on her project two hours ago.

   _____

6. Do you wait for the bus every day?

   _____

7. You wear earrings.

   _____

8. Maria has played tennis at this club since 2010.

   _____

 **Grammar Lesson**

Past Progressive Tense

The phone rang while I was taking a shower.

usage	1. To emphasize what we were doing at a certain time in the past. 2. To tell what action was happening in the past when another action interrupted it. In other words, the first had begun and was continuing when the second action occurred. 3. To describe two or more actions that were happening at the same time.	
common time words	*while, when*	
affirmative	I, he, she, it + was + VERB + –ing I was **watching** TV when my cell rang.	you, we, they + were + VERB + –ing You **were preparing** for your trip all day yesterday.
negative	I, he, she, it + was + not + VERB + –ing I was **not watching** TV when you called me.	you, we, they + were + not + VERB + –ing You **were not preparing** for your trip all day yesterday.
question	Was + I, he, she, it + VERB + –ing Was it **raining** at your house when you woke up this morning?	Were + you, we, they + VERB + –ing Were you **sleeping** when I called you last night?

<u>Rule 1</u>. Use **was** for **I/he/she/it.** Use **were** for **you/we/they.**

<u>Rule 2</u>. To make a negative, add *not*: was **not** (wasn't) or were **not** (weren't).

<u>Rule 3</u>. To make a question with past progressive tense, move **was** or **were** before the subject.

<u>Rule 4</u>. If one past action interrupts another past action, the longer action is usually in past progressive tense and the shorter action that interrupted it is in simple past tense.

<u>Rule 5</u>. We usually use **while** with 2 actions happening at the same time and **when** for the action that interrupts the other.

BE CAREFUL!

Common Learner Errors	Explanation
1. When I got my first job, I ~~was live~~ was living in Los Angeles.	Progressive tenses always need an **–ing** on the verb. Don't use two verbs in simple past if one was already in progress when the other one interrupted it.
2. From 2010 to 2011, I ~~was owning~~ owned two cars.	**Own** is not an action. Do not use **–ing** with a verb that does not show action.

EXERCISE 12. Contrasting Verb Forms in Situations

Read each sentence. Think about the time of the action, and then write the correct form of the verb on the line. Check your spelling.

1. wear

   a. They _____ jeans now.

   b. We _____ jeans yesterday.

   c. He _____ jeans tomorrow (plan).

   d. She _____ jeans every day.

   e. I _____ jeans since I was 15 years old.

2. fly

   a. Many planes _____ over the Pacific Ocean every day.

   b. Well, if you won't go with me, I _____ alone.

   c. There was a terrible storm while we _____ into Tampa last night. I didn't think we would be able to land safely.

   d. Captain Ray _____ for American Airlines since 1995.

   e. Sam's pet parrot _____ away yesterday.

3. consume

   a. Do you _____ enough water every day?

   b. It is so hot today that I went into the house and _____ an entire can of soft drink without stopping.

   c. When I walked into the kitchen, Javier _____ milk directly from the carton. I couldn't believe my eyes.

 Do Online Exercise 9.3. My score: _____ /10. _____ % correct.

EXERCISE 13. Sentence Study for Critical Reading

Read the numbered sentences. Then read the answer choices and put a check mark (✔) in the yes or no boxes in front of each sentence to show if that answer is true based on the information in the original sentence. If there is not enough information to mark something as yes, then mark it as no. Remember that more than one true answer may be possible.

1. Diana was driving her husband's car when she fell asleep and drove off the road.

   ☐ yes ☐ no a. Diana was sleeping before she drove the car.

   ☐ yes ☐ no b. The accident happened because Diana fell asleep.

   ☐ yes ☐ no c. The car was in motion at the same time that Diana fell asleep.

2. Mr. and Mrs. Kelly have been waiting for years to take a cruise. For their 40th wedding anniversary yesterday, their children gave them a gift certificate to take a cruise.

   ☐ yes ☐ no a. Mr. and Mrs. Kelly are on a cruise now.

   ☐ yes ☐ no b. Mr. and Mrs. Kelly went on a cruise.

   ☐ yes ☐ no c. Mr. And Mrs. Kelly will go on a cruise.

3. The price of corn is increasing. Mr. Mills wants to buy more farm land.

   ☐ yes ☐ no a. Mr. Mills is probably a farmer.

   ☐ yes ☐ no b. The price of corn will be lower next year.

   ☐ yes ☐ no c. Mr. Mills wants to buy more corn.

4. Lori bought a television two years ago for $800. She has just come from Alco's where the same size television was selling for $500.

   ☐ yes ☐ no a. Two years ago Alco's TVs were less expensive.

   ☐ yes ☐ no b. Lori saved $300 by shopping at Alco's.

   ☐ yes ☐ no c. The price of a TV is now $500.

5. When I find my dog, I am going to build a new fence.

   ☐ yes ☐ no a. My dog is lost now.

   ☐ yes ☐ no b. I plan to build a new fence after I find my dog.

   ☐ yes ☐ no c. I am building a fence now.

ONE-MINUTE LESSON
The verb **take** is used with many types of travel: *take a trip, take a vacation, take a cruise, take a flight.*

EXERCISE 14. Practicing Past Perfect Tense

Combine the sentences using the past perfect and the connector that is given. The first one has been done for you as an example. (See Unit 3 for a review of this verb tense.)

1. The cat was outside all night. It was tired and hungry.

   <u>The cat was tired and hungry</u>   because <u>it had been outside all night.</u>

2. He was tired for many months. He decided to take a vacation.

   _____ so _____

3. She never wanted to get married. She met Mark.

   _____ until _____

4. He finally succeeded. He tried many times to quit drinking.

   _____ before _____

5. He couldn't concentrate well at work. He was up all night with his sick baby.

   _____ because _____

6. He was young. He was very active in work for peace and justice.

   When _____—_____

7. She had a dream that showed her the solution. She thought about a problem for days.

   _____ when _____

8. He didn't want a cat. He met Sheba.

   _____ until _____

9. He decided to celebrate. He lost fifteen pounds.

   _____ because _____

10. My mother was upset. I didn't call her for ten days.

    _____ because _____

EXERCISE 15. Using Past Perfect Tense to Indicate Sequence

Which action started first? Which started second? Write 1 and 2 under the correct clause. The first one has been done for you as an example. (See Unit 3 for a review of this verb tense.)

1. I had been thinking about my brother when I received an email from him.
   _____   _____
               1   2

2. The audience had given him a standing ovation when the performance ended.
   _____   _____

3. The hot water had run out, so I took a very short shower.
   _____   _____

4. When our baby woke up, we had been enjoying a quiet, romantic dinner.
   _____   _____

5. When their son got an F in one of his classes, they became very worried about him.
   _____   _____

6. When she had done everything else she could, she tried prayer.
   _____   _____

7. She had gained a lot of weight when she had her first baby.
   _____   _____

8. She gained a lot of weight when she had her first baby.
   _____   _____

EXERCISE 16. Simple Past and Past Perfect Tenses in Context

Which action started first? Which started second? Write 1 and 2 under the correct clause. Read this passage. Underline the correct form of the verb in parentheses. (See Unit 3 for a review of this verb tense.)

Peace Pilgrim was an American woman who ❶ (lived, had lived) from 1908 to 1981. For the last 28 years of her life, she walked, spreading a message of peace. By the time she died, she ❷ (walked, had walked) more than 25,000 miles.

Before her life as Peace Pilgrim, Mildred Norman had been married and divorced. She ❸ (was, had been) interested in freedom and truth since she was young.

When she ❹ (started, had started) her trip, she already ❺ (did, had done) many things to prepare. She was physically ready for her journey because she ❻ (purified, had purified) her body by being careful about food and by getting exercise. She was mentally ready because she ❼ (made, had made) many spiritual and psychological adjustments. For example, ❽ (changed, had changed) her attitude and had simplified her life. She ❾ (didn't start, hadn't started) her actual walk yet, but she already ❿ (started, had started) her own spiritual journey.

She ⓫ (gave, had given) many talks during the years of her mission, and she touched the lives of many people. Many today are still inspired by her message of peace.

EXERCISE 17. Using Verb Tenses to Indicate Sequence

Use the past progressive and a word from the word list to complete the sentences. (See Unit 3 for a review of this verb tense.)

word list	argue	eat	look	read	take
	care	jog	pay attention	sleep	try

1. We _____ to sell our house for almost a year before we found a buyer.

2. Tom _____ for work for almost six months when he finally found a job.

3. A homeless man _____ in under our porch every night for a week before we discovered him.

4. I _____ a lot of sweets, so I wasn't surprised when the dentist found a cavity.

5. I _____ to traffic, so I didn't see that my oil light had gone on.

6. My husband and I _____ for his mother for several months before she decided to go to the nursing home.

7. The little boy was worried because his parents _____ loudly all afternoon.

8. My father _____ the newspaper when we surprised him with a birthday cake.

9. My daughter _____ tai chi classes for ten years before she became an instructor.

10. I injured my knee because I _____ on pavement.

EXERCISE 18. Using Past Perfect Progressive Tense to Indicate Sequence

Put a check mark (✓) next to the correct answer in each conversation. (See Unit 3 for a review of this verb tense.)

1. A. What caused that accident?

   a. ___ B: One of the drivers had been talking on her cell phone.

   b. ___ B: One of the drivers had talked on her cell phone.

2. A: Why was the ambulance at the Smith's house last weekend?

   a. ___ B: John had been having terrible chest pains.

   b. ___ B: John is having terrible chest pains.

3. A: Why are you so dirty?

   a. ___ B: I had been gardening.

   b. ___ B: I have been gardening.

4. A: Your brother was all dressed up the last time I saw him. He looked great.

   a. ___ B: Yeah. He'd been singing at a wedding.

   b. ___ B: Yeah. He's been singing at a wedding.

5. A: You should join the gym.

   a. ___ B: Maybe. I've been thinking about it.

   b. ___ B: Maybe. I'd been thinking about it.

6. A: Are you going to get a Mac or a PC?

   a. ___ B: I'll probably get another Mac. I've been using one for years.

   b. ___ B: I'll probably get another Mac. I'd been using one for years.

7. A: What's new?

   a. ___ B: Not much. I had been working and taking class.

   b. ___ B: Not much. I've been working and taking classes.

8. A: How did he die?

    a. ___ B: He'd been working in the yard, and he just fell down dead.

    b. ___ B: He has been working in the yard, and he just fell down dead.

9. A: Why didn't you bring a present to the birthday party?

    a. ___ B: I bought a present, but I forgot it!

    b. ___ B: I had been buying a present, but I forgot it!

10. A: Was anyone seriously hurt in the earthquake?

    a. ___ B: I don't know. But one man had been trapping for two days before he was found.

    b. ___ B: I don't know. But one man had been trapped for two days before he was found.

REVIEW ▶ **EXERCISE 19. Review Test 1: Multiple Choice**

Circle the letter of the correct answer,

1. *A.* "_____ to Tina's party on Friday night?"

   B. "I don't know yet."

       a. Do you go   c. You are going to go

       b. Are you going   d. Had you gone

2. *A.* "_____ a live panda at a zoo?"

   B. "Yes, I have. It was years ago when I was in China."

       a. Have you ever saw   c. Had you ever seen

       b. You ever have seen   d. Have you ever seen

3. *A.* "Excuse me. What time _____?"

   B. "At 6:20 PM."

       a. does Flight 87 arrive   c. is going to arrive Flight 87

       b. is Flight 87 arrive   d. Flight 87 is arriving

4. *A.* "I've been trying to call you all day. What have you been doing?"

   B. "I _____ in the garden until about 5 o'clock."

       a. have worked   c. was working

       b. had worked   d. had been working

5. *A.* "Who _____ these delicious cookies?"

   B. "Grandma did."

       a. did bake   c. baked

       b. was baking   d. had baked

6. *A.* "I have an idea. Let's take Mano to Legoland for his birthday."

   B. "No. _____ there. Let's go somewhere new."

       a. We've already taken him   c. He had already been

       b. He is already been   d. We had already been taking him

7. *A.* "Hi, is Bryce home?"

   B. "Yes, he is. But he's sleeping now."

   A. "OK. I _____ back later."

   > a. am going call   c. will call

   > d. am calling   d. call

8. *A.* "How long ago _____ *The House of Seven Gables?*"

   B. " I'm not exactly sure. Maybe 150 years ago."

   > a. has Nathaniel Hawthorne written

   > b. did Nathaniel Hawthorne write

   > c. wrote Nathaniel Hawthorne

   > d. Nathaniel Hawthorne wrote

 EXERCISE 20. Review Test 2: Production and Evaluation

Part 1.

Read this short passage. Fill in the blanks with the correct tense of the word in parentheses.

Mario and Cathy's Visit

   Mario and Cathy (live) ❶ _____ in Louisiana. They (live) ❷ _____ in Louisiana for eight years. Before that, they (live) ❸ _____ in Alaska. When they (move) ❹ _____ to Louisiana, Mario (work) ❺ _____ for an international oil drilling company. His company (transfer) ❻ _____ him to Louisiana.

   They (be) ❼ _____ happy in Alaska. They (enjoy) ❽ _____ outdoor activities such as camping and fishing in the summer and riding snowmobiles in the winter. In Louisiana they (not, can do) ❾ _____ the same outdoor activities because it (not, snow) ❿ _____ in Louisiana, and Cathy (hate) ⓫ _____ snakes, which are a possibility if you are camping in Louisiana.

Cathy really wants to move back to Alaska, but Mario always (tell)

12 _____ her that they (not, can leave) **13** _____ Louisiana because

he (have) **14** _____ a very good salary now. Consequently, Cathy (feel)

15 _____ bored all of the time.

My husband and I (invite) **16** _____ them to visit us in Idaho next

summer. They (think) **17** _____ that they (enjoy) **18** _____ the

outdoors in Idaho. We (make) **19** _____ plans now for their visit.

Part 2.

Read each sentence carefully. Look at the underlined part. If the underlined part is correct, circle the word *correct*. If it is wrong, circle the word *wrong*. Then write the correction above.

correct   wrong   1. The mechanic <u>is working</u> on my car yesterday.

correct   wrong   2. Tina <u>was playing</u> on the swing when she fell.

correct   wrong   3. Mom, you <u>are needing</u> to put gas in the car soon.

correct   wrong   4. Guess what? We <u>will be</u> in Paris one week from now!

correct   wrong   5. Luis <u>attend</u> class every day.

EXERCISE 21. Reading Practice: Who Is Going to Help?

Read this article about an organization that helps people in need. Note that the organization is real, but the two examples are fictional. After reading the passage, answer the questions that follow. In this reading passage, at least one example of each verb tense that has been reviewed in this unit is underlined for you.

Who Is Going to Help?

1   An 82-year-old single woman, Mrs. P., has been living alone in her own

2   home most of her life. She retired on a small pension 18 years ago after her

3   first heart attack. Since that time, she has had two more heart attacks and a

4   number of other debilitating ailments including high blood pressure,

5   limited vision, chronic fatigue syndrome, and loss of hearing in one ear.

6   Additionally, like most senior citizens her age, she does not have the

7   strength or flexibility she once had at a younger age.

8   Her meager pension is barely enough to cover the costs of her food,

9   medicines, electricity, yard maintenance, mortgage payment, and insurance.

10 If something falls into disrepair in her house, it usually remains that way as

11 the cost of repairs has increased considerably since her retirement. Recently,

12 she was attempting to close the curtains in her bedroom and while pulling

13 on the cord, the entire rod with curtains fell to the floor. Without the

14 agility to climb a ladder or use a screwdriver while holding the rod, the

15 entire ensemble remains on the floor and the uncovered window has

16 minimized her privacy.

17   Another senior citizen, Mr. M., age 79, has recently suffered from a

18 stroke, which has left him paralyzed below the waist and dependent on

19 a wheelchair. This condition has greatly changed his lifestyle. No longer

20 can he work in his beautiful garden or enjoy fishing on the nearby lake. In

21 fact, he can't even drive to the lake nor can he get down the steps to the

22 driveway. Inside his house, he is not able to reach the faucets on the sink

23   as the wheelchair is too low and the cabinets beneath the sink <u>prevent</u> the

24   wheelchair from getting close enough. Moreover, he is unable to pull

25   himself into the bathtub. He <u>lives</u> with his wife, who is frail, and they

26   <u>do not have</u> the finances to remodel their home.

27   These two senior citizens, Mrs. P. and Mr. M., have some things in

28   common. First, their children <u>live</u> in other states, and second, they <u>have</u>

29   limited financial resources to take care of the unexpected. The bottom

30   line is that they both <u>need</u> additional assistance.

31   Fortunately, there are compassionate citizens who volunteer thousands

32   of hours of labor to help people just like Mrs. P. and Mr. M. Sometimes

33   these people <u>volunteer</u> to join an organization that can mobilize crews and

34   equipment. One such organization is called Rebuilding Together, with

35   affiliates across the United States. Not only do citizens volunteer their time,

36   but also many U.S. corporations and private citizens <u>contribute</u> millions of

37   dollars to facilitate the purchase of construction supplies. The main

38   objectives of Rebuilding Together are to make homes safe and rebuild

39   neighborhoods that <u>are</u> in decline or that <u>have been destroyed</u> from a

40   natural disaster.

41   Mrs. P. is a prime example of the excellent work that Rebuilding

42   Together <u>is doing</u>. Thanks to these generous people, Mrs. P. <u>is having</u> a

43   new curtain rod installed and also new smoke detectors that the group

44   <u>noticed</u> were lacking. While these two repairs may seem relatively small,

45   they are not small to Mrs. P. In addition, the volunteers from Rebuilding

46   Together <u>are constructing</u> a wheelchair ramp from the driveway into the

47   house for Mr. M., and with additional donations from a local building

48   supply store, they <u>are going to install</u> a new bathroom with a wheelchair-

49   accessible shower and sink. Clearly, Rebuilding Together <u>has been making</u> a

50   valuable difference in the lives of these and many other needy people.

1. Write a check mark (✔) to indicate if each description is true for Mrs. P., Mr. M., both of them, or neither of them.

Description	Mrs. P.	Mr. M.	Neither
a. at least 80 years old			
b. health problems			
c. received help from Rebuilding Together			
d. a spouse is also in the house			
e. wealthy			
f. a senior citizen			
g. donated to Rebuilding Together			
h. a wheelchair is in the house			
i. needed assistance			
j. multiple heart attacks			

2. List at least three lifestyle changes for Mr. M. that are mentioned in the article.

a. _____

_____

b. _____

_____

c. _____

_____

3. Do an Internet search for information about the group Rebuilding Together or a similar volunteer organization. Write three important facts about this organization.

a. _____

_____

b. _____

_____

c. _____

_____

EXERCISE 22. Vocabulary Practice: Word Knowledge

Circle the answer choice that is most closely related to the vocabulary on the left. Use a dictionary to check the meaning of words you do not know.

Vocabulary	Answer Choices	
1. quote	your possessions	your words
2. fog	hard to see	hard to write
3. frail	narrow	weak
4. a parrot	fly	ride
5. pregnant	a grandmother	a mother
6. a bypass	a type of house	a type of road
7. assistance	attendance	help
8. motivated	avoid doing	want to do
9. a client	a customer	an interview
10. a patient	a sick person	a small machine
11. found out	discarded	learned
12. predict	the future	the past
13. struggle	with a gift	with a problem
14. off and on	from time to time	very easy to do
15. meager	limited	unlimited
16. moist	a little expensive	a little wet
17. a pamphlet	food	information
18. debilitating	stronger	weaker
19. resign	begin a job	leave a job
20. vary	be different	be the same
21. malaria	a disease	a machine
22. a gem	an app	a jewel
23. a pyramid	like a circle	like a triangle
24. a checkout line	at the airport	at the supermarket
25. a boarding pass	at the airport	at the supermarket
26. to be fit	exercising	intervening
27. a shake	you drink it	you organize it
28. a compliment	"Don't do that!"	"Great job!"
29. a journalist	a nurse	a writer
30. a cruise	by plane	by ship
31. lately	not early	recently
32. went off	an airplane	an alarm

EXERCISE 23. Vocabulary Practice: Collocations

Fill in each blank with the answer on the right that most naturally completes the phrase on the left. If necessary, use a dictionary to check the meaning of words you do not know.

Phrase	Answer Choices	
1. install a _____	key	lock
2. intense _____	feelings	pickles
3. verify _____	your age	your new socks
4. in the 9th _____	floor	grade
5. rake _____	animals	leaves
6. _____ asleep	fall	take
7. the _____ is boiling	meat	soup
8. earn _____	money	taxes
9. rely _____ someone	in	on
10. install a new _____	speaker	speech
11. a boarding _____	pass	turn
12. _____ about the weather	concerned	interested
13. _____ my laundry	do	make
14. _____ a problem	identify	scramble
15. a _____ carton	coffee	milk
16. in 2 more _____	day	days
17. on the _____ shelf	average	bottom
18. an application _____ a job	for	to
19. I wonder _____ it will rain	by	if
20. variety of _____	search	subjects
21. _____ up	heavy	hurry
22. once _____ month	a	the
23. an _____ hour	almost	entire
24. _____ way	no	yes
25. a _____ battery	dead	silent
26. associate X _____ Y	for	with
27. I've lived here _____ 10 years	for	since
28. where we _____ our anniversary	brought	spent
29. the _____ forecast	supermarket	weather
30. a patient in a _____	bank	hospital
31. we feel _____	absent	upset
32. concerned _____ the weather	about	for

EXERCISE 24. Writing Practice: Verb Tense Review

Part 1. Editing Student Writing

Read these sentences about Chinese New Year. Circle the 15 errors. Then write the number of the sentence with the error next to the type of error. (Some sentences have more than one error.)

_____ a. missing subject   _____ d. time expressions

_____ b. subject-verb agreement   _____ e. singular-plural of nouns

_____ c. verb tense   _____ f. negative

<table>
<tr><td colspan="2" align="center">Chinese New Year</td></tr>
<tr><td>1.</td><td>A few weeks before, I participated in a Chinese New Year celebration with six friend.</td></tr>
<tr><td>2.</td><td>This was no our first time to take part in this celebration.</td></tr>
<tr><td>3.</td><td>We know each other from our Chinese class. Have studied Chinese in the same class for the past three or four year.</td></tr>
<tr><td>4.</td><td>We are always enjoying participating in the loud celebrations that are part of Chinese New Year.</td></tr>
<tr><td>5.</td><td>My friend Justin usually take part in the lion dance, and the kids have really loved watching him dance at this year's as well as last year's celebrations.</td></tr>
<tr><td>6.</td><td>Since the 1990s, most of the students and staff from our Chinese language school has participated in the local Chinese New Year festivities.</td></tr>
<tr><td>7.</td><td>Three year ago, I start attending the celebrations, but I don't have performed in the lion dancing yet.</td></tr>
<tr><td>8.</td><td>My friends say I'm chicken, but I am thinking about being in the lion dance the next year.</td></tr>
<tr><td>9.</td><td>At last year's celebration, I have been happy to see our teacher's family.</td></tr>
<tr><td>10.</td><td>I recognized them as soon as I saw them because I have met them at last year's celebration.</td></tr>
<tr><td>11.</td><td>Participating in this celebration with so many people were so much fun.</td></tr>
<tr><td>12.</td><td>My friends and I had a great time. Are really looking forward to doing this again next year.</td></tr>
</table>

Part 2. Original Student Writing

Write a short essay about something you have always wanted and why you have wanted it. It could be your dream vacation or perfect job. Describe it and include reasons for it. You can also say what you are going to do once you have it. Use at least four different verb tenses or expressions from this list: simple present, present progressive, simple past, *be going to*, present perfect, and past progressive. Underline each verb tense so the teacher can see what you are trying to practice.

Unit 10

Review of Units 1–9

This unit contains two types of review practices for the grammar covered in *Clear Grammar 4*.

Part 1: Comprehensive Review (five tests of 25 multiple choice questions on all nine units)

Part 2: Individual Units (nine review practices, one for each of the nine units)

The multiple choice questions in the five tests in Part 1 can be used as an objective assessment of the material covered in this book. You may do this unit after completing all previous nine units, or you may take these tests after certain intervals such as every two units. Following this schedule, you would do Test 1 after Units 1 and 2, Test 2 after Units 3 and 4, etc. If you follow this schedule, your scores should be lower on Test 1 and much higher by Test 5 since you would be progressing through the material in the book and on the tests. Remember that the tests in Part 1 are comprehensive and each covers all nine units.

The completion questions in the nine tests in Part 2 cover each of the nine units one by one. Thus, there is a test for Unit 1, a test for Unit 2, etc. You may use these tests as a diagnostic pre-test to see if you need to complete a given unit. Of course the tests in Part 2 can also be used as additional assessments after you have completed the units.

Part 1: Comprehensive Review

Test 1.
Write the letter of the correct answer on the line.

1. If you'd had more time, you _____ have visited more places when you were in Alaska.

   a. must   b. could   c. may not   d. should not

2. No one is certain of how long the current program _____.

   a. exists   b. is existing   c. has existed   d. had existed

3. Unless the rain _____ stay home instead of driving to the meeting.

   a. stops we'll   b. stops, we'll   c. stop, we'll   d. stop we'll

4. At the national meeting this morning, the names of the employees _____ for the award were announced.

   a. were chosen   b. were choosing c. choosing   d. chosen

5. Question 17 on the tax form asks how much money _____ last year.

   a. you earned   b. earned you   c. earned   d. did you earn

6. I went to Bulgaria last month. It was my second trip because _____ there in 2009.

   a. I'd been   b. had I been   c. I were   d. were I

7. Can you _____ why your job is so _____?

   a. clarificate; stressful   c. clarificate; stressive

   b. clarify; stressful   d. clarify; stressive

8. At Thanksgiving, many families _____ turkey because it _____ a traditional dish.

   a. cook; considers   c. cook; is considered

   b. cooks; considers   d. cooks; is considered

9. When students _____ the final exam four months from now, we expect to see much higher scores.

   a. will take   b. takes   c. are taking   d. take

10. None of us knows where _____.

    a. Brittany lives

    b. lives Brittany

    c. does Brittany live

    d. Brittany's address

11. She has _____ any flour to make her cupcakes.

    a. hard   b. harder   c. hardly   d. hardest

12. We _____ blowfish before, but I hear it's a delicacy!

    a. has never tried   b. has never try   c. have never try   d. have never tried

13. _____ ever eaten eel before you tried it tonight at the restaurant?

    a. Did you have   b. Have you   c. Had you   d. Do you have

14. If I _____ to Miami, I will visit the aquarium.

    a. going   b. went   c. had gone   d. go

15. The clown smiled so that the children _____ scared by him.

    a. won't be   b. aren't   c. wouldn't be   d. weren't

16. If it _____ rain, we will take the kayak out to the lake this afternoon.

    a. isn't   b. don't   c. doesn't   d. can't

17. My daughter _____ snowboarding before her recent spring break trip to Colorado.

    a. was never trying

    b. had never tried

    c. has never tried

    d. never tries

18. Can you believe it? _____ we left early for the airport, we still missed our flight.

    a. Whether   b. So that   c. Although   d. After

19. How did the accident happen? Do you think _____ he lost control of the car?

    a. what   b. that   c. whether   d. if

20. I_____ been a little jumpy, but I was really scared after watching that horror movie!

    a. might   b. might have   c. should   d. should have

21. Even though she is still a child, she _____ known better.

    a. ought to have   c. ought not have

    b. ought have   d. ought

22. I studied so hard last night for my exam that I _____ this morning at my desk! Yes, I didn't sleep in my own bed last night.

    a. waked up   b. wake up   c. has woken up   d. woke up

23. José didn't make it to the meeting last night, so he _____ had to work late.

    a. must   b. mustn't   c. must have   d. must not have

24. I love my cat, but yesterday he unexpectedly _____ me when I picked him up.

    a. scratched   b. has scratched   c. was scratching   d. had scratched

25. I really liked the appetizer that we just had, but the chicken in this main dish _____ a little strange. I don't think that we should eat it.

    a. is tasting   b. has tasted   c. tastes   d. taste

Test 2.

Write the letter of the correct answer on the line.

1. We left home so late that we _____ get to the concert on time.

    a. couldn't   b. can't   c. weren't able   d. aren't able

2. Shawn knows the bus schedule better than anyone else in our office because he _____ the bus since he started his job last May.

    a. has taken   b. is taking   c. have taken   d. was taking

3. Tonight we _____ the new movie in 3-D.

    a. will have seen   c. has seen

    b. are going to see   d. don't see

4. I'm sorry! _____ asleep? I hope that I didn't wake you.

    a. Could you have   c. Were you

    b. Had you been   d. Did you

5. We could not understand the boy even though he was speaking as _____ as he could.

    a. clearer   b. clear   c. clearing   d. clearly

6. Neil _____ a few years of French before he went to Paris last September.

    a. study   b. had studied   c. had study   d. have studied

7. The kite is really _____ in the sky!

    a. high   b. higher   c. highly   d. height

8. Luckily, we _____ dinner before the power went out.

    a. have cooked   b. cooks   c. had cook   d. had cooked

9. If Stefan _____ his raincoat, he would have gotten wet.

    a. worn   b. didn't wore   c. haven't worn   d. hadn't worn

10. A popular saying is, "You shouldn't go swimming for 30 minutes _____ you eat."

    a. even though   b. after   c. unless   d. in order to

11. Can you imagine _____ Maria must feel? Her boyfriend just broke up with her.

    a. are   b. who   c. that   d. how

12. We _____ to see the opera performance last night if the tickets weren't so expensive.

    a. would have gone   c. have gone

    b. had gone   d. must have gone

13. American football players must wear helmets _____ they do not get injured.

    a. because   b. so that   c. after   d. though

14. Tammi wasn't sure _____ spring break was.

    a. if   b. when   c. how many   d. how much

15. We asked the maintenance worker _____ the bathrooms were blocked off.

    a. which   b. had   c. why   d. what

16. I did really poorly on my exam, but it _____ worse!

    a. should have been   c. could have been

    b. can have been   d. could not have been

17. I _____ to school every day this week!

    a. do walk   b. had walked   c. am walk   d. have walked

18. You look exhausted! You _____ working all night on that report!

    a. can be   b. can't have been   c. must be   d. must have been

19. Before my car _____ by the valet, he asked me for my keys.

    a. is taken   b. took   c. was taking   d. was taken

20. She just started that course, so she _____ it already.

    a. could have finished   c. could have started

    b. couldn't have finished   d. couldn't have started

21. Tina was very sensitive about her writing skills when I worked with her, so I _____ watch what I said to her.

    a. always   b. must   c. had to   d. was going to

22. That was a very dangerous and stupid prank because someone _____ gotten hurt!

    a. might   b. might have   c. must   d. must have

23. Neither of the boys _____ at home when their mother called them.

    a. were   b. was   c. is   d. has

24. Sheila _____ a really bad day yesterday, so I took her out to dinner.

    a. have   b. has   c. had   d. was

25. The police detective wasn't sure if the robber's victims _____ that their property was missing.

    a. were realizing   b. has realized   c. must realize   d. realized

Test 3.

Write the letter of the correct answer on the line.

1. Felipe wants to watch the World Cup tonight, but he's frustrated because once again his TV _____.

   a. is breaking   b. is broken   c. was breaking   d. was broken

2. The forecaster predicted snow, and I think it _____ any second now!

   a. snows   c. is going to snow

   b. has snowed   d. is snowing

3. While Dave _____ on the phone, he accidentally drove into the curb.

   a. did talk   b. were talking   c. is talking   d. was talking

4. Before she turned 30, she _____ a fortune in the publishing business.

   a. had made   b. was making   c. has made   d. do make

5. Eduardo is always helpful. For example, he _____ a set of flashcards for all of us before the test last week.

   a. has created   b. creates   c. would have created   d. created

6. Sherri might have understood the issue better if the politician _____ it better.

   a. explains   b. will explain   c. have explained d. had explained

7. You must carry your driver's license when you drive a car _____ it is illegal not to have it.

   a. because   b. before   c. so that   d. even though

8. When I was little, I _____ to a private school.

   a. go   b. gone   c. going   d. went

9. If I _____ what the server said at the beginning of the meal, perhaps I could have ordered a better dinner.

   a. was understanding   c. would understand

   b. had understood   d. would have understood

10. You should check the meat you have cooked _____ you serve it.

   a. because   b. so that   c. until   d. before

11. _____ the celebrity was eating lunch, the photographers began taking

    pictures of him.

        a. After   b. As   c. Often   d. So that

12. _____ dirty socks are these on the family room floor?

        a. How   b. Where   c. Who   d. Whose

13. _____ did Naren tell us to meet him?

        a. What   b. Which   c. Where   d. Who

14. _____ made us stop and think about our own lives.

        a. Did what he said   c. What he said

        b. Did he say what   d. What did he say

15. A party _____ on the weekend is better than one during the week if you

    are in school.

        a. holding   b. holds   c. had held   d. held

16. Marta works at the coffee shop, so she _____ smells like rich French

    Roast.

        a. always   b. rarely   c. never   d. only

17. He couldn't call his wife because someone _____ his phone.

        a. is stealing   b. has stolen   c. had stolen   d. had stealing

18. Mr. and Mrs. Johnson, _____ for twenty years, have four children.

        a. married   b. who married   c. are married   d. whose married

19. The students _____ in the history class were surprised with a quiz by

    their teacher.

        a. sat   b. sitting   c. who sitting   d. who were sat

20. The police came and _____ the criminal to jail.

        a. took   b. taking   c. will take   d. had took

21. _____ in Chicago at 12:14, Flight 222 arrived almost half an hour ahead

    of schedule.

        a. It landed   b. Landed   c. It was landing   d. Landing

22. If you had put gas in the car earlier, you _____ run out on your way to work!

    a. might not have   c. could have

    b. can not have   d. had not

23. That tooth looks terrible! You _____ had it fixed a long time ago!

    a. can have   b. can have   c. must have   d. should have

24. Jake made a good impression on all of us at dinner last night because he _____ at all of our jokes!

    a. laughed   b. had to laugh   c. laughs   d. must have laughed

25. A small percentage of students _____ unable to register for classes this week.

    a. was   b. has   c. have   d. were

Test 4.

Write the letter of the correct answer on the line.

1. Before computers, authors _____ their manuscripts page by page on a typewriter.

    a. types   b. is typing   c. type   d. typed

2. Nancy _____ at that restaurant three times.

    a. has eat   b. has ate   c. have eaten   d. has eaten

3. Hey, never mind about helping me move to my new apartment. My brother _____ going to help me.

    a. will   b. is   c. has been   d. has promised

4. Dan _____ in Cairo, but he moved to London in 2002.

    a. live   b. had been living   c. lived   d. was lived

5. When I saw Kelsey, she _____ at the party with her friends.

    a. is dancing   b. were dancing   c. am dancing   d. was dancing

6. By the time the vet _____, the cat _____ much better.

    a. has arrived, is feeling   c. is arriving, feels

    b. had arrived, felt   d. arrived, had felt

7. You would definitely get better grades if you _____ more often.

   a. study   b. studied   c. had studied   d. will study

8. Tina looked at her new book _____.

   a. happy   b. happily   c. happiest   d. happier

9. The celebrity _____ before the photographers arrived.

   a. had left   b. was leaving   c. leaves   d. has left

10. I really hate fish, so I _____ eat it.

   a. always   b. often   c. sometimes   d. never

11. While I _____ my brother on my cell, my sister Anna called me on my home phone.

   a. called   b. was calling   c. call   d. had called

12. Teresa _____ hit by that car if she had crossed the street just a few seconds later!

   a. does not get   c. would have gotten

   b. is not getting   d. was not got

13. What has Fatimah been doing _____?

   a. lately   b. later   c. late   d. lastly

14. We were late for the party _____ a horrible traffic accident on the highway.

   a. as soon as   b. due to   c. since   d. so that

15. My mom is _____ in a good mood—no one ever sees her upset.

   a. rarely   b. never   c. sometimes   d. always

16. Does your sister know _____ bike that is?

   a. whose   b. who   c. who's   d. who is

17. _____ he _____ to her must have been very nice because she is smiling.

   a. How, say   b. That, said   c. If, says   d. What, said

18. Mary _____ to the airport yesterday to pick up her brother.

    a. has gone   b. had gone   c. went   d. goes

19. Matt knows _____ you _____ solve your problem.

    a. which, could   b. if, would   c. how, can   d. why, ought

20. The dog, which _____ eating when we arrived, had surgery recently.

    a. are   b. is   c. were   d. was

21. The passenger _____ in the first row of the bus could not believe it when a deer appeared in the middle of the road.

    a. was sitting   c. who sits

    b. whom was sitting   d. sitting

22. _____ the test I have tomorrow, I don't think I'll be able to go to the movie with you today.

    a. As of   b. Despite of   c. Despite   d. Because of

23. I wouldn't put mayonnaise on that sandwich because Mike _____ it.

    a. can not like   b. must not like   c. would like   d. may not like

24. Many children in the United States _____ had all of their immunizations.

    a. has   b. had   c. have   d. is

25. The company _____ sure how many employees were enrolled in its 401K plan.

    a. wasn't   b. hasn't   c. weren't   d. hadn't

Test 5.

Write the letter of the correct answer on the line.

1. If I'm not mistaken, I believe that JoAnn _____ that she could bring an extra dozen cupcakes.

    a. should have said   c. would say

    b. said   d. says

2. Diane and Jason have just _____ a new house.

    a. buy   b. bought   c. buying   d. been buying

3. She _____ agreed to sing with us next weekend.

    a. happy   b. happily   c. happier   d. happiest

4. We _____ some water with our dinner instead of soda.

    a. are going to have   c. is going to have

    b. am going to have   d. was going to have

5. _____ you and Karina _____ when I called you last night?

    a. Was, studying   c. Were, studying

    b. Were, study   d. Are, studying

6. An hour after Srini _____ his driver's license, he _____ his dad's car for the very first time.

    a. got, drove   c. has got, drove

    b. gets, drove   d. was getting, drove

7. Speak very _____ because the baby's taking a nap.

    a. quiet   b. quieter   c. quietly   d. quite

8. The smaller birds _____ away before they _____ the hawk.

    a. had flown, saw   c. was flying, saw

    b. has flown, see   d. flies, are flying

9. If it rains, Ariel and her friends _____ to the outdoor concert.

    a. won't go   c. would not have gone

    b. wouldn't go   d. could not go

10. I think that car is really old and you shouldn't buy it _____ it is covered in rust.

    a. so that   b. before   c. since   d. though

11. My older brother doesn't ever come home to see our parents. In addition, he _____ sees the rest of the family.

    a. always   b. ever   c. often   d. seldom

12. Sharon wouldn't have fallen asleep in class if she _____ all night last night.

    a. doesn't stay up   c. haven't stayed up

    b. did stay up   d. hadn't stayed up

13. I want to make sure that I study very hard tonight _____ I don't fail my math exam tomorrow!

    a. after   b. although   c. so that   d. since

14. _____ you get into a good college or not is important for your future.

    a. Should   b. Can   c. Other   d. Whether

15. Did Debra tell you _____ she was going on vacation this year?

    a. where   b. what   c. will   d. could

16. Marco's sister _____ Ireland three times before.

    a. has visited   b. was visiting   c. is visiting   d. wants to visit

17. The best part _____ the movie was the car chase scene at the end!

    a. for   b. of   c. about   d. to

18. _____ she was the first female candidate is a major accomplishment.

    a. If   b. What   c. That   d. Who

19. The campus library, _____ at the main entrance to the university, caught on fire last week.

    a. locate   b. locating   c. located   d. locates

20. The president, who _____ only one term, was very unpopular with voters.

    a. serve   b. serves   c. serving   d. served

21. The mother distracted her child at the doctor's office _____ they were waiting.

    a. whether   b. in spite of   c. while   d. which

22. Since Marley won six games in a row, we thought that she _____ a lot this week.

    a. have practices   c. would have practiced

    b. must has practiced   d. must have practiced

23. When we couldn't find Jill when the store closed at 9 PM, we realized that she _____ taken the bus home.

    a. has   b. could have   c. might not have d. had not

24. Either insurance company _____ a good choice.

    a. are   b. were   c. is   d. have

25. Our school has zero tolerance for cheating on tests. When caught, cheaters _____ to the principal's office at once.

    a. are sending   b. send   c. have sent   d. are sent

Part 2: Individual Units

UNIT 1. Subject-Verb Agreement

If the sentence is correct, write a check mark (✓) on the line. If it is not correct, write an X on the line and circle the mistake. Then change the sentence to make it correct. Write the change above the sentence.

_____ 1. Terri, along with her three dogs, is going camping this weekend.

_____ 2. Everyone like chocolate ice cream, right?

_____ 3. Part of the library was damaged in last week's storm and cannot be used for the time being.

_____ 4. Taking advanced chemistry usually cause stress in many high school students.

_____ 5. The little boy standing alone next to the swings were not seen by the adults.

_____ 6. The fast pace of changes in prescription drugs are making it difficult for insurance companies to keep up.

_____ 7. Neither the cat nor her kittens was awake when I went to see them.

_____ 8. A number of homes were hit by the tornado.

_____ 9. Five thousand dollars are not a lot to ask for that car.

_____ 10. Each of the board members were present for the vote.

Underline the correct form of the word in parentheses.

11. In the past, many doctors (was, were) of the opinion that bleeding a patient was not only safe but actually helpful in the healing process.

12. Oftentimes new parents (do, does) not know what their babies' cries mean.

13. Anyone who (take, takes) him at his word is a fool!

14. The research on the subject (suggest, suggests) that children who watch too much TV have lower test scores.

15. A diet low in calories and fat (help, helps) to reduce your weight and often (make, makes) you feel better overall.

16. According to recent statistics, people who know not to text and drive (get, gets) in fewer accidents.

17. Last summer a lot of ducks lived in the pond behind our house. One of the ducks that visited us (was, were) a male mallard.

18. A basket of apples (is, are) sitting on the kitchen table if you feel like eating a piece of fruit.

19. Almost all of the children (need, needs) a permission slip that their parents must sign indicating that their children may take part in the school's field trip next week.

20. Everyone is so busy today. While we know that fast food (is, are) not a healthy choice for lunch, sometimes we just don't have enough time for a good meal.

UNIT 2. Word Forms

Change the words into nouns by removing a suffix.

1. dirty - _____
2. homeless - _____
3. historic - _____
4. childlike - _____
5. cautionary - _____
6. daily - _____
7. basic - _____
8. athletic - _____
9. dietary - _____
10. selfish - _____

Circle the correct word that completes the sentence.

11. The weather has been very nice and (crisp, crispy) lately!

12. Her proposal was so costly, it was (laughing, laughable).

13. Some diseases are (preventful, preventable), but certain ones are not.

14. I really love working with Jason because he is so (dependable, dependent)!

15. Marissa doesn't like to eat out with Steve at nice places because his clothes are rarely (tasty, tasteful).

16. Please be sure you do not forward that email because the contents are very (sensitive, sensible).

17. I don't feel comfortable telling you his salary because that kind of information is (confident, confidential).

18. Jim is really interested in getting an (electrical, electric) car when they are available in his town.

19. My daughter is going to join the Navy to become a hospital (medical, medic).

20. Jennifer was very (interesting, interested) in Paul's news about the bookstore closing.

UNIT 3. Past Perfect Tense

Put the given verb in the past perfect tense in each sentence.

1. When I got home, I discovered that I _____ my credit card at the restaurant. (leave)

2. My co-worker invited me to see the new action movie with him, but I _____ it last week with my sister, so I didn't go with him. (see)

3. I asked my sister to feed the baby, but she _____ him already. (feed)

4. When Eric didn't answer us, we wondered where he _____. (go)

5. Last week Joshua _____ a letter to Aunt Mary telling her about his new job, so when I called her this morning, she obviously knew about Joshua's new position. In other words, I didn't spill the beans! (write)

6. The art piece was so bad, it looked like a monkey _____ it. (paint)

7. What _____ he _____ for dinner that made him so sick? (eat)

8. When I saw Mark, the police _____ him over. (pull)

9. When he took the test, he _____ for it, so he failed it. (not study)

10. In the 2012 election, Joe didn't know much about the candidates because he _____ out of the country for the previous 18 years. (live)

11. I went to Alaska for the first time in 2009. I _____ there until then. (never be)

12. As soon as Michelle realized her glasses were on the bus, it _____. (already leave)

13. The day that I met him, Kareem told me that he _____ in both Ocean City and Atlantic City. (live)

14. When I talked with my mom last night, she was very upset because my dad _____ her birthday. (forget)

15. On their last trip driving to Florida, Antonio and Dalia got lost because their GPS didn't work correctly. They _____ about getting a new GPS but unfortunately decided against it at the last minute. (think)

16. I _____ with him long enough to recommend him for the job. (not work)

17. We drove to the airport to pick her up, but she _____ a taxi home. (take)

18. The good news is that she _____ the laundry earlier in the week, so all of her clothes were clean. (do)

19. Getting around the island on our vacation was really easy because we _____ a car. (rent)

20. The baby was all messy because he _____ his cereal all over his shirt. (spill)

UNIT 4. Conditionals (*if* clauses and *wish*)

Complete the following **if** sentences with the correct form of the verb.

1. If we (run) _____ out of flour, I can go to the store and buy more.

2. If I (have) _____ a dollar for every time that car alarm went off, I would be a very rich woman!

3. If you (take) _____ your wallet to the restaurant, you wouldn't have been embarrassed about not paying your bill!

4. We (miss) _____ seeing you at the party if you had left early.

5. Nate's using my lawn mower right now, but if he (bring) _____ it back today you can use it.

6. If she can pass the ASVAB exam, Maddy (join) _____ the Army this summer.

7. Gabbie's parents (be) _____ proud if she (make) _____ the volleyball team this season.

8. Even if Kevin (pass) _____ his final tomorrow, he (not pass) _____ History 101 because his overall grade is too low.

9. If my cat (eat) _____ too much, he (get) _____ sick.

10. I (not, think) _____ that I would make the same decision if I (have) _____ the choice.

Using the clue in the first sentence, write another sentence with **wish.**

11. Maria cannot sing well, but she wants to. (Maria)

_____.

12. My surgery is scheduled three weeks from now, and my knee hurts very much. (I)

_____.

13. I have to work early tomorrow morning, but I want to sleep in. (I)

_____.

14. My bird chirps so loudly that it actually wakes up my neighbors. (They)

_____.

15. Kathy has not had a vacation in three years because she works too much. She really wants to take one. (She)

_____.

16. My friends went camping, but I missed the trip because I was sick. (I)

_____.

17. I speak several languages, but I don't know Russian. (I)

_____.

18. The flight attendant was tired of hearing the child in seat 13B cry. (She)

_____.

19. Keith enjoyed watching Wimbledon on TV, but he really wanted to be there in person. (He)

_____.

20. Grading all the exams took five hours on Monday night. The teacher was so tired. (She)

_____.

UNIT 5. Connectors

Circle the correct connector in each sentence.

1. (Even though, Since) fettuccini alfredo is really an unhealthy dish, it is so delicious!

2. We always drink coffee with our breakfast every single morning (so, when) we get a boost of energy.

3. (Since, After) Kaley just got her license, she drives extremely carefully.

4. I have never been to Toronto, but I hear it's (so, such a) beautiful city that I want to go this summer.

5. (During, After) almost two hours of calling her uncle, Sandra still hasn't been able to reach him.

6. The dancer performed very badly during the competition (given that, despite the fact that) she had practiced four hours a day for six weeks.

7. (Although, Wherever) Miguel comes to class, he usually comes late.

8. Have you heard Keiko speak French? (When, While) Japanese is her native language, she speaks French beautifully.

9. (By the time, Given that) my car needs to be serviced at the dealership tomorrow, I have to get up early.

10. She knows how to play the piano well (so that, because) she's taken lessons for years.

Complete the sentences.

11. The cars raced down the road rapidly once _____

_____

12. She rarely fails her grammar tests if _____

_____

13. By the time he got home, _____

_____

14. After I saw the mouse, _____

_____

15. The baby was sleeping, and we talked quietly in order not to _____

_____.

16. Whether or not your grandmother is late, _____

_____.

17. The workmen whistled happily now that _____

_____.

18. Max took the test slowly so that _____

_____.

19. Despite the fact that Beck went over the totals from the day's sales carefully, ___

_____.

20. Katie always calls her husband whenever _____

_____.

UNIT 6. Noun Clauses

Combine the two sentences into one sentence by adding a noun clause.

1. I parked my car very early this morning. I can't find it now.

   I don't remember _____

   _____

2. Monica saw the accident. One car hit another. _____

   The police are asking Monica _____

   _____

3. The mayor died last night. How did he die?

   No one has been able to find out _____

   _____

4. Shawn left his shoes somewhere. His shoes are in a place where he cannot see them.

   Shawn doesn't know _____

   _____

5. William said something shocking.

_____ shocked everyone.

6. My wife is surprised. She is surprised at the amount I saved at the grocery store.

She can't believe _____

_____

7. Gasoline is now so expensive.

No one can believe _____

_____

8. She sat in her car on the highway and wondered for a long time. She did not know the cause of the accident.

She wondered _____

_____

9. The neighbors heard the noise. The noise came from the empty lot behind their houses.

They didn't know _____

_____

10. Jerry is worried. His roof needs repairing and it may cost a lot of money.

Jerry is worried about _____

_____

Circle the correct word in the parentheses to complete the sentences with noun clauses.

11. I told my husband (what, that) I would be home late after work this evening.

12. Can you figure out (if, where) the new mall is?

13. Cheryl wondered (why, that) the toaster caught on fire in the kitchen because it was brand new.

14. I did not hear (what, that) she said because the music was too loud.

15. Can you tell me (what, where) the parking lot for the courthouse is?

16. (How, That) the pyramids were created will always be a mystery.

17. Roberto is excited (with, about) where he might go to college.

18. Chelsea wondered if she (would, should) complete another assignment for extra credit.

19. Sheila was having a hard time figuring out (who, that) Felipe was.

20. We weren't sure (that, what) he did for a living, but he drove a really nice car!

UNIT 7. Reduction of Clauses

Reduce the clauses in the each sentence if possible.

1. We are adopting a dog that has been living at a shelter.

_____

_____

2. The teacher who has been working here the longest is Ms. Harrington.

_____

_____

3. The coffee that is served in most cafes is French roast.

_____

_____

4. Most of the students who participate in university events live on campus.

_____

_____

5. The restaurant that serves the best breakfast is located downtown.

_____

_____

6. Zachary Taylor and Millard Fillmore, who were both U.S. presidents, are not as well-known as George Washington or Abraham Lincoln.

_____

_____

7. Dumpster, which is a brand name, is commonly used for all large mobile garbage bins.

_____

_____

8. The Statue of Liberty, which is located in New York, has over 3 million visitors each year.

_____

_____

9. Quiche Lorraine, which is a dish made of eggs, butter, cheese, meat, and a crust, can be eaten for breakfast, lunch, or even dinner.

_____

_____

10. The Sundance Film Festival, which is held yearly each January, often shows films that have received Oscar nominations.

_____

_____

Add commas to the sentences where they are needed.

11. In order to save even more money we started shopping at a discount grocery store.

12. Guillermo who is usually the best student in the class failed the last chemistry exam.

13. Irene Sanchez the candidate with the most support won the election with just 22 percent of the overall votes.

14. A hippopotamus which can live up to 50 years weighs almost two tons.

15. The Baiji which is also known as the Yangtze River Dolphin is a very rare mammal.

16. Did you know that Germany where the printing press was invented was the home of the first mass-produced books?

17. Before we took our road trip we purchased new tires.

18. Since I was a little girl I have always loved to watch horror movies.

19. While driving I never text my friends because it's too dangerous.

20. When tired many people try to drink coffee to wake themselves up.

UNIT 8. Past Modals (includes passive forms)

Complete the second sentence in each item using a past tense modal. Use the information in the first sentence and the type of modal in parentheses at the end to determine which past tense modal to use.

1. Marty is in the hospital after crashing his car. It _____ been worse—he could be dead! (possibility)

2. Gina got 100 percent on her last exam. She _____ studied very hard for it. (strong certainty)

3. The boy cracked his tooth on the popcorn. There _____ been an unpopped kernel in the bag. (possibility)

4. Joan got pulled over by the police for running a stop sign. If she had seen the stop sign, she _____ stopped. (conditional)

5. Hannah is wearing a huge diamond ring on her left hand. She _____ gotten engaged! (strong certainty)

6. I didn't know you were going to be in Caracas last month when I was there! You _____ told me you were planning a trip! (advice or suggestion)

7. We don't know why they didn't show up to the party. They _____ been sick or had an emergency. (possibility)

8. The teacher called to say he would be 15 minutes late to class. If I had known he was going to be late, I _____ slept in a little longer. (conditional)

9. The power to all of the houses on my street is out! There _____ been a lightning strike or a broken transformer. (possibility)

10. Wow, Susan is really upset with you! You _____ told her that you couldn't finish the project on time. (advice or suggestion)

Using the first sentence and the modal in parentheses as a clue, write a sentence with a past modal.

11. If the storm had been worse, there was a possibility that the roof would leak. (might)

_____

12. Jack is pretty sure that Marie came here from Quebec. (must)

_____

13. It was possible that she took the bus. (could)

_____

14. Stan failed his exam, and he realizes that not studying was a huge mistake. (should)

_____

15. Bill did not show up for the company meeting this morning. (must)

_____

16. Luke made a mistake when he bought a used rental car. (should)

_____

17. She looks too young to be a college senior. There is no way she was born before 2005. (could)

_____

18. It is possible that we got off at the wrong subway stop. (may)

_____

19. He had an opportunity to go to medical school and become a doctor. (could)

_____

20. I ran the risk of being too late to register for classes this term. (might)

_____

UNIT 9. Review of Verb Tenses

Fill in the blanks with the correct tense of the verb.

1. She usually _____ dinner at 6:30 PM. (*eat*, simple present)

2. The restaurant _____ every night at 10 PM. (*close*, simple present)

3. My sister _____ in Miami. (*live*, simple present)

4. Which **is not** a present tense form of a verb?
   a. ate   c. meet
   b. heats   d. love

5. They _____ on fresh fruit and white cheese before lunch. (*snack*, simple past)

6. The weather during my vacation _____ beautiful! (*to be*, simple past)

7. After dinner, we _____ around the block. (*run*, simple past)

8. Which **is not** a simple past tense form of a verb?
   a. called   c. watched
   b. drove   d. think

9. _____ they _____ to the movies with us? (*come*, present progressive)

10. We _____ lunch together. (*eat*, present progressive)

11. I _____ a great book right now! (*read*, present progressive)

12. Which verb form **is** spelled correctly?
   a. begining   c. operateing
   b. dividing   d. reviewwing

13. She _____ going to _____ me move this weekend. (*help*, future)

14. Serena and I _____ each other for the past 20 years. (*know*, present perfect)

15. Ken is an amazing writer, and he _____ three books that have
    been published. (*write*, present perfect)

16. Katie _____ up late too many times in the past three months,
    so I think she's going to get fired. (*show*, present perfect)

17. Jessie _____ really hard for her exam, so I'm sure she'll get a
    good grade. (*study*, present perfect)

18. I could not hear him, so I am not sure what he _____. (*ask*,
    past progressive)

19. The phone rang while we _____ our favorite TV show. (*watch*,
    past progressive)

20. When I saw John and Pete yesterday, they _____ a new
    computer. (*purchase*, past progressive)

Appendix A: Parts of Speech

Category	Definition	Examples
noun	a name of a person, place, thing, or abstract idea	*Maria, a store, a book*
verb	shows action or state of being	*eat, take, is*
pronoun	takes the place of a noun	*he, him, myself, mine, anything*
adjective	describes a noun or pronoun	*good, delicious, green*
preposition	shows relationships	*in, with, for*
conjunction	connects	*and, because, if*
adverb	describes verbs, adjectives, or other adverbs	*quickly, very, extremely*
interjection	expresses strong emotion	*Wow! Oh! No!*

Appendix B: Verb Tenses

Tense	Example
simple present	*I* **drive** *to my office every day.*
simple past	*I* **lived** *in an apartment in 2009.*
simple future	*I* **will help** *you with that job.*
present progressive	*I* **am reading** *these verbs right now.*
past progressive	*I* **was watching** *TV during the storm last night.*
future progressive	*I* **will be flying** *to Japan at midnight tonight.*
present perfect	*I* **have been** *here since 9 AM today.*
past perfect	*I* **had been** *in France twice before.*
future perfect	*I* **will have finished** *this work by midnight.*
present perfect progressive	*I* **have been living** *in Sacramento for two years.*
past perfect progressive	*I* **had been reading** *all night.*
future perfect progressive	*I* **will have been working** *here for thirty years.*

Appendix C: Irregular Past and Past Participles of Verbs

The vast majority of verbs in English are regular verbs, which means that their past tense and their past participles end in –ed.

Present	Past	Past Participle
add	added	added
like	liked	liked
map	mapped	mapped

Other verbs, however, are irregular, which means that their past tense and past participles are formed in some other way, including internal vowel changes (*sing–sang–sung*), –en or –ne (*choose, chose, chosen* or *go-went-gone*), and no change at all (*cut-cut-cut*). (Note that the present participle has not been included here because it always ends in –*ing*.)

Though some sources claim to have more than 350 irregular verbs, these lists often include rare words such as *forego* (*forego-forwent-forgone*), *hew* (*hew-hewed-hewn/hewed*), and *unspin* (*unspin-unspun-unspun*). The following chart lists 155 of the most frequently used irregular verbs. A list of 155 items may seem daunting to ELLs, but these verbs should be introduced in much smaller groups. For example, beginning students are often given a list of 25 of the most common verbs, and this list is increased as ELLs attain intermediate proficiency. See Teaching Technique 15 in *Keys to Teaching Grammar to English Language Learners* (Folse, 2009) for specific ideas for teaching these verb forms.

Present	Past	Past Participle
arise	arose	arisen
awake	awoke	awoken
be	was / were	been
bear	bore	born / borne
beat	beat	beaten / beat
become	became	become
begin	began	begun
bend	bent	bent
bet	bet	bet
bid	bid	bid
bind	bound	bound
bite	bit	bitten
bleed	bled	bled
blow	blew	blown
break	broke	broken
bring	brought	brought
broadcast	broadcast	broadcast
build	built	built
burst	burst	burst
buy	bought	bought
cast	cast	cast
catch	caught	caught
choose	chose	chosen
come	came	come
cost	cost	cost
creep	crept	crept
cut	cut	cut
deal	dealt	dealt
dig	dug	dug
dive	dove	dived
do	did	done
draw	drew	drawn
dream	dreamed / dreamt	dreamed / dreamt
drink	drank	drunk
drive	drove	driven
eat	ate	eaten
fall	fell	fallen
feed	fed	fed
feel	felt	felt
fight	fought	fought
find	found	found
fit	fit	fit
flee	fled	fled

fly	flew	flown
forbid	forbade	forbidden
forecast	forecast	forecast
foresee	foresaw	foreseen
forget	forgot	forgotten
forgive	forgave	forgiven
forsake	forsook	forsaken
freeze	froze	frozen
get	got	gotten
give	gave	given
go	went	gone
grind	ground	ground
grow	grew	grown
hang	hung	hung
have	had	had
hear	heard	heard
hide	hid	hidden
hit	hit	hit
hold	held	held
hurt	hurt	hurt
input	input	input
keep	kept	kept
kneel	knelt	knelt
know	knew	known
lay	laid	laid
lead	led	led
leave	left	left
lend	lent	lent
let	let	let
lie	lay	lain
light	lit / lighted	lit / lighted
lose	lost	lost
make	made	made
mean	meant	meant
meet	met	met
mislead	misled	misled
mistake	mistook	mistaken
misunderstand	misunderstood	misunderstood
overcome	overcame	overcome
overdo	overdid	overdone
override	overrode	overridden
oversee	oversaw	overseen
oversleep	overslept	overslept
overtake	overtook	overtaken
overthrow	overthrew	overthrown

pay	paid	paid
prove	proved	proven / proved
put	put	put
quit	quit	quit
read	read	read
ride	rode	ridden
ring	rang	rung
rise	rose	risen
run	ran	run
say	said	said
see	saw	seen
seek	sought	sought
sell	sold	sold
send	sent	sent
set	set	set
sew	sewed	sewn / sewed
shake	shook	shaken
shed	shed	shed
shoot	shot	shot
show	showed	shown / showed
shrink	shrank	shrunk
shut	shut	shut
sing	sang	sung
sit	sat	sat
sleep	slept	slept
slide	slid	slid
sling	slung	slung
slit	slit	slit
speak	spoke	spoken
speed	sped	sped
spend	spent	spent
spin	spun	spun
split	split	split
spread	spread	spread
stand	stood	stood
steal	stole	stolen
stick	stuck	stuck
stink	stank / stunk	stunk
strike	struck	struck / stricken
string	strung	strung
swear	swore	sworn
sweep	swept	swept
swell	swelled	swollen
swim	swam	swum
swing	swung	swung

take	took	taken
teach	taught	taught
tear	tore	torn
tell	told	told
think	thought	thought
throw	threw	thrown
thrust	thrust	thrust
understand	understood	understood
undertake	undertook	undertaken
undo	undid	undone
uphold	upheld	upheld
upset	upset	upset
wake	woke	woken
wear	wore	worn
weave	wove	woven
weep	wept	wept
wet	wet	wet
win	won	won
wind	wound	wound
withdraw	withdrew	withdrawn
write	wrote	written

Appendix D: Four Types of Conditional Sentences

There are four types of conditional sentences: zero, one, two, and three. Zero conditional is not a true conditional, but it is included here because it uses the word *if*.

Type of Conditional Sentence	Example	Notes on Usage
Zero	*If it rains, I stay home.*	used for facts or situations that are always true; *when* or *whenever* can be used instead of *if*
	If it rained, I stayed home.	used for situations that were always true in the past; *when* or *whenever* can be used instead of *if*
First	*If it rains, I will stay home.*	used for an action that is likely to happen
Second	*If it rained, I would stay home.*	used for an action that is not true or that the speaker thinks is not very possible
Third	*If it had rained, I would have stayed home.*	used for a past action that is contrary to fact

Appendix E: Word Forms

Verb Endings

Word Endings for Verbs		
Ending	**Meaning**	**Example**
–ate	to cause, to become, to supply with	*motivate, oxygenate*
–en	to make something have a certain quality	*darken, lighten*
–ify	to cause or make into something	*identify, solidify, unify*
–ize	to become	*generalize, finalize*

Adjective Endings

Word Endings for Adjectives		
Ending	**Meaning**	**Examples**
–able, –ible	having a particular quality	*comfortable, reversible*
–al	of or relating to something	*musical, occasional*
–an, –ian	relating to someone or something from a place; relating to someone who has certain knowledge or belief	*American, vegetarian*
–ant, –ent	having the quality of	*defiant, persistent*
–ary	belonging to	*planetary*
–ate	having, containing, or having to do with something	*compassionate*
–ative, –itive	having the quality of	*talkative, primitive*

–ed	past participle	*confused*
–en	past participle	*stolen, written*
–en	made of	*wooden*
–ese	of a country	*Chinese*
–ful	full of	*beautiful*
–ic	of or relating to a particular thing	*periodic*
–ing	present participle	*confusing*
–ish	having qualities of, or tending to be	*childish*
–ive	having a particular quality	*expensive*
–less	without something	*useless*
–like	similar to	*childlike*
–ly	having qualities of	*manly*
–ory	relating to	*obligatory*
–ous, –ious	having qualities of	*dangerous, delicious*
–proof	protected from	*waterproof*
–y	having the character of	*curly, funny*

Adverb Endings

Word Endings for Adverbs		
Ending	**Meaning**	**Examples**
–ly	in a particular way or at times	*easily, occasionally*

NOTE: Not all words that end in **–ly** are adverbs.

early	adjective	Gary is in his *early* twenties.
	adverb	Carlos has to wake up *early*.
daily	adjective	Our library subscribes to four *daily* newspapers.
	adverb	Kumiko exercises *daily*.
oily	adjective	Irma doesn't like *oily* foods.
lonely	adjective	Ronald was a very *lonely* child.
friendly	adjective	She is such a *friendly* person.

Note: In addition, not all adverbs end in **–ly:** *fast, well, soon, always, here.*

Noun Endings

<table>
<tr><th colspan="3">Word Endings for Nouns</th></tr>
<tr><th>Ending</th><th>Meaning</th><th>Examples</th></tr>
<tr><td>–al</td><td>the act of doing something</td><td>*rehearsal, denial*</td></tr>
<tr><td>–ence, –ance, –cy</td><td>action or process; quality</td><td>*confidence, performance, lunacy*</td></tr>
<tr><td>–ent</td><td>someone or something that does something</td><td>*resident*</td></tr>
<tr><td>–er, –or, –ar, –r</td><td>someone or something that does something</td><td>*teacher, elevator, registrar, writer*</td></tr>
<tr><td>–hood</td><td>having a quality or state</td><td>*brotherhood, childhood*</td></tr>
<tr><td>–ity, –ty</td><td>having a quality</td><td>*equality, specialty*</td></tr>
<tr><td>–tion, –ion</td><td>act or result of doing something</td><td>*attention, impression*</td></tr>
<tr><td>–ism</td><td>a belief or set of ideas</td><td>*capitalism*</td></tr>
<tr><td>–ist</td><td>a person who performs a specific action; a person with certain beliefs</td><td>*typist, capitalist*</td></tr>
<tr><td>–ment</td><td>a result of doing something; a place of action</td><td>*development, department*</td></tr>
<tr><td>–ness</td><td>state or condition</td><td>*happiness*</td></tr>
<tr><td>–ure</td><td>an act or process</td><td>*failure, pressure*</td></tr>
<tr><td>–ship</td><td>a state or quality; an art or skill</td><td>*friendship, sportsmanship*</td></tr>
</table>